# On fire for God

# ON FIRE FOR GOD

Victor Budgen

EVANGELICAL PRESS

EVANGELICAL PRESS
16/18 High Street, Welwyn, Hertfordshire, AL6 9EQ, England



*First published 1983*

ISBN 0 85234 179 2

*Cover illustrations:*
*Top left – Statue of John Hus, Tabor.*
*Top right – Evangelical Church of Czech Brethren at rear of Hus' house, Husinecs.*
*Bottom – Site of Hus' birthplace and home, Husinecs.*

Typeset in Great Britain by Inset, Hertford Heath
Printed in Great Britain at The Pitman Press, Bath

To the people of God at Milnrow Evangelical Church, in gratitude for their stand for the gospel in a conflict far less heroic than that recorded in this book,
and especially to my wife, Pauline, who never wavered in her support.

'Finally, I beseech you, dearly beloved, pray for those who proclaim God's truth with his grace; also pray for me, that I may write and preach more against the malice of the Antichrist, and that when need is the greatest, God may place me in the battle-array to defend his truth.'

*(John Hus in a letter from exile to his congregation at Prague.)*

'Oh, that my name were worthy to be associated with such a man!'

*(Martin Luther speaking of John Hus.)*

# Contents

# Preface

'Did you finish your book, Sir?' asks Marcie of Peppermint Patty in the well-known Peanuts cartoon. 'No, Marcie, it had too many footnotes . . . I hate footnotes!' replies the reluctant scholar, gazing disapprovingly at the offending book. 'Why should I keep looking at the bottom of the page?' she demands, indignantly warming to her theme. Then, as she strides defiantly away, she declares, 'If they can't put the words where I'm looking, I won't read them.'

This book has notes but they are tucked away well out of sight at the end of the book. They can easily be ignored. Yet they are designed to acknowledge my indebtedness to many other writers and in particular to the monumental labours of the Hus scholar Matthew Spinka in his work both of translation and of historical commentary. This is not a work with any pretensions to learning or original research. I am heavily dependent on the labours, translations and researches of others. Where I have felt that they are spiritually helpful I have not hesitated to use works on Hus of an older vintage.

Yet as the book was nearing completion I read a brief article which was urging pastors to write and warning of the dangers when too many books were written by men who were mainly or solely academics. In a real way, this book has been written from pastoral research and from a conviction that the battle in which Hus engaged has many parallels in our century. I trust that I have not been guilty of any deliberate falsification or distortion in taking this viewpoint. There is a sense in which the story ends at chapter 23 but the two appendices are for those who, like myself, do appreciate a contemporary and pastoral application to their church history.

It is no exaggeration to say that above all else this book has been written out of a real love for John Hus himself as a true and great man of God. This admiration began almost in desperation, over twenty years ago, when in the course of a study of the barren, soul-destroying wilderness of the medieval papacy John Hus was suddenly seen as one of the few beacons of hope and gospel light. What began as hero worship has become increasingly a study of a man, 'warts and all', but the affection has deepened, not diminished.

Some three years after my meeting with Hus I met my wife, Pauline, and she too met the Bohemian reformer as she began in the first year of marriage her long process of co-operation as she typed notes from an old edition of the letters of Hus. Since then she has typed and retyped, over and over again. She has deciphered, corrected and many times endured my standing over her to snatch the most recent sheet of paper from the typewriter. I am deeply indebted to her.

I am also grateful to the many members of my own fellowship who have helped in the project. They helped initially in their own stand for the gospel some years ago, as the dedication makes plain. Some of them who attend the after-church meeting were the first to hear two simple talks on John Hus in the early days of Milnrow Evangelical Church, and from this small beginning the book sprang. In their willingness to hear it in simple story form they made a real contribution to the origin of the book. Others have helped with typing and in checking quotations and manuscripts and I am grateful for all of this.

My aim is that many may see something of the truth and beauty of Christ in Hus, and that the book may clearly show Christ reigning and triumphing in the church, not only as the flames crackle round his martyred servant, but also in all Hus's strenuous and courageous endeavours to apply Scripture with equal fidelity both to issues of personal salvation and also to the daily life and fellowship of the church itself. My prayer is that this portrait of the reformer be a spur to us to serve Christ and his church as faithfully in our day as Hus did in his.

# Introduction: 'A thing of beauty is a joy for ever'

After the First World War a cartoon appeared in Czech newspapers. The reader saw President Wilson of the United States of America sitting in front of a map of Bohemia, with his head buried in his hands, exclaiming, 'I can't find Litomyšl!'[1] He is surely not the only one not to have heard of this remote Czech town. Even fewer people would know that long ago its bishop, John 'the Iron', was a fanatical opponent of the greatest evangelical reformer the land has ever seen. Furthermore, how many realize that today's 'Republic of Czechoslovakia' is, in fact, the ancient kingdom of Bohemia, over whose map the American President pored in vain? The 'Republic of Czechoslovakia' came into being in October 1918. Along with Moravia, Slovakia and some smaller regions, it incorporated historic Bohemia. Since the *coup d'état* of 1948 the country has had a totalitarian Communist regime. However, happily, it is with the Bohemia of old that we are concerned.

'Bohemia' is a name with an almost magical ring. It is a word that poets might long to use. The very cadences are right. This would seem to be why so much of Shakespeare's *Winter's Tale* is set there. The poet is able to make full use of the word and indeed repeatedly does so. So with the chorus from his play we would say,

> Now take upon me, in the name of Time,
> To use my wings . . . Imagine me,
> Gentle spectators, that I now may be
> In fair Bohemia.[2]

Immediately our thoughts turn towards a country whose very name conjures up vistas of isolated castles on towering crags, mountainous regions, networks of rivers, stretches of beautiful woodland, an actual king called Wenceslas, an authentic Holy Roman Emperor, vividly symbolic legends and, in particular, one fervent religious reformer, John Hus, whose faithfulness unto death has undoubtedly been one of the most significant and fruitful moments in the history of the true church of Jesus Christ.

Our story will lead us to say much about this land called Bohemia and in particular its capital, Prague. There is an ancient and apt saying that when you throw a stone through a window in this city you throw with it a morsel of history. Indeed everywhere in a 'hundred-towered golden Prague' history and beauty, both man-made and natural, mingle together. Arthur Symons has well said that Prague is to a Bohemian 'still the epitome of the history of his country; he sees it, as a man sees the woman he loves, with her first beauty, and he loves it as a man loves a woman, more for what she has suffered'.[3] One modern historian has remarked, 'Prague "is" Bohemia just as Paris "is" France.'[4]

In countless ways the story of Hus is bound up with the story of Prague. Many of those stones, if they could cry out, would speak of events in the life of the reformer. The ancient squares witnessed processions, upheavals, stormy scenes and even bloodshed as conflict grew round his teachings. The hallowed halls of the university saw him enter as a humble student, unknown and literally up from the country, and eventually said its last farewell to him as a former rector of the institution. In particular, the walls of the renowned Bethlehem Chapel re-echoed to his voice as for years his preaching ministry moulded and ultimately divided the entire community of the city. Although the sufferings of Hus were consummated elsewhere, they were begun at Prague. We trust that, as with the city itself, many will come to love him both for the beauty of his life and even more for what he suffered for the gospel's sake.

A modern writer speaks of 'Bohemia, with its pronounced individuality and its central location' as appearing 'to occupy a commanding position in central Europe'. He then cites Bismark who stated, 'Whoever controls Bohemia controls Europe.'[5] Such a remark was made in a century when people hearing it would immediately think of quarrelling groups of nations or two hostile superpowers. The battle described in this book is supremely a battle in the heavenly places between Christ and Satan. Furthermore, it was a battle which was of significance not merely for Europe. It was with no empty rhetorical flourish that John Hus addressed his last letter to 'the entire Christian world'.[6] How should we regard this? Has this struggle meaning for us today?

One of the saddest episodes in recent English history was when, just before the Second World War, Chamberlain came back from Munich insisting that he had brought 'peace with honour'. After arguing that the British Empire could not involve itself in every local dispute, he spoke of what was happening in Czechoslovakia as a 'quarrel in a far away country between people of whom we know nothing'.[7] This may be the attitude of the man of the world, the politician, with regard to political events. Should it ever be the attitude of the Christian, especially where the heart of the gospel is concerned?

In a preface to the writings of Hus, Martin Luther with splendid irony powerfully stated some of the main issues involved in this struggle, when he wrote, 'Hus committed no more atrocious sin than to profess that a pope of an impious life is not the head of the church catholic. He conceded he was the head of a church, but not of the catholic church. Truly he ought to have said: "No matter how criminal and wicked the *pontifex maximus* is, yet ought he to be venerated for sanctity. He cannot err and all that he says and does is to be accepted and treated as an article of the faith." The good men at Constance disposed of three wicked popes and would not allow them to be taken to the fire; but Hus was sentenced to death.'[8]

Through the sharp, crisp pen-strokes of the Reformer yet more of the mysterious and fascinating panorama of the ancient landscape stretches before us. Was there then an era when there were three popes all ruling at the same time, all claiming the allegiance of considerable bodies of people and all evil men? How were they all deposed? What were the consequences? It is an intriguing situation which must inevitably have some bearing on the claims of Rome, which boldly asserts that it speaks with one recognizable voice in all ages. We shall look at all this in some detail. It will be helpful for the reader to bear in mind that for most of Hus's life there were two popes, one at Rome and his rival at Avignon, and that during the latter stages of the great schism there was a third pope as well. We shall look at this in more detail later.

Moreover, the prospect of visiting the greatest ecumenical council of its day, namely the Council of Constance, with its galaxy of contending theologians and its frenzied mob of merry-makers, beckons us with promise both of rich human interest and obvious contemporary relevance. Writing of what happened at the various ecumenical councils of the day, one historian with a fine and dramatic turn of phrase reminds us that 'It is necessary all along to remember Hussitism in the background – a sort of thunder, never far away, which accompanies the reformers on their task.'[9]

Even here new and exciting horizons open up. Who then were these 'reformers' who met in ecumenical council and who were so firmly opposed to Hus and all that he stood for? Why did they so fear the clear thunderclaps in the teaching of Hus? Were they in fact true reformers? This will be yet another important theme that has far-reaching implications for the church of today, especially with regard to its constant quest for unity and its love of ecumenicity, denominational mergers and seemingly never-ending ecclesiastical small-talk.

Above all, the reasons for the death of a man of God always demand investigation for those who love the Lord of the martyr church. In itself the martyrdom was a tremendously dramatic event that is well worth retelling. But because we possess such an excellent first-hand account of the gruelling trial, with all the clash of personalities and all the decisive doctrinal cleavage, it is a particularly important occurrence to study. Especially is it important, in view of later developments, to distinguish between what Hus himself advocated and did and what some Hussites sought to do after Hus's death.

For many years after the death of Hus there was indeed terrible warfare, with the crack troops of Europe quailing and fleeing before the Hussite warriors, just as the Royalist armies later fled before the Ironsides of Cromwell. The Hussites swept all before them until they themselves were largely destroyed by internal squabbles and rivalries. Nevertheless the memory of their fame lingered on. 'Without an understanding of the Hussite explosion there can be no understanding of the Czech aspirations and sufferings over the last five hundred years,' comments a modern writer.[10]

A study of this strife and the wide-ranging upheavals in Europe lies far beyond the scope of this book and we are far from suggesting that Hus would himself have approved of all the blood shed in the name of religion. There are elements in his teaching which clearly indicate that he would have disapproved strongly. Nevertheless the fame of the Hussite warriors is certainly firmly embedded in the national consciousness.

It was perhaps inevitable that Bedřich Smetana, probably the greatest of all Czech composers, should draw inspiration from these themes. He does so in his *Má Vlast* suite, a series of six tone poems which seek to portray the country's landscape, scenery, history and legend. The final two items in the suite deal almost solely with Hussite material, the penultimate one 'Tábor' being based on a famous Hussite hymn. With grim, sombre, repetitive, almost grinding intensity Smetana builds on the Hussite chorale 'Ye Warriors of God', himself speaking in a letter of the 'strong will, victorious fights, constancy and endurance and stubborn refusal to yield' which the work was intended to convey.[11] Smetana said this of the Hussite warriors, but the same could certainly be said of Hus himself.

According to legend, after their final defeat the Hussite warriors took refuge in Blaník hill, waiting in slumber for the time when, led by King Wenceslas of old, they would be summoned to the aid of their country at the time of its greatest need. 'Blaník', which draws on the legend, is the great climax of *Má Vlast*. But that this legend is very much alive even today, and not merely in the poetic imagination of a nineteenth-century composer, is shown by a recent story. During an economic crisis in the late nineteen-fifties a widely circulated joke told of the Communist President Novotný's alarm when the statue of Wenceslas in Wenceslas Square came to life and rode purposefully off in the direction of Blaník Hill. Wenceslas had the obvious intention of summoning the Hussite warriors from their long sleep.

Accompanied by his Minister of Finance, the President managed to intercept Wenceslas and the warriors as they made their way towards Prague. Novotný ordered his Minister of Finance to read out reassuring details of the country's new five-year plan in order to calm the warriors. When he had finished listening, Wenceslas turned to them and said, 'This, gentlemen, is not the hour of our country's greatest need. Back to Blaník – they will be in much greater need of us five years from now.'[12]

While we realize that the Hussite warriors are not going to return to this earth as the legend says, we may ask whether it is worth seeking to reconstruct the earthly life of the man from whom they took their name. Yet as we do so we will find that he is a man with a definite message to mankind's greatest need – a need which does not vary in any age. We will find that in John Hus we meet a servant of Christ whose genuineness and courage are beyond dispute. We may even find ourselves movingly compelled to look beyond the man himself into the very heavenly regions.

'When he opened the fifth seal, I saw under the altar the souls of those who had been slain because of the word of God and the testimony they had maintained. They called out in a loud voice, "How long, Sovereign Lord, holy and true, until you judge the inhabitants of the earth and avenge our blood?" Then each of them was given a white robe, and they were told to wait a little longer, until the number of their fellow-servants and brothers who were to be killed as they had been, was completed' (Revelation 6:9–11).

# 1.
# The peasant's son

Who then was John Hus? He was born about the year 1372 or 1373 in the hamlet of Husinec in southern Bohemia. Very little is known of his parents except that they were poor and had at least one other son who died before John. We deduce this latter fact from a letter which Hus wrote shortly before his death, where he tells his correspondent to 'apprentice to a craft' the sons of his brother, as he fears they are not particularly fitted for a spiritual career.[1] It would seem clear from this that Hus was caring for the sons of a deceased brother.

He was first known as John of Husinec but this was later abbreviated to John Hus. There is no ground for the slander of one writer that Hus took the name of his village because he had no knowledge of his father. Among many of his distinguished contemporaries it was common practice that they should be known by the name of the place of their origin. Thus one of Hus's closest friends, who came from an adjoining village somewhat larger than Husinec, was known as Christian of Prachatice.

Hus was unkindly described by one inveterate enemy as 'lowborn, base, of unknown origin', and another opponent derisively asserted that Hus and his closest friend were 'born of the lowest common rabble and were squat yokels'.[2] Since both these comments were made by men who were contemporaries it confirms the fact that Hus's peasant origin was well known and suggests that possibly he was short of stature. More than this we cannot deduce, but as the whole tone of Hus's ministry was influenced by these early years, we must pause to say something about the significance of his background. 'Meanly born but of no mean spirit' may well be our final verdict.

In Bohemia, as in the rest of Europe, the lot of many peasants was generally hard. While prosperous ones might own one field or more, there were many less fortunate who possessed less than a quarter of a field, or in some cases only the ground on which their homes stood. Everywhere the peasant was confronted with the church as the great land-owner. In fact the church possessed more than one third of the agricultural land and was often a hard task-master. But, if the church was so often lacking in sympathy towards the poor, many nobles were no better. A contemporary saying showed an all-too-common attitude of the nobility towards those who depended upon them. 'The peasant is like a willow – the more you lop it the more numerous and dense are its shoots,' hardly testifies to a kindly attitude among many whose office it was to rule![3]

Where peasants were alleged to have misbehaved there were in many places typical medieval tortures and humiliations, such as flogging or the stocks. Where there was rowdyism and tumult from a Saturday night spree which had got out of hand, some local lords chose to let these take place because of the considerable fines they could impose, rather than to prevent the trouble. They preferred the fees to administering justice, as Hus later said, commenting on such a situation. He was also in later years to comment in vigorous terms on the fact that many peasants were prevented by various devices from bequeathing their own property as they wished. Many were indeed more or less in slavery to their lord. 'They had to provide board and room for his travelling justices, make contributions to his troops on a campaign and in some cases, even though it was not included in the original contract, they had to perform labour services,' comments one who has written a detailed study of society in Bohemia at this time.[4]

Few things more effectively symbolized the seemingly inescapable hardness of their lot than the aptly named 'iron cow'. This described the custom whereby the priest loaned a poor peasant a cow for his use and for which he had to pay a regular fee. However, when the cow died, the obligation to reimburse the priest did not cease. Instead the peasant had both to replace the cow and continue to repay the fee. Obviously 'iron cow' was no misnomer. This would deeply rankle as would the fact that, when peasants brought their goods to town, merchants would often blatantly exploit them. Realizing the peasants' desperate need for ready cash, they would purchase for a low price and then wait until grain was scarce so that they could sell at a high price.

As though these measures were not sufficiently harsh and unjust, there was yet one other practice that must above all else have deepened the already simmering resentment and emphasized the gross inequity and inequality. Following medieval custom, when a peasant whose lord was a delinquent debtor brought goods to sell, the merchant was permitted to confiscate the goods which in reality belonged to the peasant. Ignoring the fact that certain popular preachers roundly condemned this practice, greedy unscrupulous merchants continued to collect from peasants debts owed them by the peasant's lord.

From this background Hus came. We note that he was vividly aware of the poverty and skimping to save experienced by many. Thus he casually referred to the last precious coin that 'an old granny has tied in her handkerchief lest a footpad or thief steal it'.[5] He was acquainted, too, with the misleading advertising of his day and the way in which people could be robbed in more subtle ways. Thus he mentioned the greedy innkeeper who, implying that his food is free, then charges the customer only for the beer but still manages to make him pay more than both the food and beer are worth together.

Drawing on the experience of these early years, Hus, in his avowal that 'The cowsheds on the church estates are more imposing than the lord's castles or the churches,' confirms our comments on the church as the big land-owner.[6] Nor were the monasteries the centres of poverty that their founders had intended. 'In reality, if one should count the persons, the ploughs, fields, fishponds, and other revenue of the monastery, he would find that the share of each monk would be between twenty or thirty *kopy* of revenue, with a plough and a fishpond to spare!' Hus declared.[7] This is the comment of a man who knew the local scene. He was aware of the value to the peasant of a field, a plough and a well-stocked fishpond, and also aware that monks rather than peasants often actually owned these.

There are glimpses in his writings of the scenes of his boyhood. He spoke of the common amusements such as bowls and chess. He wrote of the widespread craving for dice games and all forms of gambling. He referred to the boisterous, wild and often immoral dances with 'flirtation, obscene looks . . . pawing and embracing, and other indecent gestures . . . plenty of laughter, quarrels and loud shouting; plenty of pride, envy, anger, and other such irritations'.[8] He was also aware that such pastimes often led to loss of virginity and even to homosexual practices and sadly mentions such evils. 'If they are peasants, they sometimes abandon their villages and households and run away in order to be more freely able to play the dice and other games, and to lie day and night in taverns,' he wrote, describing the desperate and evil escapism that he himself had witnessed on such occasions.[9]

Those responsible for opening their estates for such revelry were, of course, the nobles, whose sole aim was to make a profit out of it all. Hus deftly depicts such lords pursuing their hunting with zest and flamboyantly indulging in wagers. He writes, 'Sometimes, the lords and their officials order perhaps a poor man to be hanged, because in his need he had stolen a goat or a cow; that is the one sin they punish instantly and promptly.'[10] Yet Hus goes on to say that when a man steals someone's daughter or wife, or rapes some maiden, this is regarded with callous indifference as a trivial matter by these same officials. In such a world of topsy-turvy morality and manifest injustices Hus himself grew up. The experiences of these years marked his outlook and moulded his thought.

He also shows us simple scenes: the annual fair with the prosperous innkeepers and their fat geese; the blacksmith with his large pincers; the avaricious monks, 'vulgarly called *dives* and the fat ones of the lord', as he describes them; the notary thinking of the amount of money that he hopes to make.[11] He is familiar with ordinary people. He can refer to 'simple folk' who imagined that the Holy Trinity was a woman and that God the Father was older than God the Son.[12] Even in his prime and after years of study he can on one and the same occasion refer colloquially to the devil as 'old Nick' and debunk a complex and unnecessarily abstract theological argument by citing what he would expect to be the reaction of 'Hodek, the baker, or Hůda, the vegetable woman' to such unnecessary wordiness.[13]

As we listen to the adult Hus, we can frequently glimpse the background of simple rural experiences and catch the tang of fresh air or even the whiff of a very different odour. To a priest who claimed that an ordinand was 'the father of God and creator of God's body', Hus roundly replied, 'Let him take all his fellow-priests and create a single louse.'[14] 'What is the purpose of all this quacking, my good story-teller?' Hus bluntly demands of another opponent.[15] As we wonder whether Hus ever had to feed the ducks and geese at his parents' home (the suggestion is not far-fetched since his name means 'Goose'), we might also wonder whether he had had other less delightful farming experiences, as he refers to the unworthy bishops, 'who are not even fit to herd swine properly'.[16]

Such vivid and striking comparisons are particularly applied to members of the church's hierarchy. Are they echoes of the complaints of the local peasants, often heard in his youth and retold in the homely vernacular in which he first heard the criticism expressed? Therefore Hus also speaks of the monks who have abundant food even to 'squander on dogs and bitches', and who have supplies of both thick and thin beer, the former to drink themselves and the latter to fob off onto casual visitors![17] Continuing in this vein, he can speak in down-to-earth, racy language of the 'clergy and prelates who eat, gorge themselves, guzzle, and feast abundantly, but in spiritual matters amount to nothing'.[18] As well as showing us something of the poor calibre of many of the clergy among whom the young Hus grew up, these sayings and the kind of imagery he so naturally uses tell us something of his own early experiences. It is significant that the resentment of the hungry towards the well-fed (even the dogs of the rich are lavishly fed) is a recurring note.

It was because of his peasant origins that Hus had such illustrations so readily at his fingertips. The same explanation can be given of the ready use of local sayings and proverbs that characterize his writings. Thus we meet bishops who are merely titular and who never preach in the diocese.

'Accordingly, the Czechs have given them the name of "barren bishops",' Hus tells us.[19] When illustrating the fact that with regard to salvation or damnation every man has his own choice confirmed, Hus writes, 'Accordingly, Czechs have a proverb, "One's will is both the paradise and hell." '[20] Yet another of Hus's allusions to 'common report' shows us not only his familiarity with the sayings and lore of the common people but also introduces us to another formative influence in his early years. 'A German is a heretic, a Czech naturally a thief,' is the saying which Hus quotes.[21]

Hus came from a part of the country which was itself not far from Bavaria, with its German people. Racial strife is often at its worst in such regions. Hus himself knew German, quoted it in his writings, and made a speech in that language at the close of his life. There can be little doubt that he initially shared in much of the hostility that dominated feelings between the two nations. Ludolph of Sagan, who studied in Prague in the 1370s summed it all up, when he wrote, 'Old is the hatred, and all too deeply rooted between German and Czech. As the Jew had once no fellowship with the Samaritans, so now the very sight of a German calls forth aversion in the Czech.'[22]

There were reasons for this. Charles IV, the father of Wenceslas, who was ruler during Hus's life, had been married to no less than three German princesses in succession. Despite his own personal love of the Czech language, Charles had ensured by his marriage and by various appointments that many in court and university circles were German. However, this would only have a limited effect upon those who dwelt far away from Prague in the countryside. It was other factors that weighed more heavily with the country folk. Causes of resentment lay much nearer at hand.

Because of insufficient manpower, large fertile areas of land had been uncultivated in Bohemia, Hungary and Poland during the twelfth, thirteenth and fourteenth centuries. At the same time internal difficulties at certain periods within Germany had meant that constant waves of German settlers had come to these lands. Many towns and rural areas were dominated by Germans. There were written contracts stating that for a fixed period, as they broke in and developed the land, the settlers were exempt from levies. After ten or fifteen years, the exemption no longer applied and payments had to be made. The prosperity of many of these 'immigrants' and the sound of a foreign language no doubt irritated local feeling even though in many cases these generous exemptions were extended to Czech peasants who were willing to cultivate new areas. There may sometimes have been the only too common envy of the lazy locals towards the industrious immigrant.

In particular, Germans came in large numbers to the silver mines at Kutná Hora, Jihlava and Příbram. One of the most ancient mining codes comes from Bohemia and was issued in the mid thirteenth century. Often the miners were allowed to run their own mines. They had their own local courts, in which twelve or fourteen miners sat as judges. As we learn that this was 'to prevent local authorities from intervening arbitrarily in mining disputes, thus risking a stoppage of mining operations, which would be against the financial interests of the overlords or lords of the soil', the seemingly distant 'medieval' scene suddenly comes very close to conditions today.[23]

The German miners were soon followed by German traders. German merchants were numerous and frequent visitors to Prachatice, the trading centre so near to Husinec. When we add to all this the fact that during the pontificate of Clement VI, the friend of Emperor Charles, many of the bulls sent to Bohemia were concerned with lesser benefices and many of these provisions concerned the appointment of foreigners and of Germans in particular, we are not then surprised to know that the nobility, who retained a memory of the time when they had so much more control, were also deeply resentful. There was an undercurrent of seething anger and anti-foreign feeling. Hus himself grew up in and imbibed this atmosphere. Knowledge of such animosities helps us to understand certain of his later attitudes and pronouncements.

Nevertheless life for Hus as a boy would not be all hard fare, scant supplies, feuding and rivalry. There were rural skills. There were workmen to watch and admire. We have seen that Hus describes the blacksmith at his work. He contends that 'The layman who carved and set up the altar performed much harder work than the bishop who consecrated and anointed it'.[24] In this very reference he refers to the 'peasants' who do such work and clearly he has admiration for their evident abilities. Indeed there may be good reasons why the young Hus would have reason for respecting the craftsmanship of such people in his own area.

Anyone who turns to practically any illustrated book on glass-making is likely to find that one of the most vivid pictures will be a fifteenth-century drawing of a glasshouse in Bohemia. The Bohemian glass was of a particularly high quality and it was produced in the thickly wooded country on the borders near Bavaria, the very area where Hus lived as a boy. It was made here largely because of the availability of wood fuel in such abundance. The picture in question in fact shows abundant trees in the background and indicates that the glasshouse was set in a forest. It also reveals the glasshouse as a veritable hive of industry and illustration of varied human skills. This fascinating drawing depicts the raw materials being mixed and carried down to the glass furnace by one group of men. In the foreground a glass-blower is 'marvering' (or smoothing) the bubble of hot glass at the end of his blowing-iron on a flat piece of rock. To his right a glass-blower is reaching for another gather of glass from the crucibles in the furnace. Various glass vessels are visible in the oven and a man behind the oven is examining one of the finished products. It is generally agreed that the glass was well worth examining with considerable pride. The 'green' glass of this area was especially attractive. It was known as 'Wald' or 'forest' glass, because the glass-makers derived their raw material from their wooded surroundings, using as alkali the ashes of bracken and other woodland plants.[25] Obviously not all the peasants in the area around Hus were empty-headed country bumpkins!

There were undoubtedly pleasures and means of relaxation for a growing boy. We have already indicated that there were the games, some of dangerous tendency, others definitely harmful, but some worthwhile and enjoyable. There was above all the countryside. An extremely popular musical piece by Bedřich Smetana underscores this. It comes again from his cycle of six tone poems, *Má Vlast* ('My Country') and is the fourth in the set picturesquely and appropriately entitled 'From Bohemia's Woods and Forests'. The piece successfully captures a mood of spring-like exuberance.

The music is intended to give a general impression of the composer's feelings on seeing the Czech countryside. On all sides fervent singing, both sad and gay, echo from forest and field. The woodlands, in a horn solo, and the merry fertile Elbe lowlands, along with other regions, exult. It is a picture of spacious rural landscapes, abundant fertility, mysterious forest life that is set forth in this joyous and dancing music, some of which is actually in the rhythm of a polka. It was a countryside with real lure and beauty, worthy of being celebrated in such rich and vibrant music.

The boundaries of Bohemia were surrounded by the hilly and mountainous terrain through which they ran. It was in fact almost surrounded by towering mountain peaks. The country, variously described as either diamond-shaped or even as having a 'lozenge shape', has a Central European type of climate. This is modified by altitude in the Bohemian highlands. During the long, cold winters there are sometimes light snowfalls while the hot summers are accompanied by frequent thunderstorms. There are few areas where drought is a problem. Thus much of the landscape is fresh and lush. Even today Bohemia still has thirty per cent of its total area under forest. In the past this covering of woodland would have been greater. In the north there are the brown coal and rich fields of sugar beet and grain. Woods, marshes, secluded valleys and artificial ponds in the south still preserve their quiet charm.

It is obvious that John Hus was born in an area which shares to the full some of the beauties typical of the country as a whole. Let a modern writer give the scene as it is today: 'Below the foothills, with the dark heads of Boubín and Bobík to the south, a pleasant road leads to Husinec. A room in the house in which it is thought John Hus was born forms part of a small museum, standing on one slope of the village street which dips and then climbs again to the church. In the square facing the church is a statue of Master John. As a boy he walked three miles to school in Prachatice, and it is tempting to think he may have trodden that same path which now follows a tinkling stream for a while, climbs through patches of woodland, and then starts a gentle descent beside an undulating line of white wayside shrines.'[26]

It is an attractive picture, with mountains looming in the background, stretches of woodland and a rippling stream. A growing boy could hardly wish for a pleasanter environment. Especially would this be so, if Husinec and the surrounding district had benefited from the wise administration which immediately preceded Hus's own birth. Sheep-farming had been encouraged in certain regions, the grape-vine planted in many country districts, and a particularly attractive touch had been the introduction of fish-ponds in many areas. These had been stocked with carp, which is to this day the traditional Czech Christmas dish. However, in view of what we have said, it would perhaps be rather too much to expect that many of the peasants would regularly sample all these things.

Charles IV, who introduced these measures, not only made roads safe for travel in many areas but resurfaced many. No effete weakling, he himself besieged a castle to catch a robber and it is said that he threw the rope himself round the victim's neck telling him that 'it was not only golden chains that he had in his gift'.[27] It is worth recording that it was said that in the early years of the reign of his son Wenceslas such perfect security and prosperity prevailed that one carrying a bag of gold on his head could have traversed Bohemia from end to end without incurring any risk. Such sayings do tell us something about the mood of the country, even though they may seem somewhat excessively idealistic.

It may be thought that Husinec and district were too far from the capital to experience any of these benefits. To be sure, Husinec was but a village. However, at only an hour's walking distance lay the busy commercial centre of Prachatice. Prachatice was certainly no back-of-beyond place. It has been estimated that each week between one hundred and one thousand wagons would enter bearing goods, for it was situated at the end of the 'golden way' to Passau, a trade centre even in Roman days. It was in fact one of the wealthiest commercial centres in Southern Bohemia.

We still have a reminder today of the sumpter mule caravans in the 'Caravan Bell', the sound of which told errant merchants the position of the town. Even up till quite recent times this bell was rung daily at 10 p.m. At Prachatice the precious salt, coming from Passau to Bohemia, was unloaded, and from here the grain and malt, corn, brandy and furs were sent from Bohemia to Germany and the West. At this commercial centre the merchants gathered in considerable numbers to swop their stories and exchange their news. Did the young boy listen to them? We can assume that he sometimes did because it was to Prachatice that he came to school.

Little is known about this period of the life of Hus. Therefore surmise and legend have been strongly at work. It has been suggested that the local monks had been trying to teach the young lad but, finding that he was far too advanced for their limited abilities, they suggested that he should be sent to Prachatice where he could find more skilled instruction. Another story, this time obviously of a legendary nature, is that his mother, who is said to have accompanied him on his walk to school, joined him under a rock as they were forced to seek shelter from a sudden and violent storm. As they crouched there, lightning struck a nearby juniper bush, setting it ablaze. When his mother declared that they ought to return home at once, young John replied, 'You will see that I also, like this bush, shall depart from this world in flames.'[28]

However, it is most appropriate, in view of the fact that John Hus came as a pupil to the grammar school here at the age of about thirteen, that the restored front of the old town hall, with arms dated 1571, should bear so significant a picture. It celebrates the dance of death, and there are allegories of Justice, in the form of Susanna, Solomon and a corrupt judge copied from Holbein. But these were not there when the young boy came for his schooling. No such solemn scenes yet confronted him. Hus was at this time more concerned with escaping the wrath of exacting schoolmasters than facing corrupt judges. He was no doubt more absorbed in the dance of life than the dance of death. That lay in the future.

## 2.
## Prague — a garden of delight

Although it has been suggested that Hus's mother seems to have been fairly devout, the evidence on which this is based is rather flimsy. Apart from the fact that Hus did gratefully recall that she had taught him to say, 'Amen, may God grant it,' which really does not tell us very much, there are no significant references to her or to his father.[1] In face of this reticence and because of what follows we may well wonder whether his parents' motives in sending him to school were of the highest kind. We first of all note some heartfelt pleas that Hus himself later addressed to readers in words that it seems fair to say do pulsate with personal undertones. In order to understand the quotation we must bear in mind that many, though not all students, automatically became priests at this time.

'It appears to me', says Hus, 'that the reason so many people send their children to school is that they may become rich, receive honour in the world, and become able to help their relatives. It is for these reasons also that the sons give themselves to study. Hence we see that afterwards they commonly live bad lives, because they have entered the priesthood unworthily. Also because the priestly possessions are constantly increasing, the number of students and priests likewise increases. For everyone desires to live well and to become rich.'[2]

Although this is put in general terms we will see in due course that it ties in directly with what Hus says in clearly personal terms about his own unworthy motives in studying and entering the priesthood. It also fits Hus's own background for he goes on to say, 'For that reason serfs are expensive, fields lie fallow, servants are lacking, since every peasant wishes to have his son become a prelate.'[3] It seems most likely that Hus is hinting at the ambition of his own parents, who desperately wanted their son to get on and to break free from the trammels of his peasant background.

Furthermore the passion in his closing plea fully supports the personal meaning that we are ascribing to this passage: 'And because both sides sin, the clergy and the lay people – fathers and mothers by the evil intent with which they send sons to school, and the sons by the evil intent in pursuing their studies – hence from both sides we benefit the holy church but little. Accordingly, father and mother! if you wish that your child become a good priest, pray God that he may endow him with gifts to his glory and your son's salvation, as well as your and holy church's benefit. And you, pupil, study with the same goal in view: for if you study in order to become rich, it leads you into avarice; if for worldly fame, it leads you to pride . . .'[4]

Ambitious parents mapping out for their son a successful career in learning and the priesthood and desiring for him opportunities which they had not had – such an attitude seems commonplace and comprehensible enough. But is this all? Hus also speaks pointedly and feelingly of those 'who in pride prefer to love their relatives more than Christ'.[5] In other words, unlike Christ himself, who did not set out to enrich his own mother – an example Hus himself adduces – sons were encouraged into the priesthood so that in turn they may help their own poor relatives to get on in the world. That real family need should be met, Hus does not dispute. What he sees as evil is the priest who has been encouraged into office and has risen merely to further the security and prosperity of his relatives.

Whatever we may think of this interpretation with reference to the motives of Hus's own parents, the son's desire for worldly fame is clearly indicated in the excerpts we have considered. And this undoubtedly sums up John Hus in the early stage of his career. He was destitute of real spiritual fervour. In fact he himself tells us that, as a boy, and therefore in all likelihood during his time at Prachatice, he took part in the customary mummery of the Christmas period in which there was direct mockery of Christian truth. The 'bishop of the Innocents' was chosen from among the boys, dressed up comically and entered the church backwards on a she-ass. Then there took place a parody of a consecration ceremony, after which they all turned their skin-coats furry side out and, miming animals, danced wildly. Hus admitted, 'While I was still young in years and understanding, I myself made one in this wild rubric.'[6]

Yet, as the fourteenth century has been designated by one important authority as the golden age of the grammar school, we may believe that Hus himself did profit much and that not all his time was taken up with horse-play and wild antics. Indeed, it is unlikely that this would have been tolerated. Since instruction in such schools was mainly oral, few text-books being available, enormous feats of memorization were expected. The aim was not to teach the child to think independently. There were long hours and no school sports – at least not officially organized ones. The aim was to teach the beginner to converse in Latin. As one writer has put it, speaking of medieval grammar schools in general, 'The fare was poor; the punishments, severe. For any misbehaviour, such as speaking one's native tongue, *vae natibus* – "woe to the buttocks!"'[7] There is no reason for thinking that the school at Prachatice was an exception to this rule and certainly Hus had learned this main lesson well, for he was later able to converse, write and preach in Latin with facility and fluency. But soon the time came to leave Prachatice.

Yet another legend deals with the next stage in Hus's career, namely his move to the University of Prague, and once more his mother features in the story. Again she is seen as accompanying him to the city, this time taking from her humble store a goose and a cake for a present to the rector. However, as she journeyed the goose flew away and could not be recaptured. The poor woman, associating this loss with the possible loss of her son and as an ill omen, fell on her knees and commended her son to God. The story draws further meaning from the significance of Hus's name.

However, with the move to Prague University we are certainly not in the realm of legend. This was a very significant moment in the life of Hus. Indeed it was as though Charles IV, who had founded the university in 1348 and who had made it such a focal point in Bohemian life and culture, was doing little more than setting the stage for the entrance and career of Prague's most distinguished student.

Therefore it is towards Prague, its town and university, that we must turn our gaze to understand the next stage in Hus's career.

For the student in those days there was little choice or indeed opportunity in the university world. But for any of the privileged few students the town and university of Prague would surely have rated as very high, probably as the highest in their scale of preference, even if there had been more competition. Much of the planning of this town was conceived in the mind of one man and, because he left his own distinctive imprint upon so much that John Hus inherited, entered into and no doubt enjoyed, we must pause to look at this man and his achievement. Charles IV was the Holy Roman Emperor and King of Bohemia, the father of Wenceslas and Sigismund, two of the men who feature so prominently in the life of Hus himself. A chronicler tells us that, in the year 1348, 'Our Lord Charles, King of the Romans and of Bohemia, laid the first stone, and founded the new city of Prague, building a very strong wall with ramparts and high towers extending from the Castle of Vyšehrad to Poric.'[8] This typified the man. He was supremely the rebuilder of Bohemia, and of Prague in particular.

Charles IV, the son of a warlike father, who characteristically died on the field of battle, was essentially a peace-loving man. In his early years, he dutifully took part in certain campaigns, but as soon as he was master in his own house the sword was laid aside in preference to the supervision of the trowel, the perusal of the scroll and the enjoyment of the choir. Although he had been away from Bohemia since he was seven and had largely forgotten the language, Charles quickly learned it on his return at the age of seventeen.

A man of many parts, who laid at least three wives to rest and accepted their loss with philosophic resignation, Charles has been variously described as 'an odd, small ugly man of genius, who saw in Bohemia both his home and the centre of a European power' or as a 'nervous, restless individual, never still', always with something in his hands, chipping away at pieces of wood (it is suggested that today he would have been a chain-smoker) passing sleepless nights in work and worry.[9]

Yet all the verdicts on Charles are unanimous on one point – he was a truly great king. Says a modern author, 'It is difficult to avoid the conclusion that Charles IV was one of the most civilized monarchs who ever lived.'[10] After a personal visit to Prague, Petrarch, a famous writer of old, commented, 'I own that nowhere and never have I seen anyone so cultured as the emperor and various illustrious men around him, men of prominence and deserving of the highest praise, as could have been born citizens of Athens in Athens.'[11]

Charles sought to create a Czech state and did so with outstanding success, earning himself quite justifiably the title of 'the father of his country'.[12] Perhaps it is customary for men taking up office to magnify somewhat the faults of their predecessors in order to enhance their own achievement, but from what we know of the careless, spendthrift nature of his father, there would seem ample justification for what Charles asserted in his autobiography with regard to his succession to the Bohemian throne. 'We found this kingdom so neglected', he wrote, 'that on our travels we met with no castle which had not been mortgaged, and all its crown lands with it, so that there was no choice but to lodge in a house in the town, like any other citizen. Worst of all, the castle at Prague, deserted since the time of King Ottaker, had fallen into such rubble and ruin that it was beyond repair. We therefore caused to be built at great expense a fine new palace, the palace men see there today.'[13]

Building projects abounded in his reign. Skilled architects were brought into the country. In particular, Peter Parler of Germany and the Frenchman Matthew of Arras have many achievements to their names. The raising of the city of Prague to the status of an archbishopric prompted the building of the Gothic cathedral. Everywhere spires and steeples dominated the skyline. It was appropriately and almost inevitably at this time that the phrase 'hundred-towered Prague' was coined. Yet nothing was haphazard. There were careful planning techniques. The system of streets was symmetrically arranged in relation to three market-places. The height of ordinary roof levels was fixed so that churches and cloisters might tower above them.

As Charles himself caused acres of vineyards to be planted, attractively intertwined among the buildings, it is no surprise that the emperor himself called Prague 'a garden of delight', or that a more impartial observer, the Nuncio Rudolph, enchanted by its beauty, should write as follows: 'There are few countries in the world that can boast of a town whose beauty even remotely approaches that of Prague. I would even say that the Bohemian capital surpasses Nuremberg, Vienna and Wroclaw, even the old Cologne, and I really don't know if such cities as Rome, Venice, Florence and other towns in the world can rival the beauty of this gem set in the heart of Europe.'[14]

We must pause to underline the fact that Hus himself entered into this heritage, a good deal of which has survived to this day. Arguing that Prague is a synthesis of natural beauty and human creativeness, the author of a guide to the art treasures in Eastern Europe says that it is the most beautiful of all cities. Conceding that such claims are made for many more places, he writes that Prague's claim must rest on the abundance of art and architecture concentrated within a small space and also that 'In the old town, with its labyrinth of narrow streets around the ancient Jewish synagogue, the wanderer is transported at a step into the early Middle Ages.'[15] Supporting this, the author of a modern book on architecture states that 'The streets which John Hus knew we walk today.'[16] In face of this, we may well recall the words of the poet who exclaimed as he looked down from a bridge upon another great city,

> Dull would he be of soul who could pass by
> A sight so touching in its majesty.[17]

We have no reason to believe that John Hus was dull of sight. He must surely, though there is little evidence of his feelings in this sphere, have entered into some of the vast artistic inheritance which was, at least in part, available for inspection. The years as a student are usually the years for exploration in these realms and Charles IV had provided through his love of the arts, which was sincere and extensive, an abundance of material. The emperor was the founder of a guild of artists of which painters, sculptors, wood-carvers and goldsmiths were members. It was during this time that the style known as 'the beautiful style', the Czech school of painting and sculpture, originated. A portrait of Peter Parler the younger, stemming from this time, is probably the first self-portrait of an artist known to us. Karlštejn Castle, twenty-three miles from Prague, served both as a country retreat and as a repository for the imperial and royal jewellery, for Charles shared with the Black Prince of England a love of precious stones. Even the emperor's personal physician was a renowned clockmaker, who designed a clock, the complexity of which was such as had never been seen before his time. Talented men seemd to gravitate towards the king.[18]

New schemes were for ever germinating in the Emperor Charles's fertile mind. At the meeting of the Estates at Prague in 1343 Charles made the following statement: 'One of our greatest endeavours is that Bohemia our kingdom, for which we feel greater affection than for any of our other lands, should, through our action, be adorned by a great number of learned men; thus will the faithful inhabitants of that kingdom, who incessantly thirst for the fruits of learning, be no longer obliged to beg for foreign alms, rather will they find a table prepared for them in their own kingdom . . .'[19]

This was but the prelude to his announcement that he was going to found the University of Prague. It immediately attracted many students. The comment of one contemporary chronicler is interesting. 'The university became so great that nothing equal to it existed in Germany, and students came there from all parts of the world – from England, France, Lombardy and Poland, and all the surrounding countries, sons of nobles and princes, and prelates of the church from all parts of the world.'[20] Soon this illustrious centre, drawing from so many nations, was to rival the older institutions of Paris, Bologna and Oxford.

Not all the students were young men. Wealthy men, with their many servants, sometimes enrolled, more with the intention of enjoying the beauties of the city than for the purpose of serious study. The university, like Prague itself, was skilfully planned. For example, when the new university was founded, the New Town was also carefully and deliberately built so that its quiet streets should be freed from the hum of noise caused by the trades and handicrafts carried on in the Old Town. There would be much in the setting for the wealthy to enjoy. There was also the opportunity for real study if they so desired.

There seems little doubt about the emperor's own genuine love of learning. In his autobiography he speaks of 'that love of study which I have tenaciously preserved in my heart'.[21] He had attended in person some lectures at the University of Paris and was relatively widely read. He was, for instance, acquainted with such writers as Boccaccio and Petrarch. The Collegius Carolinum or Charles College, with its excellent library, showed his real practical commitment to the whole project of the university. He would often attend the examination and disputations, dressed in his royal robes, escorted by officers and nobles, sometimes remaining for three or four hours at a time. Apparently he often became so absorbed in listening that upon being reminded by hungry courtiers that it was mealtime, he would reply, 'Go, get your supper – my food is here.'[22]

It has been well argued that, although the emperor left many imposing monuments, none was so significant as the university. It was described later even by those who regretted the influence that Hus had brought to it, as having been originally 'that noble university' which was 'numbered amongst the greatest jewels of our world'.[23] This was not an exaggerated claim. Not surprisingly, John Hus himself could refer to 'the foundation privilege of the University of Prague' in a backward glance at the emperor's love of learning and in an appreciative comment on the emperor's desire that the table should be spread for Czech students in their own kingdom.[24] In a commemoration sermon he was also to refer to Charles as a 'protector of the church, lover of the clergy, builder of churches'.[25] We can envisage the young man up from the country drinking in the beauties of the city itself and counting himself highly privileged to be at the seat of learning, the country's only university city.

What kind of institution would Hus have found when he came up as a freshman? It would surely have been a university already conscious of its own status and achievement. Unlike the other universities which had grown up more haphazardly, it had been founded deliberately. Most of the masters who taught kept houses in which students could lodge, and carried on their teaching there. In this way the image of the vast impersonal institution would have been considerably softened. There would have been much more intimacy in this kind of system. Teachers would know some students very well.

However, there were also the beginnings of a collegiate system, even in Hus's day. As far back as 1366 Charles had founded the Charles College, which housed a dozen men. His own son, Wenceslas IV, founded a college in 1380. This also bore his own name and seemed to be exclusively for art students and theologians, who had living-quarters and lecture rooms in it. This college, to which Hus eventually went as a mature student, was to prove a breeding-ground for the reform movement.

In a contemporary note we find this brief allusion to Hus's sojourn there: 'Therefore we, the young Bohemian students of Prague – John Hus and Jerome of Prague along with Jakoubek of Stříbro and Marek of Hradec and others – dwelt in the College of King Wenceslas.'[26] It is a fascinating glimpse especially because Jerome was such a firm friend of Hus throughout the years that lay ahead and was himself to be burned by the same council which condemned Hus. Jakoubek also was to be a staunch supporter of reform until his death some fifteen years after that of Hus himself. But here we see them no longer as 'freshmen' – for friendships had been formed – but still as young men, and in all likelihood conscious of the fact, living together, dreaming dreams, the world at their feet, the future stretching invitingly before them. Like all students they indulged in nicknames and word-plays. Hence Jakoubek became Jacobellus, which is a diminutive, and it is most likely that Hus's frequent punning on his own name, which means 'Goose', was lavishly employed here.

The university possessed all four faculties – law, medicine, arts and theology. This was rare at this time. There were also – and this, too, was unusual – elements of democracy insofar as, theoretically at least, sovereign authority rested with a general congregation of all the members of the university. Such meetings were to be held twice a year and only the congregation was permitted to alter the statutes of the university. Since it was difficult to carry out decisions in so large and democratic a body, eventually its control passed over to a 'council' of eight persons elected by all the 'nations'. Nevertheless the democratic temper may well have acted as a stimulus to the student body to think vigorously and question established institutions.

Certainly we must not underestimate the importance of the university in the life of the town. The judgement of a modern historian would seem to be in accordance with the facts when he writes, 'Shortly after its foundation, the student body was more than 7,000 in a city of some 40,000, and inevitably began to be considered as an important social and political factor.'[27] Hus had come to a place which was to have a shaping influence first on the whole town of Prague, then on the whole Bohemian kingdom and ultimately on most countries of Europe. He could not have foreseen this. But it is hard not to imagine that he felt and knew that he had come to one of the vital centres of the nation's life. Indeed, a scholar who has written a monumental study of universities of Europe in the Middle Ages points to 'the importance of universities as centres for the growth of reformation movements, particularly the universities which possessed a faculty of theology'.[28] Consequently we may see the university as precisely the place of God's appointing for John Hus.

Nor must we forget the intimate and important link with the town in general. Sometimes it might be in the form of indignation and even legislation against rioting students and we have evidence of this. Street brawls were commonplace. In 1374 the authorities of the university came to an agreement with the powers-that-be in the city whereby the city-guards were empowered to arrest and hand over to the rector turbulent and rioting students. Such scenes were not peculiar to Prague. 'Violence was an almost inescapable condition of medieval life including that of students at the university,' comments one authority, adding that in their merry pranks and jovial pastimes 'They fought not only among themselves, quarrelling over dogs, slashing off one another's fingers with swords, and rushing, with their tonsured heads unprotected, into conflicts, that would have made a fully armed knight hesitate, but they also broke into houses, attacked citizens and abused women.'[29] Such incidents among students are not, as is well known, confined to medieval times.

Although Hus himself was later to view a city torn with riots because of his own ministry in it, this still lay on the distant horizon. More important for him during the next years, with regard to this link-up between town and gown, was the simple fact that the leading theologians of Prague held parochial cures in the town, and preached in Czech to townsmen and students. It is also clear that many of the more controversial university debates were indeed rapidly reported to the local people, who were genuinely keen to hear the news, even waiting for the latest bits of information to be conveyed to them. John Hus had indeed moved to the centre of things and much was to happen at that centre over the next two decades.

# 3.
# The student years

What else would John Hus have found in the early years of his time in Prague? He would soon have realized that the peaceful days under Charles IV had passed. It was a turbulent time. Wenceslas IV had succeeded to the kingdom of his father in 1378. He is often seen as a kind of Caliban, 'half-clownish, half-vicious' and the judgement does seem apt that there were two apparently irreconcilable aspects of the king: 'the one serious, benevolent, just; and the other furious, full of contradictory caprices'.[1]

Some of the stories about Wenceslas are, it is to be hoped, the exaggerations of opponents who fiercely resented the fact that later he gave a real measure of support and protection to Hus. Although friends claimed that he was handsome, others said that he was sired by a cobbler, born ugly and deformed, and responsible for the death of his mother at birth. Such wild fabrications can be ignored. He has also been depicted as a kind of wild boar, constantly on the rampage at night, accompanied by frenzied companions, bursting into the homes of respectable citizens in order to rape their wives and on one occasion roasting a cook who served him a burnt meal. In some of this there is an element of truth (he did roam the streets disguised and with wild companions) but also much exaggeration. Other crude stories about him are scarcely repeatable.

Yet it would seem that his second wife, Sophia of Bavaria, showed true insight into his character when on her marriage to him in 1389 she brought with her to Prague a waggon-load of skilful conjurers and jugglers. It was certainly the kind of wedding present that would have appealed to him. He loved pleasure, spending months in the woods and forests, to the neglect of government, and in all likelihood the seasons of wild rage were due to the fact that he was an alcoholic. With reckless abandon he had with a stroke of the pen sold large tracts of land. For cart-loads of his favourite wine, it seemed that he would assent to almost any hair-brained scheme.

In 1398 it was his responsibility in his office of Holy Roman Emperor to discuss with the King of France and the Avignon pope the problem of the papacy and the existence of two rival popes. One historian has vividly described the amusing and yet tragic nature of this encounter, a scene surely typical in some measure of so many round-table conferences between leaders. 'The Emperor, Wenceslas,' writes G. C. Coulton, 'was a confirmed drunkard, and could do no business but quite early in the morning. The King, Charles VI, was seldom sane, but there was most sense in him later in the day when he had eaten and drunken. The Pope (or anti-Pope), sober and sane enough in other ways, was less sane politically, less able to listen to reason where his own power and dignity were concerned, than either the drunkard or the lunatic.'[2]

In 1389, a year before Hus was at the university, there was a notorious pogrom among the Jews. It was alleged that a priest leading a procession through the Jewish quarter of Prague was stoned by a Jewish child, causing the townspeople to slaughter a large number of the Jewish community. However, when the survivors pleaded with the king for justice he declared that they deserved their punishment and then fined the survivors, rather than those who were responsible for the outrage. There was another incident when the king tortured a group of priests who had opposed his will and had the body of one who had failed to survive the ordeal unceremoniously dumped in the Vltava river. There was a real and frightening undercurrent of violence at this time. Sadly true justice could in no wise be expected from the king in any consistent manner. Vehemently and publicly he had clashed with both Jewish and Roman Catholic leaders.

Nor was Wenceslas popular with the majority of his own nobility. He had battles with them over the administration of the law as he sought increasingly to limit their powers. They in turn came back with their demands and even imprisoned the king for a period. They also strongly resented the fact that in his numerous escapades and hunting expeditions he preferred the company of low-born grooms to their own. All through these years these dissensions rumbled on and flared up spasmodically. Thus in 1397 the nobles openly expressed disapproval of his manner of governing, contrasting him unfavourably with his father Charles who, they asserted, 'did not summon a cohort of burghers and labourers to serve in his high council'.[3] Between 1394 and 1403, the nobles, concluding a series of armed leagues, forced the king, albeit reluctantly, to accept their point of view.

What all this meant was that, because there were frequent distractions and unsettled conditions, Wenceslas, even if he had had the inclination, had little time for looking into the movement for reform that was, under the sovereign hand of God, developing at his university. It is also important to realize that, despite her marriage gift, Queen Sophia was certainly a devout and eager hearer of the Word of God during the greater part of Hus's own ministry. We cannot tell at what period her thoughts turned in a true and genuine way to the living God, but, if it were during this early period, it would obviously have meant that any preachers, lecturers or students beginning to dig earnestly into the truths of sacred Scripture would have had a friendly voice speaking on their behalf in the ear of the king.

The young Hus would also have found that, apart from all this, the main cause of the rivalry and hostility of his boyhood years had not evaporated in the rarified atmosphere of study in Prague university. Far from it! The cleavage between Czech and German was writ large on the university scene. There was considerable resentment by the Czechs of the German dominance, and there were obvious grounds for this. Because of the founder's desire to attract people from all nations, the university was a very cosmopolitan place but, because votes were given to each of the Saxon, Bavarian and Polish nations, as well as to the Czech nationals, and because Germans predominated in both the Bavarian and Polish group, ultimately they outnumbered the Bohemians by three to one.

These rivalries affected many aspects of university life. They even affected academic disputes. It has been argued with cogency that because the Germans as a whole accepted one point of view in theology, namely nominalism, the Czechs automatically took the rival view and embraced the realist position. This would seem to be a very abstract matter and we shall not engage in an explanation of the rival theological systems. Suffice it to say that it is but an illustration of the way the two groups tended to polarize automatically and oppose each other at every point, regardless of the issue itself.

As competition for university places and for a place to live was even stronger then than it is today, there were other aspects of the German dominance which would have caused dismay among the Czechs. Not only the Carolinum, but also the college founded by Wenceslas was being filled by Germans against the express intentions of the founders. The same thing was to happen in the new college founded in 1397 by Queen Hedwig of Poland, which was intended specifically for poor students from Lithuania.

But it was not just a question of securing proper entry and accommodation. The Czechs were constantly confronted with these issues during the study courses and also in the very mundane matter of finding employment at the end of the course. All the jobs seemed to be going to one side. Since we take the following statement from a close and warm personal friend of Hus, one who grew up with him as a student in this divided community, we are obviously listening in to the kind of debates and murmurings that agitated the student world of the day and the circles where Hus himself moved. The following paragraph gives the heartfelt utterance of Jerome of Prague. His indignation is unconcealed. At the beginning of his speech he is, of course, speaking of the emperor.

'This same Charles, being King of Bohemia, saw that it was a rich country, not lacking in food, gold or silver, but only in educated men, and that his subjects had to go outside the realm to acquire learning, to Paris and other places to get the degree of master or doctor. Therefore the Lord Charles, wishing to endow the kingdom of Bohemia and the city of Prague, founded and built a university there. In that university many Germans secured prebends and fellowships, so that the Czechs had nothing. And when a Czech had graduated in arts, if he had no other means of livelihood, he had to go to the towns and villages and earn his living by teaching in some private school. The Germans were in complete control of the University of Prague and of all its benefices; they held the seal of the foundation and all the insignia. Also they had three votes in the university . . . Whatever the Germans wanted in the university was as good as done. The Bohemians could do nothing.'[4]

In actual fact it could not be said that the Bohemians were totally excluded from every sphere. From early days there had been some Czech teachers, although they were in the minority. To some extent there was a growth in the Czech element. For example, in the arts faculty during the 1380s about twenty-five per cent of the graduates were from the Bohemian nation. By the year 1400 it had risen to thirty-six per cent. 'Where the Bohemian nation in early years had provided some ten per cent of the deans in the faculty – an elective office – they were providing almost forty per cent by the years 1391 to 1408,' is an interesting statistic and especially so since it covers the years when Hus himself was studying there.[5] Hus himself was to occupy this very office. The local people, with their acute national consciousness, must have been aware of their own growing strength in the university's affairs, as well as their frustration.

Not only did the rivalries of his early years pursue Hus to the university but in addition the poverty of those years did not relinquish its grip, at least in his early years. The bull granted by the pope for the founding of the university mentioned that Prague was 'abounding in food, and the other necessaries of life'.[6] It may well have been so when the bull was granted (1347) though even then it was highly unlikely that everyone partook of this lavish spread. Yet it must be admitted that even towards the end of the century the Italian humanist, Umberto Decembrio, wrote of Prague: 'Never have I seen so many people, nor a town so rich and overflowing with all kinds of goods.'[7]

However, by the time of Hus's sojourn there was considerable poverty. The stagnant Czech balance of trade, compensated for occasionally by the exportation of native silver, gradually began to crush the rural population, the local aristocracy and the poor of the cities. Contemporary records show that many prices were rising, that butchers were often charging the poor people far too high prices, and that the profits of a dealer in Italian cloth dropped so markedly between 1383 and 1401 that he had to sell up and leave Prague. Most interesting of all is the information that a holder of a benefice at St Vitus Cathedral received almost twenty times as much daily as a bricklayer. Much of the prosperity, as well as the peace, of the reign of Charles had vanished.

Certain provisions were made for the poor student. He was generally exempted from the strict requirements concerning academic dress. 'At Prague the criterion was simply financial. All students with an income of less than twelve florins per year were classified as "poor" provided they could take an oath to this effect to their master or to the rector,' observes one modern writer.[8] The same authority goes on to say that masters who were clearly out for financial rewards were often forbidden to withhold tuition from poor students who could not pay the fees. Yet at Prague in 1400 action had to be taken against masters who were seeking to find loopholes in this. Quite clearly not all academics were imbued with altruism or sheer love of study. There were also fees to be paid for the certificate of graduation, with the proviso that they would be waived for very poor students.

Students have always resented means tests. Hus was no exception. Much of this was felt as a humiliation. We shall see when we look at his conversion that he had a love of the academic robes and regalia and of the easy life. To be at a disadvantage because of poverty would be a smarting experience. Hus certainly was at a disadvantage. We know that in his early years as a student he certainly did not partake of rich fare. In his quaint manner Hus tells us of the time when his only food was made up of a scant diet of bread and peas. 'As I,' he wrote, 'when I was a hungry little student, made a spoon out of bread till I had eaten the peas, and then I ate the spoon also.'[9] It was a poignant and deeply felt recollection.

In our own century a group of English historians presented a series of essays to the Caroline University of Prague on the occasion of its six-hundredth anniversary. Writing of Hus's own period, one contributor says, 'Students expected support from rich patrons, from benefices, and from the higher clergy as well as from the court; some lived by begging, letter-writing, or servile attendance upon richer companions.'[10] It has been inferred by at least one writer that Hus had at one stage to resort to begging, and had to sleep on the bare ground. If this were so, it must have completed the sense of humiliation from which the poor student must have suffered.

Presumably Hus had at this time sought to supplement his inadequate income by earning a little money singing in some church choir. In later life he referred to this. 'When I was a student and sang vigils with others, we sang them rapidly just to get the job done quickly,' he said.[11] Quite clearly singing in the choir was often done then with as little seriousness as it is done in many cases today. But it is interesting that he also went on to say that they often were robbed of their income by the man in charge of them. Obviously this was money he could ill afford to lose. It was no doubt from strong personal feelings that later, after writing of various modes of extortion, he added, 'The masters who torment the poor students are guilty of the same sin.'[12]

In religious terms John Hus was surrounded by medievalism and what must unambiguously be labelled 'spurious Christianity'. In great measure Charles IV, despite his support of some reformist preachers, was responsible for this. To be sure, he was an assiduous builder of churches. Characteristically he had also set out to collect all the religious orders not found in the city. 'The variety of architectural styles which these churches displayed was as great as that of the robes their clergy wore,' is one apt description which links together his prime concern for architecture and religious orders.[13]

Religious feelings and economic interests combined to make him a relic collector *par excellence*. In fact, relics were added to his treasure almost yearly, from both the empire and the kingdom, so that Prague gradually became a place of pilgrimage for the whole of Europe. That he had the walls of Saint Wenceslas's Chapel in the cathedral and of the Chapels at Karlštejn decorated with a polished masonry of blue and red stones set in gilded plaster was typical of him and very revealing. Here he kept a vast collection of relics, including the 'piece of the true cross' in the Chapel of the Holy Rood. Apparently the castle was erected according to a progression of degrees of holiness and the external might of each tower was related to the value of what it was intended to preserve and defend. The Chapel of the Virgin was painted with scenes depicting Charles' collection of relics, including one of him receiving the relic of the true cross. He also loved to gather illuminated manuscripts, and a standard encyclopedia of music affirms that this was the 'golden age of the arts in Bohemia' – incidentally pinpointing the fact that the liturgical music was largely a cultural exercise, as it so often is.[14]

Although the jibes against Charles, that he was but 'the parson's king' or 'the Pope's errand boy', would seem to be unwarranted, it must be conceded that for the most part he was orthodox and loyal in the medieval sense. In 1323 he had been sent as a boy to be brought up in Paris. Years later he met again his former tutor Peter Roger, who was now a cardinal. In his autobiography Charles narrates how the cardinal said to him, 'You will one day be king of the Romans' and how he replied, 'But before that you will be pope.'[15] Both predictions came true and Charles was ever a loyal friend of the pope.

In fact Charles was careful to secure papal support for his university. This was given in the form of a bull in January 1347. The university was intended to be a bastion of Roman Catholic orthodoxy with the Archbishop of Prague appointed as chancellor. To be sure Charles did encourage reformist preachers, even forgiving one for castigating him publicly as the Antichrist, but the evidence is strong for his enthusiasm for ritual rather than for personal devotion to Christ. In this connection it must not be forgotten that he was the author of stern decrees against beghards, a group opposed to Roman Catholic claims, and was in favour of the Inquisition. Therefore much of his enlightenment would appear to have been cultural rather than Christian.

A layman who wrote at this very time, and who was an exact contemporary of Hus, threatened with the pains of hell those who 'collect bones beneath the gallows or cut bits off the flesh of those who have been hanged; those who baptize frogs, mandragoras or bones, or who consecrate mistletoe'.[16] There certainly were some strange practices and the same writer vehemently castigates those who, like the heathen, honoured saints merely for temporal gain, pointing out the folly of those who appealed to St Stephen so that they might have success with horses. In his view, St Stephen had something better to do than concern himself with horses!

Clearly not all were at home in this medievalism, at least not with true heartfelt fervour. Among the objects most frequently pawned by unemployed labourers were crucifixes. While this may provide evidence of the fact that many people possessed them, it does not provide much evidence of the esteem with which they were supposed to be held. Yet at first John Hus himself was undoubtedly at home in this atmosphere. It was but a more flamboyant and rich expression of the religion of his boyhood. It may be that the emperor's interests had in some degree affected religion in the rural areas. There certainly had been influence: for example, when Charles built the Saint Vitus Cathedral in Prague, the owners of the Kutná Hora silver mines decided to erect a magnificent Church of Saint Barbara, the patron saint of the mining folk of the town. But whether or not Hus had been strongly influenced in his own home area by the emperor's particular measures, he certainly shared the outlook that it typified.

In 1393 there was a special indulgence available since it was a jubilee year. There were in fact scandalous arrangements between Pope Boniface IX and King Wenceslas, according to which the jubilee indulgence was granted to pilgrims visiting four Prague churches. A half of their offerings at the church of St Peter on the Vyšehrad were granted to the king. If later events in the time of Luther are anything to go by, Hus and others would probably be ignorant of this transaction. But at this time Hus was in ignorance generally. He went unthinkingly along with the crowd and, poor though he was, spent his last four pennies in the purchase of an indulgence. As it was his last bit of income we see that he must have believed in the whole procedure. With reference to the period when he accepted all this ritualism and even felt it was right to kneel before the pope and kiss his golden slippers, he confessed that since in his heart 'I did not know the Scriptures well and life of my Saviour, I thought it well done'.[17]

Yet there were other influences of which Hus could not fail to be aware. Milič was a reformist preacher whose ministry in earlier years had been so successful among the immoral that a refuge for penitent prostitutes was erected. It was called 'Jerusalem'. That Milič's ministry had been effective among all classes can be seen from the fact that, after his death, among those seeking to preserve this refuge for its original purpose were to be numbered Angelo 'the apothecary', Machuta 'the cloth-cutter' and Kříž 'the shopkeeper' along with a lord and various priests.

Kříž was also a principal moving force in the founding of the Bethlehem Chapel in 1391, when Hus was a youthful student. The very founding of this chapel is an indication of two things. One is that there had been some biblical preachers in Prague, and that their ministry had been fruitful. Kříž had obviously been deeply influenced, as had another follower of Milič. The one donated the ground and the other made provision for the payment of the preacher, taking into account his need of books and also optimistically envisaging a time when perhaps two preachers of the gospel might be supported. The other truly amazing thing indicated by this event was in fact the dire need in the area for the preaching of the gospel. The foundation charter for the building stated that although there were numerous buildings in the area for sacred services there was no one single place where the Word of God might be preached. It went on to declare that 'The preachers in Czech are, for the most part, forced to make use of houses and hiding places – which is unworthy.'[18] Even Charles IV had ultimately joined with the pope of his day in proclaiming a decree against all books, texts and sermons written in the vernacular. The decree declared that such should be burned.

However, it was specified that in the Bethlehem Chapel preaching must be in the native language. A small house was built for the preacher. The chapel was most appropriately called 'Bethlehem', which means 'house of bread', in order that, as it was stated in the foundation charter, believers might 'be refreshed by the bread of holy preaching'.[19] Expectations were more than realized. The place was thronged regularly. There was an evident hunger for the Word of God in the hearts of many.

Particularly would this hunger of people to hear the Word of God have been met under the fervent preaching of Matthew of Janov, who occupied another pulpit in the town of Prague. He was a man with a very decided conversion experience. Here is part of his own testimony: 'As long as the "thick wall" of desire for riches and worldly fame surrounded me and obscured the atmosphere, up to that time as a prisoner or a drunkard, I reposed softly. My only endeavour was to dwell splendidly "in painted tents", and as one who dwelleth in an inn, I reflected and thought of nothing but that which attracts the eyes and rejoices the ears. This lasted till it pleased the Lord Jesus to snatch me away from these walls, as a burning brand plucked out of the fire . . . And the Lord led me to the dwelling of sorrow, adversity, shame, and contempt. Now, only when I had become poor and of a contrite spirit, and trembled at the word of the Lord, I began to wonder at the truths of Holy Scripture, and how they have been necessarily, irrevocably and continually fulfilled in the whole and in all parts.'[20]

Like Milič before him, who spoke of Scripture as 'uncreated truth', Matthew was clear about his source of authority. The ultimate appeal must not be to the 'wisdom of this world or of the princes of this world, which perishes, but to the wisdom, which is from God, and the divinely inspired Scripture, which is serviceable for teaching, for expounding, for reproving and for instructing in justice, so that the perfected man of God may be made ready for every good work'.[21] Here the preacher is quoting the apostle Paul's great statement on the inspiration and authority of Scripture in 2 Timothy 3:14–17. Elsewhere, in more personal vein, he wrote, 'The Bible from my youth have I greatly loved and called my very friend and bride . . . soon was my spirit fixed in lasting love of the Bible. And indeed I confess that, from my youth up into old age and decline, whether on the road or at home, when busy or when idle, still this love has not left me.'[22]

There would be no doubts in the minds of his hearers

about the pointedness of the preacher's message and its direct application. Bohemians were roundly challenged as being prone above all else to 'gluttony'. Women with their 'horned' appearance looked like 'perfect beasts'. Their head-dresses were built up into three horns, they made two horns out of their breasts by making them stick out and they had two horns on their feet 'in the shape of the long pointed shoes they wear'. Those nobles who fight duels with edged weapons were castigated for refusing to be reconciled and for persisting in a fight, 'knowing full well that one or the other of them must be killed and go to hell'.[23]

Yet there would also be more clearly recognizable evangelical notes that would confront the young Hus if he listened to Matthew. He would hear that baptismal grace was not enough and that, in effect, a person who had been christened as a child needed to be converted. Superstitious veneration of images and statues of the Saviour, the Virgin Mary and the saints was firmly opposed. Matthew deplored the fact that common people put greater trust in prayers to the saints than to Jesus Christ. To use his own words, the preacher looked forward to the time when the 'works of men, ordinances, and ceremonies will be utterly extirpated, cut up by the roots and cease – and God alone will be exalted, and his word will abide for ever'.[24]

This would be strong stuff and heady wine for one reared on the ritualism and pomp of medievalism. Matthew, as might be expected, was frequently in trouble with the authorities, and there is evidence that on one occasion he did recant, albeit insincerely. This would be when he was arraigned before the synod in 1388. In 1392, when Hus was still in his first years at the university, Matthew was twice summoned before the authorities. Two years later he died. But as he was a prolific writer as well as a stirring preacher, it is well nigh inconceivable that Hus would not know of the biblical forthrightness and stirring challenge of his ministry. What ideas were thus being sown in the mind of the young student? The next chapter provides the answer.

# 4.
# The dawn of grace

In 1390, at about the age of eighteen, Hus became a member of the student body. He seems to have been a fairly diligent student. The cautious bent to his mind, the careful weighing of all aspects of a problem, so evident later on, seems to have been already present in those days for, as he tells us in a moment of reminiscence, in his work on the Trinity, 'From the earliest time of my studies I have set up for myself the rule that whenever I discern a sounder opinion on any matter whatsoever, I gladly and humbly abandon the earlier one. For I know that those things I have learned are but the least in comparison with what I do not know.'[1] He was certainly no idler, even if not in the very top rank of scholarship.

In the university syllabus, as in that of the grammar school, there was much learning by rote. The aim of medieval education was not in the first place to bring about independence of thought. It was rather to enable the student to grasp and grapple with all the accumulated wisdom of the past and then more or less reproduce it as one's own thought. Originality, far from being the prime requirement, was often frowned upon. 'If you borrow from one man they call it "plagiarism"; if you borrow from a thousand, they call it research,' is a modern saying. In the medieval context such vast and thorough-going borrowing would have been called first-rate scholarship and proper learning.

In the curriculum Hus studied Aristotle, Virgil and Cato, along with other authors, and it was customary to prove one's point by citing many authorities – the more the better. In addition to attending two more formal lectures a day, the student was given private tuition by the teacher in the latter's room. Because of the strong emphasis on disputation, ability to make fine distinctions was often the dubious recipe for success. Some of the distinctions were exceedingly finicky and hair-splitting, to say the least. At the final examination, after the examiners had been satisfied that the prescribed books had been read, each student had to undergo a public assessment and show aptitude for debate.

During the 1390s some students were bringing over from England works by one called John Wyclif, a man with a great passion for biblical reform. The sister of Wenceslas, Anne, had married Richard II of England. This marriage had been arranged at the instigation of the Roman Pope Urban VI, who dreaded lest Bohemia should ally itself with France and thus acknowledge his rival at Avignon. By a stroke of divine irony this scheming was to rebound on the papacy with devastating effect. It greatly strengthened the connection between the two countries and ensured that many brought over from England what was already regarded by Rome as subversive literature of a very dangerous type.

A song composed in the years that followed put the issue very clearly from Rome's standpoint:

> The devil sent us Englis;
> He walks stealthily through Prague,
> Spreading doctrines from England
> That are not wholesome for the Bohemians.[2]

The connection between Oxford and Prague University was for a period quite close because of this marriage alliance. Hus himself wrote in 1411 that he had been reading Wyclif's works for twenty years or more, which would mean that soon after entry into the university in 1391 he had been exposed to the influence of the English reformer.

Since the works of Wyclif then available at Prague were mainly his philosophical, rather than his theological works, we cannot deduce with clear warrant that Hus at this early stage was markedly influenced in an evangelical direction. It is nevertheless hard to believe that some seeds were not being sown. Thus in a manuscript of Wyclif copied by Hus in 1398, and now kept at Stockholm, Hus had written in the margin: 'Wyclif, Wyclif, you will unsettle many a man's mind'; or 'What you have now read is worth a gulden . . .'; and 'May God grant Wyclif the kingdom of heaven.'[3] What we do know is that, in his maturity, Hus, stating that Anne, wife of King Richard II, had taken with her to England the Scriptures in Latin, Bohemian and German, thoroughly commended her for this and affirmed that to accuse her of heresy for possessing these translations was 'Luciferan silliness' or, as we might say, diabolical stupidity.[4] It may be that in Anne we have an unsung heroine of this whole story, but the evidence is too slight for us to say more.

In 1393 Hus received his Bachelor of Arts degree. If he were then teaching as a bachelor, as was common, he would be restricted as to what he could teach. Yet there are no grounds for believing that at this time he wished to be other than conformist. He was eager to get on. Indeed the man who promoted him for his bachelor's degree mentioned that Hus had been ill because he had put his studies and the cultivation of his mind before care for his body. During this next period Hus, on becoming a servant, which must be seen as a much coveted promotion rather than a despised menial position, found that his living conditions were vastly improved, for, on receiving this post, he went to live in the Carolinum, the largest of all the colleges. He was given the use of a free room and all his meals. Gone now were the days when he had to eke out a meagre allowance of peas eaten with a bread spoon.

There would also be access to books in the library and perhaps most significantly of all, in view of God's ultimate purpose of public ministry, he would be able to listen in regularly to the conversations of the leading men within the university and theological life of the city. He was thus getting the feel of the nation's pulse and also learning to face the issues which were of paramount importance in the church of his day, as well as receiving his first unpleasant, though necessary, lessons in ecclesiastical politics. The importance of this last aspect must not be under-estimated.

Hus went on to study for his master's degree, which he received in 1396. Since fees had to be paid before the reception of both the bachelor's and master's degrees, and since the candidate had also to hold a banquet at his own expense for all the participants, it would seem that Hus had managed to get together this sum of money by some means or other. As there were other expenses to be met, such as the little matter of giving the presiding master and promoter each a pair of gloves, it was something that an impecunious student would be very relieved to see behind him. Hus might well be pleased to have a little of all this returned on becoming a master. On that occasion he himself 'received a silken master's biretta, a pair of gloves, a golden ring, an open book, and – for good measure – a kiss' as Matthew Spinka finely puts it.[5]

There is clear evidence that in the same year that Hus received his master's degree he was teaching in the Faculty of Arts. Indeed, when the degree was received, the master had to promise that he would teach at Prague University for two years and at no other during that time. As yet Hus was only in his early twenties. His mind was fresh and alert. It needed to be, for as a master he continued to study for his doctorate, a lengthy course often lasting some ten years and one which he never completed because of the turn of events. During this period he lectured on several books of the Bible. Hus was also grappling with the well-known and frequently studied writings of Peter Lombard. By now Hus was probably not reading uncritically. At least we do know that this was not so when he had to write about Lombard on a later occasion. Confronted with abstract comments on matters of no real value, such as whether angels were capable of paternity or maternity, or whether the heavens are like a barrel or a sphere, Hus tersely remarked, 'Let them sleep.'[6] In other words, Hus acknowledged that the issues were remote and unreal and better left alone.

What of his religious life at this time? Those who write about Hus in his early life often speak as though he were without gross sin and when he mentions sin seem to assess it as many speak of Bunyan's early failings – as exaggerated peccadilloes or as an almost pathological sense of guilt. Indeed, as regards immorality, drunkenness or sins of a glaring nature, it would certainly seem that Hus was without offence. If he had been guilty of such, his detractors, and they were many, would have dredged them up and broadcast them to the world, and it is noteworthy that they could find nothing.

All would seem to have agreed in attributing to him an outwardly pure character. Especially interesting is the tribute of the Jesuit writer, Balbinus, who could not in any way be expected to be favourably disposed towards Hus. He testifies, 'John Hus was even more remarkable for his acuteness than his eloquence; but the modesty and severity of his conduct, his austere and irreproachable life, his pale and melancholy features, his gentleness and affability to all, even the most humble, persuaded more than the greatest eloquence.'[7] Another testimony is that of Aeneas Sylvius, a man destined to occupy the papal chair, who wrote that Hus was 'a powerful speaker, and distinguished for the reputation of a life of remarkable purity'.[8]

Such testimonies, though clearly referring primarily to his later ministry, do also support the view that his early life was without obvious taint or weakness. It is even told how as a student he loved to pore over stories of martyrs. Once, apparently, while reading the history of one who was put to death by being roasted on a gridiron, Hus thrust his hand into the fire to test his own constancy and power of endurance and see whether he would be able to endure the torture of martyrdom. A friend who was present intervened and prevented any real harm. If this story were true, it would indicate a morbid religious sensibility, even fanaticism of the medieval kind, rather than furnishing a prophetic view of forthcoming events, as is often claimed.

Yet Hus also tells us, in a revealing passage in a letter, of his regrets for wasted hours before he entered the priesthood. The occasion may seem trivial but it is of real significance. Writing to a fellow priest, Hus appealed thus: 'I beg you, however, for the sake of the mercies of Jesus Christ, not to follow me in any levity that you have seen in me. You know that – alas! – before I became a priest, I had gladly and often played chess, had wasted time, and by that play had frequently unhappily provoked to anger both myself and others. Therefore, on account also of countless other faults which I have committed, I entrust myself, by your prayers, to the most merciful Lord for his pardon . . .'[9]

That Hus should have a conscience about matters of this nature might seem ridiculous to some, although in our own day we have seen enough evidence that sport can lead to bitterness, hostility and even violence. Even chess contests between Russians loyal to the regime and those in exile can be the source of endless intrigue and argument. Certainly throughout this whole period chess games often seemed a source of trouble, however absurd this may seem. One writer describing life in Chaucer's England tells how they regularly led to gambling and quarrels. There is extant a picture of a game of chess which appears in a book dealing with the Middle Ages. It shows a violent quarrel between the two players. Chess pieces are strewn all over the floor. A small group of onlookers gaze with consternation as one of the infuriated players raises aloft the chess board with the obvious intent of bringing it crashing down on his opponent's head.[10]

However, as well as the bitterness engendered, Hus seems also to have in mind the waste of time involved. He had not been serving God aright. His attitude to chess simply illustrated but one facet of his general rebellion against God. Likewise his attitude to God's providential dealings had not been submissive and truly 'of faith', for, as he relates elsewhere: 'I confess that before I had known better, I grieved for the death of a good man or grumbled about bad weather, as if I could do better than the Almighty.'[11] He had a complaining spirit, being guilty of the sin of 'murmuring' against God and his ways – a sin which Scripture so strongly condemns.

Yet it may be that Hus himself gives us another clue to the still deeper significance of the chess-playing incident in his own life. He speaks on one occasion of the evil practices of lay patrons in dealing out offices to unworthy clergymen and in so doing describes those who 'appoint a priest for the sake of companionship, since he can go hunting with the patron, or can play chess or other games with him'.[12] The interpretation we are giving is supported by a brief but fascinating book, which gives the history of the game of chess. After pointing out that chess was listed by one medieval writer as being among the seven knightly accomplishments, the writer gives a whole list of examples of nobility playing chess, as recorded in medieval literature and then concludes, 'This association of the nobility with chess was so characteristic that for one of the lower rank to admit a knowledge of chess was sufficient to raise suspicions as to his identity.'[13]

The same writer also observes that 'Among chess-players of noble rank from the period 1100–1500 may be named Pope Gregory XI (1370–8, or was it Gregory XII, 1406–9?), whose valuable chessboard passed later into the possession of the kings of France . . .'[14] If it were indeed Gregory XII, then this is the very pope who, as we shall see, was prominently involved at the time when Hus himself was first in conflict with the church authorities. It would seem that in the case of Gregory chess-playing, together with skilful manoeuvres of other kinds, had brought much success in the promotion battle. In the eyes of some this would have been the ultimate in success! No doubt many humble clerics set their targets lower.

Therefore is it not extremely likely that Hus felt such strong revulsion towards what seems a fairly innocuous game because it was a game played mostly by the upper classes and that, in his own youth, Hus had seen his skill in it as one of the ways of ingratiating himself with some well-to-do person and thus obtaining preferment unworthily? Does this not satisfactorily explain what otherwise might seem to be excessive feelings? This argument is also supported by what he says of his wrong motives in entering the priesthood, as we will see in a moment.

The exact date of Hus's conversion cannot be ascertained with certainty. We have seen how in his first years at university he had accepted Roman dogma and practice with complete loyalty and been largely ignorant of the Scriptures. It is clear that as long as wealth and security were tied up with being a loyal Roman Catholic Hus had of himself no desire to break rank. We have seen how the church was the great land-owner and how the incomes of many clergymen far exceeded that of other men. Hus is quite frank about his motives in entering holy orders. He declared in one of his last works: 'I confess to have entertained an evil desire when I was a young student, for I had thought to become a priest quickly in order to secure a good livelihood and dress and to be held in esteem by men. But I recognized this as an evil desire when I comprehended the Scriptures.'[15]

Just before he penned these words Hus spoke of the

security and indeed abundance that characterized the lives of monks, stating that 'Kings, lords, and princes do not always have drink and food so wholesome and so certain. The cellars of lay people are sometimes exhausted; but theirs never! The king and the lords sometimes lack in baked and cooked food, or in bread; but for them bread of the finest and whitest flour is never lacking.'[16]

Yet it was not only monks who had ample security and warmth. Priests could often aim as high. According to Hus himself, 'They buy much unnecessary household furnishing such as silver plate, cups, spoons, pillows, magnificent beds, and many other things . . . they build excessively expensive houses; they pull down good dwellings in which they could live comfortably and build new ones. And as soon as they dislike these latter, they promptly again pull them down and erect others.'[17] Here is what our own age has called 'psychological obsolescence' with a vengeance. It was a tempting prospect for anyone without real spiritual moorings and principles of cross-bearing.

It will have been noticed how earlier we recorded his observations on the priests who 'eat, gorge themselves, guzzle, and feast abundantly'.[18] For many, then, the priesthood was as much a question of getting to the top and comfortable living standards as certain occupations are for the executive, director or managerial groups in our own day. Hus does admit that he feasted excessively and devoured the labour of the poor. Also very relevant in this connection are some words that Hus addressed to a fellow priest in 1414. One paragraph of the letter concludes like this: 'See to it that you are a builder of a spiritual building, being kind to the poor and humble, not spending your goods on feasts.'[19] And then, as though the word 'feasts' sets up an association of ideas, Hus continued to warn the young man: 'I also fear that, if you mend not your life by giving up splendid and superfluous garments, you shall be severely rebuked by the Lord; as I, too, a miserable wretch, am being rebuked for having made use of such things, having been seduced by men's evil custom and praise. By these things I was wounded by the spirit of pride against God.'[20] Many ridiculous fashions among men prevailed at this time. With the long pointed shoes, 'the laced waists; the balloon-shaped sleeves standing up to the shoulders' and other such excesses, the effect was bizarre.[21] While it is unlikely that Hus's income would stretch to the purchase of extravagances such as these, it would seem that he was particularly 'clothes-conscious'. This emerges in several references in his writings.

Therefore, if we are to be just in our assessment of Hus, we must take seriously his own recorded confessions. They point consistently in one direction. We take two further illustrations, the one from his position in the academic world and the other from the early days of his preaching, both of which underline that he was not a true priest in early days. University and parochial cures were closely bound together throughout all these years and Hus comments on the decidedly unholy scrambling for position that he had often witnessed in these supposedly hallowed halls. He alludes to an incident in the latter part of his life when one monk actually 'secured a papal bull to the effect that he be granted a place above all other masters'.[22] Not surprisingly, the other masters deeply resented this blatant attempt to jump to the head of the academic queue and would not yield precedence to him in any way. Hus saw pride on both sides.

Yet he did not see it from a distance of aloofness and superiority. The whole incident struck chords within his own breast and prompted him to the following candid confession of his own earlier ambitions and his place-seeking mentality. After condemning sinful pride in learning he wrote, 'Alas! I too had gowns, robes with wings, and hoods with white fur; for they so hemmed in the master's grade with their regulations that no one is able to obtain the degree unless he possess such an outfit.'[23]

Coupled with this pride of position was a most unchristian contempt for the poor and a wrongful distinction of persons. 'Woe is me! How many times I have transgressed this Holy Word, rising and doffing my hood, or bowing to a rich man but not a poor one, and rather sending a *gross* to the rich man for drinking than giving a *heller* to the poor! I trust, however, our merciful Jesus, our Saviour, that he will forgive me and preserve me henceforth from such conduct,' lamented Hus in one sermon.[24] For one reared in a small hamlet and spending the early years as a student in poverty, the very fact that, when he entered on the course for his master's degree, he also became a servant in the largest of the university colleges and with this received the free use of a room and all his meals must have seemed like heaven on earth. His rapid rise in the academic world could also have pandered to pride.

Hus not only admitted to wrong motivation in entering the priesthood, but also clearly admitted that he was by no means a faithful preacher at the outset of his own ministry. He writes, 'But I have found that ordinary poor priests and poor laymen – even women – defend the truth more zealously than the doctors of the Holy Scriptures, who out of fear run away from the truth and have not courage to defend it. I myself – alas – had been one of them, for I did not dare to preach the truth plainly and openly. And why are we like that? Solely because some of us are timid, fearing to lose worldly favour and praise, and others of us fear to lose benefices; for we fear to be held in contempt by the people for the truth's sake, and to suffer bodily pain.'[25]

This would appear to show that, however frequently and earnestly Hus had with others debated, discussed and been provoked and stimulated by Wyclif, his own conversion was not in his early years at the university but rather towards the end of the fourteenth century, after the time when he actually began to preach. This must be so if, for a time at least, he was not a faithful preacher. He was probably preaching just before or during the year 1400 and certainly by 1402, for reasons which we shall shortly give, he must have been a faithful preacher of the Word.

As Hus himself states in a passage of vital pastoral importance, 'Man is by nature more inclined to one sin than to another.'[26] It would seem that his particular sin was love of ease, desire for position and security rooted in a proud refusal to trust in God. This is perhaps why he can urge so powerfully the poor priest to trust in God, do right and leave the Almighty to clothe him and provide the wherewithal to purchase books.[27] Was not Hus here speaking from experience? Had not he taken this stand himself at a crucial point in his life?

Yet as with all those who are truly converted, however many specific sins there may be to be confessed, and however glaring a cardinal sin there may be in the personality, ultimately the soul's great need is that of being humbled to the dust and redeemed by the Saviour. It would seem clear that this was a vital and basic experience that Hus had undergone. He knew that the basic sin is pride. Harking back again to his experience in the university, he writes, 'I myself have intently listened to their lectures in schools when they discoursed concerning humility, patience, poverty, courage, and other virtues which they celebrated so persuasively and eloquently that no one could do it better, as if they themselves had practised all of them. But later I found none of these virtues actually among them, for they were full of pride, avarice, impatience, and cowardice.'[28]

What applied to others he had also found applicable to his own heart. A phrase in the sentence which follows the above charge reveals much in little. He simply refers to 'the dear Christ'. Christ had become truly precious to him. It was supremely through the Scriptures that this was so. Whether Hus had personally listened to Matthew of Janov or not, the emphasis on scriptural authority was the same in both. After the change in his life the phrase 'Search the Scriptures' was for ever on Hus's lips. There was still much false and dangerous belief to be cast aside but Hus now had the root of the matter in him.

The predominant emphasis in his ministry can perhaps best be summed up in an illustration which he used and which he most likely took from his participation in the peasant games of his boyhood. Hus wrote, 'For men ought to adhere to those who live in conformity with the law and life of Christ, rather than to a thousand others whose lives do not so conform. For example, when men bowl, they first set up the target and then they throw the ball; and whoever comes closest to the target wins. And when they cannot discern who is the closest, they take a ruler and measure the distance from the ball to the target, and thus determine which ball is closer. Similarly, Christ and his truth . . .'[29] It is Christ in his Word that is our supreme rule. That was the firm conclusion that Hus had reached. In heart he was truly evangelical though many of the implications of this were yet to be worked out.

# 5.
# Leading halting souls to the King's supper

At the turn of the century, John Hus was a figure of growing importance, a man to be reckoned with. He had for some time now been closely associated with a circle of Bohemian students, many of whom were to become prominent and vocal in the years that lay ahead. From 1398–1402, Hus took part in frequent discussions on the burning issues of the day in the home of Christian of Prachatice, who was himself a lifelong supporter of Hus. Many years later an opponent charged Hus with denying the commonly held eucharistic teaching in a home in 1399. From what we know of Hus's views, we know that this charge was untrue, and yet the false accusation almost certainly springs from an important and genuine glimpse of the reformer avidly discussing these momentous issues among his concerned colleagues. These small gatherings were of great significance.

Within the university circles Hus enjoyed, for the most part, status, approval and increasing respect. In 1401 he was appointed for the first time Dean of the Faculty of Arts. By no stretch of the imagination could he now be described as a junior member of staff. His gifts were recognized by his colleagues. But it was particularly among the students themselves that Hus could display his undoubted talents. Within this world he was popular, settled and not without a happy, humorous turn of mind — the latter is shown in the light-hearted banter and familiar tones in the speeches he made to his students when they graduated. Many of these speeches have survived and they are marked by puckish wit. More than once Hus refers jocularly to the laziness of the particular student and even mentions having to get one of them out of bed regularly. This does at least tell us that Hus himself was no sluggard. It is also interesting to note that these references must have been taken in good part, since, with one exception, all the students mentioned in these speeches continued loyal friends of Hus through the stormy days that lay ahead.

The year 1401 is the first when we have clear references to his preaching activities. It is particularly interesting to note that he was preaching at this time at the Church of St Michael by permission of Bernard, a monk who himself was a strong opponent of church reform. Hus was often a welcome guest at this man's dinner table. As yet the lines of battle were certainly not clearly drawn, for this would not have been possible a few years later. From the beginning it would seem that Hus's sermons were held in high repute, for he could refer to copies made of some 'in the first year of my preaching'.[1]

It is also interesting to note that in 1409 a document was produced by opponents of Hus which revealed that a vast system of espionage had been operated against him for many years. In fact there are references to incriminating things which he was supposed to have said when he occupied this very pulpit at St Michael in 1401. This fascinating document contains marginal notes penned by Hus in answer to the accusations. But at present the important aspect to grasp is that almost from the very outset he was in some circles a marked man. His utterances must have been fervent and stirring even at this early stage of his ministry. Like C. H. Spurgeon, he must have developed far more rapidly than many preachers, although, as we make this comparison, we must bear in mind that Hus was no teenager, but about thirty years of age. Moreover he had had the experience of lecturing for some years prior to this. When he began to preach he was not speaking in public for the first time in his life.

When we consider preaching in Prague during this whole period, we must not imagine that it was invariably a static, orderly solo performance. There were often interjections and interruptions during the service. Sometimes documents were read out for the approval of the congregation, who also acted as witnesses. Comments on current affairs and topical references were not absent. Preachers, Hus included, were not above playing to the gallery in ways which hardly seem justifiable in the light of apostolic guide-lines. Some notes for his own delivery show the immediate emotional rapport he had with his hearers, but also seem to reveal dubious histrionic intentions. Hence we find the note: 'And then, as the audience responds, speak against idolatry'; and, again, 'This is the judgement of the letter. And then amplify if the attitude of the people justifies it.'[2]

Such an approach might make for exciting drama, but it also savours of unbiblical men-pleasing. We must concede that excessive regard was paid to the reaction of the hearers. Nevertheless we must also stress that his sermons were carefully, even meticulously, prepared. They were first written in Latin and then delivered in Czech. It must not be thought that they were merely wild, tub-thumping, empty orations. They were logical, coherent and increasingly biblical. The melodrama was an aberration. It was neither the whole story nor even the most significant part.

As an illustration of the fact that not only strictly 'religious themes' were discussed from the pulpit and also that there was often a visible response, we take a sermon of Nicholas of Dresden who, in 1403, spoke out passionately against the sins of the city fathers and rich men of Prague. Pointing to the rich merchants present, he cried out, 'Either these villains will be punished by God or they will be slain by their own servants. Their heads will be drenched in blood.' At this the city fathers rose in anger and left the church, with the intrepid preacher calling after them, 'Behold, my brethren, the devil himself drives them out of the temple.'[3] There is little evidence that Hus faced mass walk-outs of this nature. Indeed we have already inferred his initial popularity with the vast majority. Yet he was certainly pointed and definite, as well as topical and contemporary in some of his discourses.

In one of the earliest sermons preached in 1401 we detect strong nationalistic elements and echoes of the conflicts of his early years. The background to the reference is that a party of German troops had attacked from Bavaria and Meissen, pillaging and killing in the villages and even penetrating as far as Prague. Hus expressed the national indignation in his utterances from the pulpit: 'The Czechs are in this matter more wretched than dogs and snakes, for they do not defend their country, although their cause is just.'[4] Then, broadening his argument, the preacher went on to say that native Bohemians should occupy the key offices in Bohemia, just as the French did in France.

Such remarks would be understood readily by all as a reference to the situation at the university and other places where the Germans held so many key positions. But that Hus was not speaking from any attitude of ugly racism can be seen by what follows in the sermon: 'To what advantage is it to anyone if a Czech ignorant of German becomes a priest or bishop in Germany? It is about as useful as a dumb dog, who cannot bark, is to a herd. A German is worth as much to us Czechs.'[5] Here was above all the concern of a man that the gospel should be heard by the hearers in their own language. It was a gospel emphasis, not a racist tirade.

Yet Hus cannot be defended in all his utterances on this matter. He obviously had a mistrust of the Germans and this comes out quite unmistakably. 'The Germans', he later wrote, 'who are in Bohemia should go to their king [Wenceslas] and swear that they will be faithful to him and to the country, but this will only come to pass when a serpent warms itself on the ice.'[6] In that last vivid expression we see again not only the colloquial pungency of Hus's language, but also his deep-seated suspicion of Germans in general. Politically there may have been some justification for his attitude. However, as a Christian pastor his statements on this theme leave much to be desired.

This judgement applies in particular to a sermon he preached on Nehemiah 13:23–27. The passage deals with Nehemiah's cursing of Jews who had intermarried with pagan and Gentile people and whose children consequently spoke a mixed dialect. It must be pointed out that whereas the Bible actually says that Nehemiah 'beat some of the men and pulled out their hair', which seems severe enough, for some reason the version which Hus used for his own exposition stated that Nehemiah 'cursed them, and smote certain of them, and beheaded some'.

Hus briefly explained that Nehemiah was deeply concerned about this question of intermarriage, firstly, because the people were likely to be led into idolatry and then, secondly, because there was a great danger that the Hebrew language would perish. He then inexplicably widened his passage and applied it to the way in which men should treat adulterous wives. Allowing that 'Christ the merciful king' spared the adulteress and thereby abrogated the Old Testament death penalty for such offences, Hus nevertheless harshly advocated beating and whipping as the appropriate punishment in such circumstances on the basis of the severe notes in the scriptural passage.

Then the preacher sought to give his passage contemporary application as he stated, 'Thus also should we behave that the Bohemian language perish not. If a Bohemian marries a German, the children must immediately learn Bohemian and not divide their speech in two [speak partly Bohemian, partly German]. For this division causes but jealousy, dissension, anger and quarrels. Therefore did the Emperor Charles, King of Bohemia, of holy memory, order the citizens of Prague to teach their children Bohemian, to speak it, and to plead at law in Bohemian in the town hall, which the Germans call "Rathaus".'[7]

It was his forcibly expressed view that those citizens of Prague deserve a whipping who decorate their speech with large numbers of German words. He then provided a list of Bohemian words, adding after each the corrupted word derived from the German which was replacing it in common speech. This may have been an attempt to give relevant contemporary application to the Word of God, but many see it rather as a preacher abandoning his proper role and pandering in considerable degree to popular prejudice. As a Christian Hus would have to learn by the grace of God that he was wrong in some of his attitudes. This was a lesson which he was only going to learn fully in the last year of his life. As a preacher he would also have to learn to expound the Word more faithfully.

Yet Hus's popularity cannot be gainsaid. Many a noble and Bohemian patriot would fervently have said a vociferous and vigorous 'Amen' to the anti-Germanic polemic, however unspiritual and mistaken this assent would have been. Support was in fact during this early period from the throne downwards – insofar as Wenceslas was able to express his mind freely on any topic at the beginning of Hus's ministry.

The simple fact was that, after many more squabbles with his own nobility, from the spring of 1402 until November of 1403, Wenceslas was again in prison, this time in Vienna. This particular imprisonment was planned and carried out by his own brother Sigismund with the co-operation of a group of Czech nobles and Bishop John of Litomyšl.

There is little doubt, however, that Wenceslas would have supported the sentiments of Hus, for we know that, despite all his extravagances and weaknesses, the king loved Bohemia. He might, like many more, have been a misguided patriot, but a patriot he was. It was in fact simply because he did not like the thought of leaving his own much loved land that he never actually travelled for any official crowning as Holy Roman Emperor. Indeed he never was crowned since, in face of accusations for his various misdemeanours and wild acts, he was formally deprived of the office in 1400. Shortly after this he was also deprived of liberty in the way we have described and forcibly removed from Bohemia. Consequently he did not witness the promotion of John Hus to the most important of all his offices in his own native land.

In 1402 Hus was appointed rector and preacher in the renowned Bethlehem Chapel. This must be seen both as confirmation of what we have said with regard to Hus's personal experience of conversion and also as proof that in his preaching it was the clearly recognizable biblical and gospel notes that were paramount, rather than the somewhat undesirable political undertones. According to Spinka, who does not shrink from describing Hus's earlier experience as 'conversion', it was supremely through study of Scripture that the change had come. As Hus himself put it in one of his confessions towards the end of his life, 'When I was young in years and reason, I too belonged to the foolish sect. But when the Lord gave me the knowledge of Scripture, I discharged that kind of stupidity from my foolish mind.'[8]

This whole experience manifestly fitted him for the task of biblical ministry and, commenting on the fact that Hus was given a leading pulpit only one year after ordination, at about thirty-three years of age, the Czech scholar says, 'In fact, the conscientious and earnest young university professor must have been considered a remarkably gifted preacher, as well as possessed of unusual reformatory zeal, to be chosen for such a responsible post."[9] We note that by this time, with regard to his teaching and lecturing commitments, Hus can also accurately be described as a professor.

The congregation at Bethlehem spanned all walks of life. We know that from the beginning there were those sympathetic to reform among the higher classes. In the very year of Hus's appointment one noble lady, in endowing a living nearby, stipulated that the preaching of the Word of God must be honoured above all else. At the Bethlehem Chapel itself Anežha Štitný, daughter of a famous writer of devotional literature, was among the first of the nobility to become part of the congregation. She was the first of many. Soon devout women gathered in numbers and occupied a house nearby to hear the gifted young preacher regularly. The queen herself became one of Hus's most regular and keen hearers.

Student priests were present in large numbers. So were other clergymen, some for their own edification, others to spy and report on the outspoken preacher. We know from Hus's correspondence that there were burghers, craftsmen, masters, mistresses, servants and students all represented in the large assembly. As his ministry progressed he could affirm that the light of truth was 'under the direction of our Saviour . . . ardently received by the multitude, the lords, knights, burghers, and the common people.'[10] He also declared that he taught nothing in secret and that his 'ministry was attended mostly by masters, bachelors, priests, barons, knights and many others'.[11] At the opposite end of the scale he could address one letter to his congregation in Prague and begin it, 'My beloved brothers in Christ, cobblers, tailors, and scribes'.[12] It was by far the most influential pulpit in the life of the entire nation.

The king himself had in fact sanctioned the endowment of the Bethlehem Chapel, with the Archbishop of Prague laying the foundation-stone. At a later stage the pope himself confirmed the foundation. Evidently even the local authorities were favourably and generously disposed, since they released the ground without demanding the customary tax and also declared it free from all future city taxes and assessments. In a way this underlines the significance which this preaching place had in the life of the nation.

There were various pictures on the walls of the chapel. If we give the content of one, it will suffice as typifying the tone of all. One part showed the pope resplendent in papal pomp astride a large horse, while its counterpart portrayed Christ in poverty carrying his cross. All the pictures were in this vein. The people would have had no difficulty in seeing what the message was. Other writings on the wall of the chapel openly attacked the false theology of the Roman Catholic Church. This helps us to understand an otherwise obscure remark of Hus in one of his works. In the process of insisting that a bishop should not excommunicate anyone until he knows that those disciplined are excommunicated by God, Hus wrote, 'Of this I have written in another place. And, if thou wilt not believe it, learn it on the wall of Bethlehem.'[13]

Hus was here referring to six inscriptions written on the wall of the chapel which were intended to contradict six Roman errors. The fifth one, to which he refers, was on the theme of wrongful excommunication. It is important to note that Hus himself was personally responsible for putting up these inscriptions. In 1949, when the chapel was being reconstructed, parts of the inscription were found under a protective covering of plaster and were in a fairly good state of preservation. This is amazing, since there were many attempts by opponents to expunge the provocative writing.

The singing of hymns soon became an important feature of congregational worship. Both Hus and Jerome of Prague introduced the notorious 'new hymns' and versifications of parts of the liturgy in Czech. There were various places of accommodation erected for students who were under Hus's supervision. Most of these students were to continue loyal to him in the days that lay ahead, and one of them, Peter of Mladoňovice, would become the faithful chronicler of his final trial and sufferings. Much charitable work was also carried out in Christ's name. Yet while Hus was there the prime function of the chapel was never forgotten. Hus continued to be involved in the affairs of the university but preaching was now his main task. It has been estimated that he preached some 3,000 sermons there. Apart from the seasons of Lent and Advent, when only one sermon was given, Hus preached twice each Sunday and saint's day.

The sermons of Hus for the period 1401–3 have been published. What would the people have heard? In the first place it must be conceded that they would at this time have heard very little polemic against Roman error and, on the other hand, sadly, they would have been taught typical medieval and unscriptural errors about the Virgin Mary. For the most part the illustrative element would have been deficient. There would also have been absurd allegorizing in the medieval fashion. Thus the text, 'And he entered a village', was taken to mean that Jesus Christ entered the womb of Mary and was incarnated.[14]

Yet there would have been forthrightness and strong exhortations. The priests themselves would not have been spared. 'Our bishops and priests of today, and especially our cathedral canons, and lazy mass-celebrators', he thundered forth, 'hardly wait for the close of the service to hurry out of church, one part to the tavern and the other part hither and thither to engage in amusements unworthy of a priest, yea, even to dance. The monks prepare dances and entertainments in the public houses in the hope of winning the people and being entrusted with masses . . .'[15] Even in those days unscrupulous and unfaithful priests were seeking to lure people to church by organizing dances. There is no new thing under the sun. Hus also unsparingly condemned the dancing and lewd behaviour in courts and palaces. The moral earnestness of the preacher was unmistakable. But was there more?

Matthew Spinka is certain that there was much more. Arguing against a scholar who claimed that they were 'mere moralistic appeals', Spinka retorts that they were 'an urgent demand for genuine spiritual transformation. Hus deals with various aspects of moral conduct, but always stresses motives rather than outward actions.' Spinka aptly cites Hus's warning in one sermon that 'All other speaking is vain if this uncreated Word [Christ] will not speak within the heart and teach the soul.'[16] Despite other elements, the underlying evangelistic aim could not be missed.

This is very plain in these sermons, both in the terms in which Hus depicts the preacher, and in one of his references to salvation. 'Thus all who are sent by God may be recognized by the fact whether they seek the glory of God and the salvation of men. It matters little to enquire whether one is sent by a pope or bishop or whether he has certain papers or confirmations. Instead we should recognize that he is sent of God when he diligently seeks the salvation of men and the praise of God,' he declared. He also described as foolish those who 'buy indulgences, masses, and entrance into monastic orders, wishing to be pious by the piety of others, to be good by the goodness of others, and to be righteous by the righteousness of others . . . Therefore, the indulgences, masses and monkish orders will profit them nothing.'[17] Luther himself could hardly have put this better.

It is also interesting to note that he was already saying, even at this early stage, that Peter is not the rock but Christ is, and mentioning frequently God's electing purposes. Such sayings were to be remembered against him. Well might he also declare at this time, preaching on Christ's parable of the tares in Matthew 13:24–30, that even tares might be useful to the good because they can protect the good against the wind and thus enable them to stand upright. It is an unusual insight, but one by which Hus himself would need to live increasingly and with ever deepening trust in Christ himself.

Hus loved preaching. He was not lengthy. In fact he instructed one priest to preach 'assiduously, but briefly'.[18] However, on the role of the preacher he entertained no doubts. 'Preachers in my judgement count in the church for more than prelates,' he declared.[19] And from his pen comes one of the finest descriptions of true gospel preaching that has ever been put to paper when he said, 'By the help of God I have preached, still am preaching, and if his grace will allow, shall continue to preach; if perchance I may be able to lead some poor, tired, or halting soul into the house of Christ to the King's supper.'[20] Can this be bettered?

# 6.
# The influence of Wyclif

We are now reaching a point where we must deal with a very significant clash between two groups in Prague University over the teachings of John Wyclif. We have already briefly mentioned how the connection between Bohemia and England through the royal marriage facilitated the spread of Wyclif's teachings, though in the 1390s it was largely his philosophical works that were read. In 1402 Jerome of Prague brought over two even more subversive works. All this aroused interest. There was an eager desire to know more about Wyclif. We ought therefore to say something more about the English reformer. What kind of man was he?

Wyclif has often been called 'the Morning Star of the Reformation'. He exercised his ministry until his death in 1384 at first very much in court circles, with the protection and patronage of John of Gaunt, then among academic circles at Oxford and in the latter period in the comparative seclusion of his rectory at Lutterworth. Although he died in peace and in the bosom of the church, after surviving a stroke for a short while, by the time of Hus his name was widely abominated within the Roman fold.

Many have said that Wyclif's whole personality is elusive and there are conflicting opinions about him. To some he was far more of a convinced biblical reformer than Hus himself. To others he was a somewhat sour, distant, prejudiced academic, thwarted in public life and finally turning to seek in reform a kind of fame in compensation for what he had missed in court circles. To such he is an austere, repelling figure, jaundiced and without real warmth. For example, one modern scholar feels that Wyclif's writings are chiefly denunciatory and that his personality remains 'in some ways unattractive'.[1]

An older writer put this point of view very strongly when he wrote about Wyclif as follows: 'His philosophy is not original and he appeals invariably to the head; there is no sentiment or pathos or unction about him, not a grain of amusement to be extracted from his books, and we may reckon this a serious defect – not a grain of poetry, and this is more serious still. He had none of the qualities of a great preacher, or a great leader of the people, and as far as we can see, he never attempted to be either one or the other.'[2]

That this is a totally unjustifiable charge the ensuing pages will make clear. At this point we take up two aspects which we shall not deal with in depth, and comment briefly on them. The above writer comments on the lack of humour. Every man must be judged in the context of his own times. Wyclif felt, and felt rightly and strongly, that congregations and spectators of miracle plays had a surfeit of humour. On solemn and serious themes they often had little else. No doubt there was reaction against this. But it should also be said that absence of humour in published sermons by no means indicates absence of humour in the personality of the writer. The critic also refers to the absence of poetry as the most reprehensible trait of all. While we might regard this as a deficiency, it is certainly not a vital one. In his comments the critic merely displays his own ignorance of the preacher's calling and task.

It may be admitted that Wyclif's sermons lack illustration and 'flesh'. It may be that he does not express the doctrine of justification by faith with sufficient clarity, though it has recently been well argued that the substance of this doctrine is quite definitely in his writings. He wrote, 'Some men receive him [Christ] not to the health of their soul for they were unstable as water, and soon did away Christ's knowledge. But other men were stable as land, who held the knowledge that Christ put in them. And by the ground of such faith they went fully the way to heaven.'[3]

The biblical concept of divine predestination was certainly written large and clear across his whole theology. The church was the congregation of the predestined. Wyclif argued that 'Neither place nor human election makes a person a member of the church but divine predestination in respect of whoever with perseverance follows Christ in love, and in abandoning all his worldly goods suffers to defend his law.'[4] Of course, such views could inevitably lead to a lack of respect for the hierarchy, who may not even be among the saved, and ultimately to a diminution of the priest's role in the administration of the sacraments. In such vein Wyclif says, 'The ship of Peter is the church militant . . . nor do I see why the said ship of Peter might not in time consist purely of laymen.'[5] Thus the mediating priesthood gave way to the priesthood of all believers in his teaching. And most important of all he denied the dogma of transubstantiation. This teaching, that the priest is able to 'make' Christ's body in the sacrifice of the mass, had become an accepted dogma of faith in 1215 at the Fourth Lateran Council.

In addition to all this, Wyclif not only wrote powerfully and compellingly on the supreme authority of Scripture, especially in his work *On the Truth of Holy Scripture,* but he also sought to apply this truth and ultimately encouraged friends to begin what was to become a justly famous vernacular version of the Bible. In one of the first of his works, brought over to Prague by Jerome of Prague, we find him asserting, 'Therefore, if there were a hundred popes, and all the friars were turned into cardinals, their opinions in matters of faith should be believed only in so far as they are founded in Scripture.'[6] He thereby resolutely repudiated all dependence on tradition, papal decrees and canon law not founded on the Bible.

Barbara Tuchman, in a widely read modern work, has written attractively and powerfully with reference to the widespread appeal of his version of the Scriptures. She puts it like this: 'In the future fierce reaction after the Peasants' Revolt, when Lollardy was harried as the brother of subversion, and mere possession of a Bible in English could convict a man of heresy, the making of multiple copies of the manuscript Bible was a labour of risk and courage. In view of 175 copies that still survive and the number that must have been destroyed during the persecutions and lost over the centuries, many hundreds must have been laboriously and secretively copied out by hand.'[7] This seems a perfectly fair deduction and does show the eagerness of hungry people for the Word of God, together with the impact of the Wyclifite Bible.

Wyclif burned to pass on this message. He was convinced of the primacy of preaching, declaring in his work *The Pastoral Office* that 'Preaching the gospel exceeds prayer and administration of the sacraments, to an infinite degree.'[8] Therefore Wyclif sent out his justly famous 'poor preachers' to spread the gospel. That such a man could be described as unconcerned about leading others in the ways of truth staggers the imagination. Above all he was a translator and expositor of the Bible, who saw it as his mission to encourage others in the same calling. His sermons were plain and true to Scripture. Wherever men exalted themselves and their skill in telling racy tales, as the friars did, then according to Wyclif, such practices came from nothing else but the pride of man, with everyone seeking his own honour and everyone preaching himself and not Jesus Christ. Not surprisingly, the friars were among his most fervent opponents. Yet his work was not unavailing.

Because Wyclif was falsely linked with John Ball and the ill-fated Peasants' Revolt of 1381, some have unjustly described him as a revolutionary. Although he did make dangerous statements, it would appear that taken as a whole and in proper context his teaching did stress obedience to authorities. What he did make clear was that the crimes and misdeeds of clerics should be dealt with by the powers that be and that their religious garb should not procure them exemption from justice.

Of course, this theology found its outlet with Wyclif in many plain, practical down-to-earth applications. He was unsparing in the severity of his attacks on the prevalence of pilgrimages and image worship. The fasts of the church which substituted fish for flesh were 'fool fastings'. Bishops and presbyters were equal in rank. Church music could please aesthetically but could also lure people away from the urgency of the truth being spoken. He quoted Augustine's dictum: 'As oft as the song delighteth me more than that is songen, so oft I acknowledge I trespass grievously.'[9] This was an oft-quoted saying among his followers.

Obviously his targets were wide-ranging. Moreover, although his language might lack the poetic element, it was not without vivacity and pointedness. In savage terms he had ridiculed the worship of the saints as undermining the work of Christ, the only mediator and intercessor. He imputed the frequency of canonization to sheer greed or simple ignorance of the true faith. The possession of saints' bones usually secured a good income. When Rome consented to canonization, fees were forthcoming. But, argued Wyclif, some would choose a king's fool to intercede for them with his master. These saints therefore were but the fools, the buffoons of heaven. He held up Mary in her life as an example to all, but did not exhort people to pray to her.

Still more central to the thrust and appeal of Wyclif's ministry is the following assertion. He spoke of Avignon, the abode of the popes during his lifetime, as a 'terrestrial hell, a residence of fiends and devils, a receptacle of all that is wicked and abominable'. 'Why', he asked, 'should I speak of truth, where not only the houses, palaces, courts, churches, and the thrones of popes and cardinals, but the very earth and air appear to teem with lies? A future state, heaven, hell and judgement, are openly turned into ridicule as childish fables . . .'[10]

Here we come to the main issue and the heart of the reason for Hus's close identification with Wyclif. V. H. H. Green makes an amazingly common, but spiritually imperceptive observation when he describes the medieval period as follows: 'No churchman doubted for a moment that the Bible was composed under the direct inspiration of God and that its content, though not necessarily of equal value, provided a pathway for man through the maze of life.'[11] This is the kind of statement that we hear about many other eras. Such a claim is always false. Wyclif himself gives the lie to it.

But at Prague there were those who wished to give the lie to Wyclif and to silence his teachings once and for all. Just as the native Bohemians had more or less as a body been attracted to the teachings of Wyclif, so the Germans had been furiously opposed to them. Hence it is not surprising that it was a German, John Hübner, who led the accusation that the Wyclifism embraced by the Czechs was indeed a heresy. Stanislav, a revered teacher of Hus himself, was singled out in the attack and to the twenty-four articles condemned by the Blackfriars Synod, held in London in 1382, Hübner added another twenty-one articles extracted from Wyclif's works.

The first ten articles pronounced as heretical at this synod included the following: 'That the substance of material bread and wine remain in the sacrament of the altar after consecration', (This is what was commonly called the doctrine of 'remanence'. It was obviously a denial of transubstantiation); 'That if a bishop or a priest be in mortal sin, he doth not ordain, consecrate, nor baptize'; 'That if a man be duly contrite, all exterior confession is to him superfluous and invalid'; 'That God ought to obey the devil'; and 'That after Urban VI none other is to be received for pope, but that Christendom ought to live, after the manner of the Greeks, under its own laws.'[12]

Other articles touched on the question of tithes (which could, according to Wyclif, be withheld), argued that secular powers could legitimately take possessions from habitually delinquent clergy, and urged that friars should earn their living by the labour of their own hands and not by begging. Articles on excommunication asserted that a prelate should not excommunicate anyone unless he knew the person to be excommunicated by God and also stated, 'That they who cease to preach or to hear the Word of God or the gospel, for fear of such excommunication, are already excommunicate, and in the day of judgement shall be counted traitors to God.'[13] The Roman church was also belligerently termed a 'synagogue of Satan'.

In May 1403, under the chairmanship of a Bavarian rector, a meeting was called to discuss these articles. To quote a contemporary account, it was 'a full and general convocation of all the masters of the University of Prague'.[14] It was an uproarious and acrimonious meeting. 'Theological bedlam' would not be an inept description. The Czechs stood more or less unitedly in opposition to the move of Hübner. They refused to believe in the first place that the articles had been correctly extracted and fairly represented Wyclif's thought. First of all, Nicholas of Litomyšl, Hus's main teacher, roundly accused Hübner of sheer dishonesty, exclaiming, 'Thou hast falsely and unjustly drawn from these books statements that are not contained in them.'[15]

At this point Hus intervened. He thoroughly supported the point of Nicholas but outdid him in his fervent indignation. 'Such falsifiers of books,' he truculently urged, 'better deserve to be burnt than those adulterators of saffron, Berlin, and Wlaska'.[16] In this rather obscure allusion Hus was referring to a recent incident when two men had tampered with (and therefore 'falsified') some foodstuffs and had both been executed for this offence. Before we pronounce summary sentence on the social barbarism of the age, as one writer does with reference to this incident, we ought to know more about the extent of the tampering. In our own day large numbers of people have been poisoned and even killed by such activities. But what the incident does show us is that Hus stood solidly with his Czech brethren.

Indeed the next step really amounted to the throwing down of the gauntlet as Stephen Páleč, close friend of Hus and frequent spokesman for the Bohemians, threw a book of Wyclif upon the table and challenged, 'Let who will stand up and speak against any word contained in this book! I will defend it!'[17] The battle-lines were now beginning to be drawn clearly. In a parody of the genealogy in the Gospel, the Germans sneeringly concocted their own Wyclifite genealogy which declared that 'Stanislav begat Peter [of Znojmo], Peter begat Páleč, and Páleč begat Hus.'[18]

It must be emphasized that, while radical leaders such as Stanislav did adhere to the doctrine of remanence in the Lord's Supper, as expounded by Wyclif, Hus himself remained loyal to the Roman dogma. Nevertheless, this difference notwithstanding, the Czechs were at this time united in their defence of Wyclif. In January of the following year Hübner returned to this theme, denouncing Wyclif as a heretic and accusing him of having called the church 'a synagogue of Satan'. This was clearly a dispute which was not going to die a natural death or fade into academic oblivion.

Indeed Hus himself once more stepped into the fray, for one of the very earliest of his surviving letters is fittingly entitled 'A protest to John Hübner about the charges against Wyclif.' The letter does not scale great theological heights, but some of the arguments are interesting. Hus begins by admitting that Wyclif refers to heresies in his books, but counters this by pointing out that Augustine and others did similarly, quoting others only to discuss and refute them. His argument on Wyclif's reference to the synagogue of Satan is simple. 'For if the Roman curia is the synagogue of Satan, it does not follow that the holy mother church is the synagogue of Satan,' he wrote.[19]

As at the earlier meeting Hus also suggests that the articles were falsely extracted. But he goes further, implying that the accusers were motivated by bad feelings, being like blind men who cannot judge of colours and 'being all and almost every one simoniacs'.[20] Then for the larger part of his letter Hus develops this theme, showing even at this early stage the fervour of his opposition against trafficking in holy things for money and with greedy and insincere motives. He links together simony, blasphemy and apostasy as being against the Holy Trinity and singles out the former as being particularly a sin against the Holy Spirit. He also strongly objects to Hübner's position that the pope is beyond rebuke, retorting, 'You also say that the supreme pontiff must be obeyed absolutely and we ought in no wise reprove him. You contradict the canons and hence are a heretic, if you hold this positively and persistently.'[21]

After arguing that men sin more in the era of grace than in that of the law, Hus alleges that the canons teach 'that simony is the first and the principal heresy' and concludes, 'I wish, therefore, good and worthy master, that you leave off circumlocution and extraneous glosses, and in true love with Christ Jesus preach the poverty which our Lord and his disciples also taught by words and example,' citing Bernard to the effect that a cleric who has his portion on earth shall have no portion in heaven.[22]

In all this there is more than meets the eye. Not all Hus's arguments, it must be admitted, are satisfactory. Probably largely through ignorance, he does not admit the extent of Wyclif's divergence from Rome. He relies rather too much on the 'canons' than on Scripture, although he does refer to the Bible, instancing Christ's twofold cleansing of the money-changers from the temple as relevant to the issue. Yet above all, as early as this, Hus sees and says that the whole issue of true conversion and motive in ministry is at stake.

Therefore, although the early years were very much

successful evangelism and thrilling gospel proclamation, they were not solely so. The conflict with Hübner pointed to the way ahead, as did other incidents. Hus was being prepared to enter into various controversies. There must have been reasons why spies were sent so early in his ministry. We glimpse the kinds of conflict he experienced on a personal level in three references in one of his major works to events which he does not date. These experiences could well have come from this early period and certainly by 1404, in only the second of his letters to be preserved, he was referring to some of the issues central to these incidents. All his experiences as a boy in Husinec would have reinforced his concern about the issues in question.

He describes how the greedy, grasping monks seek to get certain parishes from the pope or nobles by offering money or gifts. He notes that they only desire the rich parishes and steer clear of the poor ones. He continues, 'I had an occasion once to say to certain monks, "Why do you desire the possession of such and such a parish?" for they had paid the priest thirty *kopy* and a lifelong pension in order that he might cede the parish to them so that it would henceforth remain in their possession. They answered me by saying that it lay adjacent to their own properties and bordered them.'[23]

Hus was not to be fobbed off by this reply and thus returned to the attack: 'I said to them, "If that is the whole reason, why do you not secure the one still nearer?" They kept silent. Then I said, "Is it not rather that the latter yields less revenue and has less endowments?" And I said further: "Now you desire this particular parish because it lies adjacent to your property; but when you secure it, then some other parish will be adjacent to that, and you will desire to possess that as well; and so forth and so on, until you will desire to possess the whole world." They felt ashamed.' Ashamed and abashed they might well be, but if such rebuke did not lead to true repentance, we may be sure that resentment against the one challenging them would fester and grow.

The second example reveals more the struggle that Hus experienced in seeking to convince a sincere priest to bear the cross and engage in conflict with others. It is a passage rich in dialogue and almost certainly drawn from the many discussions which Hus had with those who sought his counsel. Hus provides the nervous and vacillating priest with the very words to take to his superiors, who demand money for the benefice. He pictures the queries of the priest, 'But again you reply, "If I do not pay, another will." My answer is that if you wish thus to excuse yourself, then the executioner, the catchpole, or the prostitute could likewise be excused. For each could say: "If I should refuse to be an executioner, or a catchpole, another would. If I should not be a prostitute, another would."'[24] The priest should not sin either because others do, or because it is the common custom.

Another conflict shows how Hus was often involved with many others. Let him again tell it to us in his own words. 'Once I advised a certain priest', he writes, 'in the presence of his lord, who had granted him a parish for God's sake [i.e. freely], not to pay anything for confirmation. Thereupon a master of the sacred Scriptures who was present said: "What are you talking about? Should they render him service without pay? Why shouldn't he pay?" Thereupon I answered him: "The certificate is unnecessary. They should examine the priest only as to whether he be of good life and of virtuous morals, whether he is given good testimony by the people, and whether no one knows anything against his life; and whether he knows how to minister to the people in regard to the Word . . ."'[25] Such a man, declared Hus, should be entrusted in God's name with the care of souls. The written certificate, apparently necessary in these cases, should be given freely. At this Hus was asked indignantly what the notaries were then going to live on, and immediately retorted that the archbishop, with his revenue of several thousands, could easily provide for their needs rather than squander his income on proud retinue and crowds of hangers-on and retainers, as was so commonly the practice.

'Thereupon the master became angry with me and said, "You always want things according to your will." But I answered, "Not according to my will, but according to Christ's will . . . and according to the apostolic will, as well as that of other saints." He then left me in anger.'[26] Already Hus was deemed a self-opinionated man, thrusting his views on others. Already he was stirring up real anger and opposition. Such conflicts were perhaps less frequent at the beginning of his ministry, but they were not absent. They prompted deeper reflection on his part, showed him that the path would not be easy and taught him to dig deeper into the Word of God. Our next chapter will seek to portray another of the early major doctrinal cleavages in which Hus was personally involved.

# 7.
# The archbishop's favour

Not only were the national leaders favourably disposed to Hus, and not only was he highly regarded by the Czech community at the university, but in addition the favour and patronage of the newly appointed Archbishop of Prague rested upon him at the beginning of his ministry. Zbyněk, who occupied this position, had secured the much-coveted appointment (some said with the payment of bribes) in 1402, but did not actually take up his duties until the following year. Thus he came into prominence during the theological battle over the teaching of Wyclif without, it would seem, being drawn into the controversy itself.

Zbyněk must not be seen as an elderly father figure. When he secured the appointment he was himself only twenty-five years of age. He was trained as a soldier and, having shown loyalty to Wenceslas, he was now very much in the confidence of the king. He had only a limited theological education and only a very poor grasp of theological issues. Throughout his life he was more at home in the saddle of a horse than in the seat of learning, and more familiar with the sword of iron than with the sword of the Spirit. In fact one of the earlier tasks in which Hus gladly co-operated with the archbishop was the bringing of a robber leader to a profession of penitence prior to his execution. Hus apprehended the man with the Word after Zbyněk had apprehended him with the sword. These were not the only warlike exploits in which he engaged.

As archbishop he was none the less sympathetic to reform. There may have been family reasons for this. It is interesting in this connection to note that his own sister was married to one of the founders of the Bethlehem Chapel. It would also seem fair to state that Zbyněk was genuinely disturbed and dismayed by the generally low standards and even immorality among the Prague clergy. There was much in Hus that appealed to the archbishop and initially Hus had ready access to his ear. Words which Hus wrote to Zbyněk a year or so later sum up their early relationship: 'Very often I repeat to myself that not long ago after your enthronement Your Paternity had set up the rule that whenever I should observe some defect in the administration, that I should instantly report such defect in person, or in your absence by writing.'[1]

Confirmation of the new archbishop's initial trust in Hus was soon forthcoming. Early in 1405 Hus was asked to take part in an important three-man commission of inquiry into proceedings at a shrine in Wilsnack. A local priest had asserted that, after a fire, he had found the host in the fire unconsumed and sprinkled with drops of blood. It was claimed by the priests at the shrine and believed by many that this was none other than the blood of Jesus Christ. Many cures were attributed to the power manifested at this shrine and it was becoming an increasingly popular place of pilgrimage.

Apparently a knight named Henry was about to fight an adversary called Frederick. Before the encounter Henry vowed that he would dedicate his armour to the holy blood of Wilsnack. This enabled him to win and kill his enemy. More remarkably still it was narrated that a robber and murderer called Peter, being confined in prison, made a similar vow and found that he was miraculously freed from all his fetters and able to escape forthwith. People longed for miracles and deliverances of this type. And, as these and many such stories circulated, crowds from all over Europe, including many from Bohemia, flocked to this shrine.

All this must be seen not as an isolated occurrence but in its proper medieval context. It was a very vital matter that Hus and his two colleagues were called upon to investigate. They were looking at something which typified the outlook and deep-rooted convictions of many in the church in that day, and in many another day. For example, we may see from a reference in Luther's address to the German nobility that Wilsnack was still a place of pilgrimage in the German Reformer's lifetime. This was therefore to be a pivotal experience in the formation of many of Hus's own convictions. Through this visit he would be compelled to think about and pronounce on issues that perhaps he had not, as yet, deeply considered.

Let us hear what one person has written about this general trafficking in relics: 'Wandering friars and impostors in clerical dress sold pigs' bones as those of saints, slivers of the True Cross, and drops of the Virgin's milk at country fairs. Said San Bernardino of Siena: "All the buffalo cows of Lombardy would not have as much milk as is shown about the world." Because Saint Appollonia was considered especially effective in treating toothaches, Saint Appollonia's teeth abounded. Henry VI of England is said to have collected a ton of them. Said Thomas Fuller, a seventeenth-century divine: "Were her stomach proportionate to her teeth, a country would scarce afford her a meal."'[2]

Prophets, prophetesses, visionaries and seers proliferated in this atmosphere. Different groups sought to prove the authenticity of their own stance or teaching because a particular highly regarded visionary was of their camp. The result was tremendous confusion, especially when such criteria were applied to the question of the correctness of the claims of the papal rivals during the great schism. It so happened that although Urban could claim miracle workers such as Catherine of Siena, Catherine of Sweden and Peter of Aragon, his rival at Avignon was followed by Vincent Ferrer, Peter of Luxemburg and Colette of Corbie.

Although Catherine of Siena was famous for her trances and raptures and her claim to have received after communion the stigmata of the five wounds of Christ on hands, feet and heart, anyone with Vincent Ferrer in his camp did have a decided advantage! He was alleged to perform such slight feats as sprouting wings in the middle of a sermon and floating away. (Some might wish that more preachers would do this!) One description caps all others in this amazing repertoire of wonders. 'Even more noteworthy was the time when Vincent had promised his superior to stop performing miracles and a builder fell off a scaffold. "Wait!", he cried to the hurtling workman. "Wait till I ask permission!" The builder duly waited in mid-hurtle. Vincent ran for permission and rescued him from afar.'[3]

Although no friend of Hus, Gerson, the famous French theologian, set little store by the visions and revelations which were so universally spoken of and so widely accepted. He tells us how he visited such a woman visionary, who won the admiration of a gullible populace merely by going completely without food over a period. Gerson found her vain and arrogant and her visions meaningless. He wondered whether she was insane. He even refers to the case of an epileptic woman who was of the opinion that each twinge of pain felt in her corns was a sign that a soul descended to hell!

Therefore when the commission set to work they were indeed having to investigate something which was believed fervently and treasured avidly by the people in general. Yet they made short shrift of the whole procedure. Their findings were monotonously negative and consistently critical. In face of their careful examinations, the alleged wonders simply evaporated. They averred that two women who were reported to have received their sight swore before a notary that they had never been blind, and that a boy who was alleged to have claimed that his foot was healed was in fact far worse off after going to Wilsnack than before he went.

But perhaps the most striking of all these cases was that of a citizen of Prague, Peter of Ach, who had undertaken a pilgrimage to Wilsnack in the hope of having his maimed hand healed. On arrival he dedicated a silver hand to the Holy Blood. When he failed to find relief in any way, he lingered, an unknown, forlorn and forgotten figure among the crowds. To his amazement, a few days later, he witnessed a priest ascend the pulpit and announce, 'Listen, children, to this miracle. The hand of our neighbour from Prague has been healed by the Holy Blood, and he has offered this silver hand as a thanksgiving.' Filled with indignation, Peter stood up and, showing his maimed hand, shouted, 'Priest, thou liest; here is my hand maimed as it always was.'[4]

Hus and his two colleagues duly catalogued these fraudulent and blasphemous proceedings, exposing their real nature. More importantly, they widened the whole line of attack, as they correctly discerned the important nature of the whole issue, and they stigmatized as deceitful a whole host of similar practices. Thus Hus himself in a later work declared with regard to a similar so-called miracle at Litomyšl that some priests themselves dipped the wafer in blood and claimed that it had been miraculously transformed. He found repugnant the thought that Christ's foreskin was reportedly exhibited in Rome and bluntly said so. The claim that Christ's beard was genuinely shown in Prague he labelled as false. On another occasion, he wrote, 'As to such deceptions, I see nothing more strange in them than what is practised here in Prague, of exhibiting the blood of Jesus Christ mingled with the milk of the Virgin Mary.'[5]

In tracts and writings penned after this investigation Hus also went to the root of the whole question and brought a series of weighty biblical objections to this whole quest for miracles, visions and wonder-working shrines. He dogmatically asserted that Christ's resurrection 'glorified' all the blood of his body so that none remained on earth except that which existed sacramentally (but not materially) in the eucharist. Therefore, he urged, none should venerate either the blood or hair of Christ said to exist in some local church or shrine. He used several passages of Scripture to prove that the whole body of Christ had been glorified. Indeed, his mode of argument was sound and scriptural to the core, as it was when he also put stress on faith, quoting the words of Christ to Thomas, when the latter refused to believe until he had touched Christ's wounds and Christ replied, 'Blessed are those who have not seen and yet have believed' (John 20:27).

Hus likewise saw that such deceivers of the people ought properly to be exposed and that for a true messenger of God to sit on the fence on such an issue was both cowardly and reprehensible. Therefore he himself denounced those priests who hawked about 'false indulgences and relics for the deception of the people and those who concocted visions and other miracles' and, seeing the all-too-common mood of 'spiritual one-upmanship' that lay behind such incidents, he exhorted other preachers to preach 'against the seeking of miracles in the Lord's blood and in seeing in the host his physical body; for many desire it, regarding themselves to be thus holier than others'.[6] This was, according to Hus, actually far from the case. The reverse was in fact true. 'Thence it is obvious that the true Christian should not seek proofs for his faith, but rather be firmly content with Scripture . . . those who need miracles are men of little faith,' he rightly concluded.[7]

It is noteworthy that Stanislav was one of the other commissioners and that there is no hint that he and Hus were in disagreement on the findings. Furthermore, not only did Zbyněk gladly appoint Hus to this commission, but there was no reluctance to accept the findings. In fact the archbishop directed, on pain of excommunication, that no one should visit Wilsnack. The local priests were ordered to proclaim this decree. Moreover, far from abating at this period, episcopal approval of Hus rather increased. For, in 1405, Hus was invited by Zbyněk to preach the sermons at the synod. He willingly accepted this request.

Zbyněk must have realized what to expect, for in 1403 Hus had thundered forth against the vices of the clergy in no uncertain manner, berating them particularly for rushing through their duties in order to visit taverns and dance halls. There was no toning down of the strictures in these gatherings of august church dignitaries. In the first of his synod sermons on Matthew 22:37 he strongly castigated the clergy. Yet amid the strictures there were more wooing and challenging notes as he cried, as though the Saviour was pleading through him, 'All ye who pass by, stop and see if any sorrow is like my sorrow, I cry aloud in rags: my priests are clothed in scarlet. I agonize with bloody sweat: they delight in luxurious baths. I pass the night spit upon and mocked: they in feasts and drunkenness. I groan upon the cross: they snore on softest down.'[8]

Since the choice fell upon Hus for such preaching engagements — and he spoke at many more important gatherings — it is beyond dispute that he was an outstanding preacher. At the Bethlehem Chapel the crowds continued to gather. It was largely a success story, although there are indications that God did take measures to humble the preacher for youthful pride and unwise pronouncements. Hus seems to have fallen into the trap that has ensnared many, namely that of publicly advertising a 'star convert'. In his century attention could not be drawn to converted 'pop stars' or former world-famous tennis heroes, but when a member of the nobility seemed to turn to the Saviour the temptation could not be resisted.

The zealous young preacher could not refrain from publicly proclaiming the penitence of Lord John Chudoba of Vartenberk and Ralsko. With a title like this, who could fail to be impressed? This was no stonemason, woodcarver or washerwoman from the back streets of Prague. With deep sorrow Hus was soon regretting his public statements as he learned that the seeming penitent had returned to robbing and pillaging on a wide scale. The heartfelt personal nature of his plea cannot be missed as he writes, 'For alas! They very often reproach me to my face, saying: "Behold, your devoted son Chudoba, whom you wished to extol to heaven, and whose penitence you dared publicly to proclaim, is now a fine penitent! What formerly he could not steal he now steals; he received knighthood in order to rob more audaciously." Such talk pierces my heart.'[9]

From this we see that Hus did not escape the heartache and sorrow that are peculiar to a preacher's calling, and no more so than when he saw the former part of the parable of the sower enacted before his eyes and knew his hopes dashed, his arrogance humbled and his joy turned to deep sorrow. Hus goes on to say that even graver charges were made against him as a preacher at this time and, since the incident comes from 1405, we can see that tongues were beginning to wag maliciously and that it was not all applause and warm approval. Yet there was much popularity. The crowds did gather. While the prime reason was that God himself was active in bringing men and women under the sound of the gospel, we are right to ask how such a greatly used preacher set about his task.

Once more we must admit that in published sermons from the period 30 November 1404 to 22 November 1405 the 'spiritualizing' aspect was still very evident. For example, the five loaves in Christ's miracle of the feeding of the 5,000 become 'the knowledge of sins, sorrow for the loss of good, shame of committing wrong, the efficient keeping of the heart, and the solicitude for salvation'.[10] Yet we can understand why, as well as converts who fell away, there were also those who truly believed and persevered, when we find the preacher speaking of the one who is elect as one 'who is the son of promise by the grace of predestination, the son of a free mother by the grace of the call, the spiritual son by the grace of justification, and the son of paternal inheritance by the grace of glorification'.[11]

How would he have preached? Surely the large and very mixed gatherings who attended his ministry for many years, together with the tone of his writings, give us the clue. For a brief survey of some of his typical utterances we feel justified in drawing on writings as well as sermons since Hus himself said of his own work, 'Let him who wishes to read know that I write in the manner in which I am in the habit of speaking.'[12] We shall draw on writings and sermons given outside this early period but we may be sure that from the beginning there was a foreshadowing of things to come, even though there was need for real maturing in this as in other spheres.

Hus was plain, down-to-earth and scriptural. Writing of the question of indulgences, he pointed out that mortal man cannot forgive sins. Yet he did not use abstract language. 'What a strange thing! They cannot rid themselves of fleas and flies, and yet want to rid others of the torments of hell . . .!' is his racy comment.[13] Some proposals of the clergy who were opposed to reform were in his view as dangerous 'as a snake in the grass'.[14] Although Hus did much to encourage hymn singing, he did complain in one sermon of those who gabble through with indecent haste, as one who 'grinds his words without using his lips or teeth'.[15]

On one occasion Hus recounted an incident reported by an Englishman who had been a student at Oxford and who had brought some treatises of Wyclif to Prague. A certain cook, known to the Englishman, was summoned by the bishop to explain why he had defied the prohibition about reading the Scriptures in English. As the cook defended himself, the bishop said, '"Do you know with whom you are speaking?" The cook answered that with a man, a bishop. The bishop then angrily shouted, "How dare you, a miserable layman, quote Scripture to me?" Then the cook: "I know that you are no greater than Christ and hope that I am no worse than the devil. Since the gracious Christ quietly heard the Word from the devil [in the temptation], why would you, being less than Christ, not hear it from me, a man?"'[16]

Always Hus was seeking to bring the theological arguments down to the level of the man in the pew. We have seen how he refers to 'Old Nick', as he colloquially describes the devil, and 'Hodek, the baker, or Hůda, the vegetable woman'.[17] While this may not make for very refined and dignified theological writing of the all-too-familiar, deplorably remote and non-committal academic type, it is very effective and it shows why the preacher was heeded by all stratas of society. Not surprisingly he had the ear of the cook, the baker and the vegetable woman.

Hus was blunt, pointed and arresting. Moreover he dealt with issues of the day. One of the features of his era (and of many others) was the elaborate pomp and circumstance at funerals, especially at the funerals of the rich. There were various priests and singers, the loud pealing of church bells, lavish display of wealth in the funeral processions, then a long mass followed by a sumptuous feast and drinking bouts. Hus attacked the whole procedure from beginning to end saying that it was both a waste of money and a sheer display of pride. Pointedly and effectively he quoted a Latin tag: 'Disease gratifies the physician, death the priest.'[18]

Down-to-earth, simple and often vivid utterance typified his ministry at all levels. No one could remain ignorant of his meaning. 'Robbers, usurers and receivers of stolen goods deceive themselves vastly if they imagine they please God when, having gathered much together by evil means, they give a little to the poor or build altars or set up chaplains.' 'To give a farthing to God while one is alive and well avails one's soul far more than in giving all the gold in heaven and earth after one's death.'[19] Empty confessions and futile reliance on leaving money for the saying of masses for one's soul are thus virtually undermined.

Nor were meaningless penances, unnecessary pilgrimages and other purely human inventions spared in his pointed attacks: 'He who bears patiently a cross word does more for his soul than if he beat his back with all the rods that might grow in the largest forest.' 'He who abases himself before the lowest does more good for his soul than he who makes a pilgrimage to the farthest corner of the earth.' 'He who holds God above all creation helps his soul more than if the Mother of God and all the saints prayed for him.'[20]

Throughout his exposition of the Ten Commandments the practical note is paramount. In the exposition of the first commandment he warns against empty worship and alludes to the veneration of relics. Then, as Spinka puts it, 'He recounts what he himself heard in a sermon preached in a church in New Town. Three devils went to a festival: one to close the hearts against repentance, another to prevent prayers, and the third to close people's purses. The third, the preacher declared, is the worst.'[21] Obviously Hus sees this as a travesty of preaching. But it is again a down-to-earth vivid example that he uses.

On the question of the sabbath he takes a very strict view. All games and agricultural labour and craftsmanship are to be put aside. There should be no dancing, loose language, buying and selling or worldly amusements. With regard to various sexual perversions and acts of adultery common in his day he is detailed and unrelenting in his condemnation. Stealing can take many forms. Hus describes some of them – taking goods by force, non-payment of debts, simony, usury and business deceit.

In all these expositions he is direct and easily understood, as he is also when he writes on the Lord's prayer and warns against mechanical devotions: 'What does it profit when we howl like puppies in a sack, not understanding what we howl, having our minds in the street or in a pub, while our bodies are in the church?'[22] he asks. One can at least say, that as far as human beings can control this, Hus did his best to prevent the mind of his congregation wandering into the pub during the service. He seemed to have succeeded in this very well.

# 8.
# Friends among high and low

We have so far surveyed Hus mainly in his public role during these early years of his ministry. But there was another side. This is well caught in a tribute given to his memory by the University of Prague on 13 May 1416 which is not just fulsome eulogy or empty panegyric. This is how the tribute runs: 'O matchless man shining above all by the example of splendid sanctity! O humble man flashing with the ray of great piety, who contemned riches, and ministered to the poor even to the opening out of his bosom; who did not refuse to bend his knees at the beds of the sick, who brought with tears the hardened to repentance and composed and softened untamed minds by his unspeakable sweetness; who burned against the vices of all men and especially the rich and proud clergy, basing his appeals upon the old and forgotten remedies of the Scriptures as by a new and unheard of motive . . . showing in all things the works of love, pure faith, and undeviating truth!'[1]

If at first sight this may seem to our matter-of-fact twentieth-century minds rather cloying and even smacking of Victorian sentimentality, it is nevertheless, when we probe behind the verbiage, a remarkable tribute. We see Hus not merely before kings, or having especial access to episcopal ears, or engaging in vigorous university debates, but rather caring for the poor, at the bedside of the needy, seeking to evangelize all men. This is a picture that is supported to a considerable degree by some of the earliest of Hus's letters.

Beyond any doubt, as we consider the legacy bequeathed by Hus, the warm, intimate, open and personal letters must be given high place. It is remarkable that so many of these have survived, especially when we consider what one historian has written about the slowness and uncertainty of correspondence in this time. After mentioning that letters were sometimes marginally quicker in arriving than formerly, Margaret Aston has thus described the difficulties, citing the problems of certain correspondents: '"My dearest Giovanni, each time you write to say that you have not had a letter from me it is like a knife-blow, for I have written to you six times in the last year", Machiavelli wrote to his nephew in Pera (a quarter of Constantinople) in 1516. The frustrations of private correspondence were still much the same as they had been 150 years earlier, when Petrarch was annoyed to discover that three letters, which he had written to Boccaccio over seven months before, were still in the possession of the man to whom he had entrusted them.'[2]

Obviously Hus's letters had to survive more than normal hazards before they could be read by men in the twentieth century. This was particularly true of the later letters written at a time when Hus was hated by increasing numbers. In the National Museum at Prague some years ago there could be seen a considerably damaged letter written by Hus in 1411 against his calumniators. In 1546 a Hussite writer added to it a few words, alluding to 'the divine John Hus of sacred and pious memory'. Then it fell into Roman Catholic hands, but instead of being confined to the flames it was put behind glass in 1711 so that the readers 'may curse the baseness of a heretic', as the accompanying caption urged.[3] We may be glad that God in his providence has preserved so many letters through such vicissitudes.

A feature of these letters, although it does not always emerge with the same clarity in the earlier ones, confirms the truthfulness of the tribute which speaks of Hus 'basing his appeals upon the forgotten remedies of the Scriptures as by a new and unheard of motive'. It is, of course, the skilful and thorough-going way in which Hus quotes and applies Scripture that constitutes the very basis of his counselling. At his best he does this powerfully and incisively. Where he is inconsistent or less than fully scriptural, we must not lose sight of his pioneering role. These were 'forgotten remedies' which he was, with others, restoring to the light of day.

The first of the letters stands appropriately in its pre-eminent position at the head of Hus's surviving correspondence. It is addressed to a priest, who was taking the common course of seeking secular employment to supplement the income from his priestly duties. The opening words tell us that he was doing this against Hus's advice. At once Hus scents the motive of greed. Therefore, after urging the priest not to grasp after gifts, Hus underlines this by writing, 'Do not seek the death even of an unjust man for profit, as you have learned Cato's exhortation: "On the death of your neighbour you must not place your hope."'[4] Living in the hope of stepping into dead men's shoes or in the expectation of inheriting a legacy at a friend's death are age-old evils, but Hus does not let their venerable pedigree spare them from exposure.

The letter also contains an appeal for the priest to pursue his true calling properly, to seek to reconcile people at variance and to attack evil. Hus strongly asserts that 'it were better' for the man 'not to assume the office rather than to accept and by its means not to break up iniquity'.[5] He therefore did not take the widely held view that priestly ordination conveyed some indelible character so that, after its reception, it did not really matter how the priest lived. He demanded loyalty to a calling. It was to be an incessant and uncompromising demand throughout his whole ministry and was to earn him many enemies.

To the priest Hus was frank and straightforward. 'See to it that you receive not persons; make available the service of your office equally to the rich and the poor,' was both his command in this letter and his practice in his own life.[6] There is little evidence of any time-serving or place-seeking mentality in Hus. This was because he was a servant of the Word of God, which is no respecter of persons. The correspondence will abundantly confirm this trait. We note that in this relatively brief opening letter there are no less than four clear scriptural quotations.

The next letter we have already examined. It is the theological protest to John Hübner. At times the argument is tortuous and it must be conceded that, although Scripture is employed, it is not used sufficiently or clearly enough, but the letter is none the less the fervent outpouring of one who insists on fair play towards Wyclif and who has himself a real concern for truth, in contrast to the pleasure-loving clergy challenged in the course of his argument. The closing prayer is that 'we pray the Lord with the church, that he may be pleased to guard us from the heresy and wickedness of simony'.[7]

A noble lady was the early recipient of a fiery missive against dancing and gaming, which apparently were being permitted on her estates. Among other things, Hus is concerned about the desecration of the Lord's day, when men should be preparing themselves to 'contemplate the Lord God sweetly'. Despite the fact that some obviously justify the permissiveness from the fact that many priests are known to dance, Hus is unbending in his own opposition. He uses the incident of Aaron and the golden calf to show the evil consequences of wild dancing and states categorically, 'Dance is a very grave and mortal sin.'[8]

This was his consistent stance on this issue. Thus once, preaching on Zacchaeus in Luke 19:1–10, he said, 'Those householders are manifest sinners who allow immorality or dice-playing in their houses. I say the same of dancing, by which they mock God on Sundays.'[9] Strictures in this vein show that he made no attempt to curry favour with the people by pandering to popular tastes. He would certainly have believed that the praying knee and dancing foot rarely, if ever, belonged together and no fear of being in a minority position prevented him from saying so.

However, this particular letter is not solely negative and denunciatory. Within the letter there is shown much concern for the peasants themselves. For example, the writer inveighs against their being hanged for mere peccadilloes, and implies that many lords open their estates for wild revelry not because they have a true love for the peasants' welfare but simply because they want to rake in the profits. Hus warns that unjust lords, greedy for more and more, and callously indifferent towards those upon whom they trample, may suddenly be judged by God and fall dead in that awesome state of impenitence. His appeal to the noble lady is frank and direct as he urges that she herself be a good steward of the estate that God has bestowed upon her.

The next surviving letter, which is to the lord who had

abandoned his profession of faith, reveals Hus as a caring evangelist, as we have seen. It also underlines his concern for the downtrodden and oppressed, for he joins with others in a petition to the lord for one called William whom 'Your Nobility had jailed in Bolonia'. Salvation comes first but justice must not be disregarded and we can read with profit Hus's entreaty that 'If Your Grace seized him for no cause, that you free him with all his belongings with which you captured him. We know from Scripture that he who unjustly deprives another of anything harms himself more than the one he has wronged.'[10]

We may pause to underline that, despite the fact that Hus was sufficiently bedazzled by the title to announce this man's 'conversion' from the pulpit, he did make amends by this letter. His popularity with the nobility in general, which was considerable, was not based on obsequious deference or oily flattery. Speaking of the all-too-common tendency of undue deference to the rich and titled among eighteenth-century evangelicals, one historian, perhaps a little unjustly, says that John Wesley was one of the few who wrote to the Countess of Huntingdon 'with no hint of approaching her on all fours'.[11] Hus was free from this fault. His letters were respectful, without ceasing to be forthright, manly and courageous.

A very long letter to a nobleman concerning death duties, written about 1407 from Prague, not only evinces these qualities of frankness and impartiality but reveals an ever-deepening compassion for the peasants and the outcasts of society. It also displays a clear grasp of biblical principles and shows that Hus realized that the Word of God called for justice in its broadest sense and not merely for 'law and order' in the shape of punitive measures and harsh practices. Obviously Hus was not ploughing a lone furrow in all this for the 1405 synod, at which he had been preacher, had stated that 'Whoever buys the year's produce or wine at harvest or vintage cheaper, so that they can sell for a higher price later, such persons shall have sinned mortally.'[12]

The letter, with its passages of question and answer, is obviously from one who had listened to and taken part in many discussions on this topic. There are echoes of these debates as Hus expresses his strong abhorrence of the common practice whereby a lord, on the death of a peasant, sought to seize the peasant's inheritance in the way of death duties. Hus movingly pictures the friendless and helpless peasant shrugging his shoulders in a futile gesture of resignation as he says, 'However the lord disposes of my property, so be it!'[13] Hus insists that his property is the result of his labour and that he ought to be the owner of it and the disposer of it at his death.

In a powerful series of scriptural references Hus pronounces against 'those who claim the right for themselves to fleece their peasants'.[14] He calls as witness Isaiah, who denounces those making iniquitous decrees (Isaiah 10:1–3). He summons the help of John the Baptist, who warned hearers against exacting from needy people more than they should (Luke 3:13). And, in a lengthy discussion of another scriptural passage, he appeals to the incident in Numbers 27, where the daughters of Zelophehad successfully plead with Moses to secure for them the inheritance of their father who had died without male heir. 'You hear the law of God, issued by himself, a holy law, not a distorted one; an eternal law, not subject to change by human will; a plain law, not difficult to understand!' is his irresistible and cogent argument.[15]

He then widens the attack to include the plight of the orphan, using the words of Augustine to accuse those who, a few days before the death of the parent, professed to be dear friends, but afterwards cannot wait to get their hands on the property. What if these scoundrels then 'endow a church and give thanks to God'? It will not fool God at all, for 'they sin the more by wishing to make God an accomplice of their robbing'.[16] The religious veneer makes this practice all the more thoroughly reprehensible. Using Augustine again, he shows from the words of Christ in Matthew 25:42, 43 that, if there is condemnation for refusal to share one's possessions, how much greater will be the condemnation for robbing the needy? Dorothy L. Sayers saw the common and culpable blindness of Christians in this whole matter when she wrote, 'Doubtless it would have needed courage to turn Dives from the church door along with Mary Magdalen; (has any prosperously fraudulent banker, I wonder, ever been refused Communion on the grounds that he was, in the words of the English Prayer-book, "an open and notorious evil liver"?)'[17] Hus was free from this type of blindness.

No one can fail to detect the fervour of his final challenges. 'I also admonish you when you hold judgement, that you do not chase after money, as many do, who condemn poor simple folk for one word spoken in simplicity, demanding money and sometimes even inflicting death,' he writes.[18] Hus argues that a wise judge should discriminate. If the offence was just an insolent word, let the spokesman be put in the stocks to cool off. (Hus obviously accepted this form of punishment.) If one man actually wounds another, then a fine or proper compensation to the victim should be paid. (Have we today grasped this principle?) If it were murder, then Hus, it would seem, feels that the judge should not be bribed into releasing the criminal for this heinous crime. (It would seem that he expected capital punishment to take place.)

Yet, when a lord has to impose a fine, he should not pocket the money. To safeguard against avarice and consequent injustice, let him 'take the fine and distribute among the poor, or repair a road, or otherwise use it for common good'.[19] He should be particularly aware of the terrible temptation to encourage temptations so that he can draw large profits from those who fall. Moreover justice must be executed speedily. Hus vividly pictures the dithering judge, who clearly sees what is right but does not wish to be in the bad books of either party, and either seeks to play for time and say nothing definite or, more commonly, takes the line of least resistance by oppressing the powerless poorer party.

'These things, it seems to me, are commonly done among the nobility,' is the sentence which begins the last paragraph of this fine and perceptive letter. Was it, one may ask, all hot air, fine-sounding phrases, or a preacher's pious platitudes? We do not know of the reaction of the recipient of the letter, although the fact that the letter has survived and not been violently torn to shreds does augur for the fact that it was well received. What we do know is that in Bohemia God was working powerfully at this time and there is clear evidence that a considerable group of lords did heed such warnings and endeavour to give their peasants fairer treatment over the next decade. Thus the Hussite Lord John of Hradec in 1407 granted his peasants the freedom to dispose of their own land, stating candidly as he did this that he also hoped to attract settlers to his villages. Another noble, Čeněk, who was a close adherent of Hus's teaching, also gave his peasants the liberty to sell their possessions at any time and move from his village to another one or to the city.

'At the moment when Henry V's soldiers were hunting down Oldcastle's conspirators, many of the Bohemian nobles were displaying their solidarity with the cause of their native reform leader John Hus,' is a verdict which would seem to sum up accurately the trend of much of Hus's ministry among the higher class and show the contrast between the two lands.[20] There were those who fell away and disappointed, there were those who opposed and those who showed little interest, but there were a surprisingly large number of this group who did seem to make a sincere response to the gospel offer. Like the Countess of Huntingdon, whom we have already mentioned, they would have been grateful for the 'm' in 'many' when the apostle Paul, cataloguing the converts, stated that 'not *many*' were of noble birth (1 Corinthians 1:26).

We have also given evidence from three letters to demonstrate that Hus had not forgotten his own early experiences among the peasants. That he had a real and heartfelt burden for the underprivileged is abundantly clear. Not for him the supercilious and superior attitude of Shakespeare's Coriolanus towards the 'rank-scented many', as he contemptuously termed them.[21] Hus did not look down on the peasants. He knew that many were skilled workmen. He realized that some had far more spiritual gumption than better-educated people and therefore wrote, with reference to the ability of some to detect a false shepherd and simoniacal clergyman, 'Even a peasant can understand that he who has never fed sheep is not to be called a shepherd.'[22]

What a refutation all this is of the cynical judgement of the Czech writer who summed up the Hussite revolt in this epigrammatic but misleading manner: 'Why did the Hussite troubles occur? They really wanted to know whether the divine body should be eaten with or without sauce'![23] Not surprisingly, this saying is quoted by a Communist historian. Hus himself was a peasant, but a peasant whose mind had been opened by the living God and who inevitably believed that God could do the same work in many of his contemporaries. This was his main task. Yet as he pursued this calling, he did not omit to call for the implementation of biblical justice in many situations. This surely is the true way.

The last of the early letters which we shall examine is quite different in tone and content from those hitherto discussed. It bears the intriguing title: 'To Some Young Women Living in a Country Retreat'. In the opening we see Hus at both his best and worst. He is at his best as he extols the great worth of Christ himself as the heavenly Bridegroom who 'does not defile, violate, or trouble his wives, does not grow old, never becomes faithless to them'.[24] This could be based on firm scriptural foundation, in that Christ is the Bridegroom and his people are compared with the bride or virgins (Ephesians 5:22–33; 2 Corinthians 11:2; Revelation 19:7, 8). So far, so good.

Indeed in the light of the customary medieval attitude much of the letter is highly commendable and far in advance of the general churlish approach. Medieval monks delighted in denouncing women: 'What else is woman but a foe to friendship, an inevitable penance, a necessary evil, a natural temptation, a coveted calamity, a domestic peril? . . . Wherefore it is a sin to desert her, but a torment to keep her.'[25] Reams could be quoted in this jaundiced vein. Writing just a little before Hus, Chaucer makes his Wife of Bath say,

> For take my word for it, there is no libel
> On women that the clergy will not paint,
> Except when writing of a woman-saint,
> But never good of other women, though.[26]

In other words, a cleric will never have anything good to say about a woman unless she is actually a supersaint. 'Women in the Middle Ages found themselves perpetually oscillating between a pit and pedestal,' comments one historian.[27]

Where it suits, Hus can join in this general denunciation. Here is his regular advice to a priest: 'Avoid young women in every way. Do not believe their devotion; for St Augustine says: "The more devout they are, the more prone to lasciviousness: and under the pretext of piety is hidden deceit or venom of fornication."'[28] There are women who under the guise of seeking pastoral counsel move from spiritual flirtation to a more dangerous kind of flirtation. But that this is the whole story of spirituality in women or that Augustine is a reliable guide in this sphere is totally unacceptable. Also unacceptable is the illustration given (without comment) by Hus of the saint who 'cut off his hand because he had felt a carnal desire when he had touched the lips of a woman during the administration of the body of God'.[29] Of course, we are not saying that this should not be a matter for watchfulness, but the emphasis is wrong.

In his letter to the group of women, Hus's opening prayer had been to 'the Lord Jesus, to grant you his grace and to strengthen you in grace and virginity'. He then catalogues the qualities of marriage: 'If he is good-looking, you will fear that he would go after another; if he is ugly, there is distress; if he is a drunkard, irascible, or otherwise evilly disposed, there is hell enough. If he sires a child, there is suffering in pregnancy, in the birth and the upbringing; if there is no issue, it brings disgrace, sorrow, and useless cohabitation. If a child is born, you will worry about it being still-born or somehow deformed.'[30] There would, if this gloomy counsel were heeded, hardly have been a rush to marry!

Then Hus brings the example of Christ and the Virgin Mary, along with the teaching of the Saviour in Matthew 19:12 and the apostle Paul in 1 Corinthians 7, to support his argument for celibacy. While there is a proper place for the latter two scriptural passages, we would have to say that regrettably he affirms quite explicitly the unscriptural doctrine of the perpetual virginity of Mary. He also urges the virgins to hold on to their virginity as they will receive a special crown in the reward to come.

The last section of the letter, on a slightly different theme, is interesting and provides a sidelight on what went on among the different groups attached to the Bethlehem Chapel, as it seems clear that Hus is referring to one of the practices there. He writes, 'I am sending you a song which we sing at the afternoon service of the holy virgins, that considering the words, you may rejoice in your heart and sing it with your voices. However, let not men overhear you, lest they be moved by an evil incentive and you fall into sin of pride and of scandal.'[31] Oddly enough, Hus's opponents later were to comment critically on the fact that both men and women shared in the singing of the church. One wonders whether Hus later changed his mind on this or whether he offered this kind of counsel only to young women dedicated to celibacy.

Although it is not really known which song it was that was to be sung by these women, it is interesting to speculate. There were three hymns ascribed to Hus in the Bohemian hymn book of 1576. In the Moravian hymn book of 1891 there is only one. It contains this clear gospel verse:

> To avert from men God's wrath
> Jesus suffered in our stead;
> By an ignominious death
> He a full atonement made.[32]

Any Christian women singing this were singing about the heart of the gospel. It must not be overlooked that despite weak elements in the reasoning (Hus fittingly signs himself 'a weakling priest') the very fact of his concern and his sending the song shows that he did accept their spiritual standing in Christ. Nor must the gatherings of the pious women and the support of Queen Sophia be forgotten in our assessment of his attitude. Hus wrote a beautiful little tract *The Daughter* for such.

People of all kinds were embraced under his ministry. In an exposition of the faith written in Czech Hus wrote, 'The first Czech who explained the Greek word ἐκκλήσια understood it wrongly, for he stupidly translated it by the word "kostel" or "cierkev", which would mean that the bride of the Lord Jesus Christ is a stone church or a building made of wood. But if he had explained that this word ἐκκλήσια means an assembly [sbor] they would not have made this mistake.'[33] Not only did Hus grasp this evangelical insight, but also in one of his Bethlehem sermons he declared, anticipating the insights of the Reformers later, that 'Every holy man is a priest, but not every priest is a holy man.'[34] The letters give practical expression both to his concept of the church as people, and to his belief in the priesthood of all believers.

His concern for the common people in general had long been evident in the type of sermons he preached. We have now seen it in the letters he wrote. We close the chapter by mentioning one other aspect – his concern for the vernacular. At Bethlehem he preached in Czech not only because it was stipulated in the foundation, but because it was his conviction. As the years went by he was to express himself increasingly in his native language both from the pulpit and with the pen. This was not a total innovation but there were not many precursors. The large numbers of works in Czech produced at the close of his ministry are the logical outcome of all this.

It has been argued that outside theology Hus's greatest achievement was in the development of the Czech language. His interest and influence were certainly considerable for, as one authority has pointed out, 'While at the Bethlehem Chapel, Hus began a reform of the Czech language, in order to transform it from a mere spoken vernacular into a useful literary medium. He introduced the diacritical marks ˇ ´ and ° to replace clumsy combinations of letters; so that, for example, the word for "line", previously spelled "czaara" henceforth became "čára". Czech as it is written today is largely Hus's handiwork.'[35] Hus was a man of many parts with many talents. But ultimately it must be acknowledged that all, including his interest in the Czech language, were used that he might bring 'the hardened to repentance', as the university tribute puts it.

# 9.
# Signs of growing opposition

The year 1408 was to be a significant year for Hus. Events of the previous year had given little hint of what lay ahead. In 1407 Hus had again been asked to preach the synod sermon. With Archbishop Zbyněk in full support, from a text in the sixth chapter of Ephesians, he had branded as heretics the sons of Eli who both forgot the duties of their priestly office and were guilty of gross evils, such as fornication. This was in the same vein as the synod sermon two years before where Hus had castigated many as little more than wanton womanizers. 'When the blood becomes heated, they talk of woman and acts of lust in most wanton language,' he had said.[1]

After the sermon in 1407 the archbishop did not stride away in fury. On the contrary, he even issued a decree himself condemning such priest fornicators as heretics. It has been suggested that Zbyněk sought to limit Hus's influence by confining him to church assemblies. But this is far-fetched. Hus was preaching and saying such things far more frequently to the common people. Yet, despite episcopal favour, Hus could not have been unaware of the possible consequences. That there must have been a period of conflict and see-sawing of emotions as he foresaw the inevitable conflict is evident. In one letter he speaks of the period when he was afraid to speak out against obvious evils. He was afraid of excommunication or death. But he added, 'But the gracious Saviour, who admitted me to his office, now gives me courage not to fear, but to speak the truth against everyone who opposes the law of Jesus Christ.'[2] It must have been particularly hard to foresee that he would lose friends and face hostility in this world where he was so loved and respected.

But were Hus's tirades against the clergy in fact right or necessary? We must seek to answer this question in general terms. It has, for example, been argued repeatedly by a French Roman Catholic scholar that Hus's attacks on the clergy were misplaced and an offence to pious ears, especially when given to the common people. Others who said similar things are excused because they did it discreetly in Latin to a select gathering![3] In this De Vooght only echoes the arguments of many of Hus's contemporaries.

How far the lust for money dominated the clergy of the day is revealed in the 'Prologue' to Chaucer's *Canterbury Tales,* written some half a century before Hus's day. Everywhere Chaucer shows us the glitter of gold, the chink of coins, the fleecing of unsuspecting layfolk. His sleek, fat monk, with his shining bald head, had round his sleeve 'fine grey fur, the finest in the land' and near his chin 'a wrought gold cunningly fashioned pin'. Next to him the friar gave only light penances as long as the fee was forthcoming. Nor was the summoner a man of finer conscience:

> He would allow — just for a quart of wine —
> Any good lad to keep a concubine.

Moreover, the pardoner, Chaucer tells us, in 'one short day' drew more money than the parson in many a long month.[4]

This was not abusive caricature by a critic hostile to the church. Chaucer himself lived and died a devout Roman Catholic. Also, in his picture of the poor parson he does present the other side of the picture, even though his insincere clergy greatly outnumber the genuine ones. As to the value of this type of writing as evidence of historical fact, Mark Pattison has an apt comment when he writes, 'Satire to be popular must exaggerate, but it must be an exaggeration of known and recognized facts.'[5]

Other chroniclers contemporary with Hus recognized and deplored the facts. One of them declared that 'Benefices which ought to provide alms for the poor have become the patrimony of the rich. One holds eighteen, another twenty, a third twenty-four; while the poor man is despised, his knowledge and his holy life are of no account.' A man who had been secretary to the Pope of Avignon, Nicholas de

Clemanges, wrote that the clergy 'would endure with greater calmness the loss of ten thousand souls than of ten thousand shillings'.[6]

That the pope himself was in the forefront of this spirit of covetousness is beyond dispute. There had been a steady unapostolic succession. Pope after pope competed in devising new ways of raising money. If it was not a jubilee, then it was an indulgence. And ever present was the desire to control and allocate the various benefices and pocket some of the fees. Therefore it is no surprise that when Hus began his attack on the simony of the church he began with the pope. Referring to an incident of 1402 when an archbishop took office for a short period before Zbyněk, he says, 'The third form of papal simony is the appointment of bishops and priests for money. A proof of this is at present plainly to be seen in the payment of many thousand gulden for the archbishopric of Prague.'[7] The pope himself had benefited considerably from this particular transaction, as he did when this archbishop died a speedy death, enabling him to obtain only one year later another 2,800 gulden from Zbyněk.

Earlier we noted that Hus himself originally entered the priesthood for the wrong reasons. He wanted an easy life. We have also seen how he describes the life of a monk and obviously sees it as one of the best occupations of his day. He further writes, 'Cold does not bite them, for they have boots and greatcoats; heat does not scorch them, for they have cool cells and cloisters, that is, courts of paradise. Therefore

> Whoever wishes to live well
> Let him enter the monks' cell.'[8]

The above extract is from his work *On Simony*. Apart from writing a long tract on this, Hus mentions simony again and again in his letters and says it is as bad as heresy. He argues that Gehazi in the Old Testament and Simon Magus in the New are the ancestors of 'all who demand reward in exchange for spiritual gifts'.[9] Simon Magus it is who gives 'simony' its name.

In all this he was not saying that the preachers should live on nothing. He insists in one letter that the congregation should provide them with a 'necessary livelihood'.[10] What he had particularly in mind and often mentions is the priest haggling for money for his fees for funerals, baptisms and weddings and refusing to give spiritual ministry until he had received payment. Having said this, we must also admit that Hus would argue more strenuously for clerical poverty than many would today. He feels that the preacher should be able to point to himself as an example and quotes Acts 20:33, 34, and 2 Corinthians 11:7–9, 29 to support this. Yet there are places where he does say that more than the bare minimum may be given. He does leave room for grace and generosity, but the preacher must not seek after these.

Another of his charges was that immorality was widespread. Again we must ask whether he was exaggerating. Apparently not. A visitation in 1379 in Bohemia convicted of immorality sixteen clergymen out of thirty who were visited.[11] At the height of Hus's own subsequent conflict, when his opponents among the clergy were becoming unpopular, we learn that numerous attacks were launched on the homes of parish priests, who had to fly with their concubines. 'We have here again evidence of the almost universal immorality of the parochial clergy of Prague,' comments one authority.[12]

'Their fornication has become so customary that they keep their women openly and without shame, some hypocritically calling them sisters . . .', was Hus's strong and unpleasant stricture.[13] We have already seen that Hus denounced the priests of the day for organizing dances to lure people to church. He saw the priests as sapping the morals of the community in this way. Unfortunately, Hus argued, the bishops themselves, who should be rebuking this immorality, were frequently among the worst offenders. His view was that any priest guilty of such behaviour should be deposed. Without naming people or places, he gives examples of priests adorning their mistresses more lavishly than church altars, and of evil practices in Bohemia, Moravia and Hungary. In the latter country the priest, supposedly celibate, paid a stated sum to the bishop for each child he had. There is further independent confirmation of the tragically low standards in the fact that Gerson, himself a loyal son of the Roman church, bewailed the fact that in some churches prostitutes came in search of customers and lewd pictures were openly sold. Such facts are sordid but they must be seen as the background for Hus's indignation. One would have hoped that support for him would have been whole-hearted and universal among the clergy, whereas the reverse was the case.[14]

Most important of all, the unity that there had been among the Czech brethren, especially in face of German hostility and opposition to the teaching of Wyclif, was not to exist for much longer. Up till now there had been little foreshadowing of the coming divisions and hostilities within the movement. Perhaps one hint of things to come had been when Stanislav, the revered teacher of Hus himself, and one who was at the forefront of the movement, was challenged about his denial of transubstantiation. He had written a tract which clearly reflected Wyclifite 'heresy'. Not only did Stanislav recant, but he even professed at the time that his own tract on this theme was in actual fact incomplete and that he had intended to finish it in an orthodox way.

Hus's close friend Jakoubek of Stříbro was particularly angered by the cowardice and subterfuge of Stanislav. The recantation which took place in Stanislav's private rooms in 1406 did not allay suspicions and in 1407 the Czech was still under attack from a Saxon scholar who was also seeking the help of a German university and of Rome itself. Whether Hus now suspected the reality of Stanislav's faith we do not know. Stephen Páleč testified that originally Hus held Stanislav 'as if there was no one like him under the sun' and Hus never denied this.[15] Indeed Hus was as closely and warmly bound to Páleč himself.

Yet the works of Wyclif still continued to appeal strongly to many of the Bohemians. Although the bringing over of books was often a risky business, there were those who volunteered for the task. Jerome of Prague himself transcribed and brought over material, as he himself admitted. Two other Bohemian students were surreptitiously gathering texts in England in 1406 and 1407. We have a glimpse of them paying a pious visit to Wyclif's tomb in Leicestershire *en route* (and taking a fragment of the tomb), probably visiting Sir John Oldcastle, a prominent Lollard of high rank, and then going on to do their main copying in Lollard hide-outs in country villages in Northamptonshire and Gloucestershire. Since Oxford was a place closely watched, they only stopped there briefly in order to correct their texts. There was an eager readership waiting for this highly explosive theological material, for this time a lot of theological works were brought back. Hus was among the keenest of the readers. By the end of his life he himself had accumulated copies of nearly all Wyclif's writings. This was no mean feat. It denoted a genuine enthusiasm for the works of the English reformer.

This enthusiasm in itself earned Hus enmity. At first this was principally among the German element. But by 1408 there were many of his own countrymen who had far from friendly feelings towards Hus. A contemporary chronicler saw it like this: 'It was commonly said that as long as he preached against the lords, knights and squires, the citizens and the artisans all praised him and felt kindly towards him. But when he attacked the clergy, the pope and others of the ecclesiastical estate, then many deserted him.'[16] Although this is an oversimplification, insofar as it was a clash of doctrine above all else, yet there were also the personal animosities.

We recall the numerous clashes which Hus had with monks, with clergy and with notaries. There were those who had old scores to settle among these. We have seen that some of his letters were very pointed and strong. Not every recipient was grateful for the candid rebuke. We have observed that in his two synod sermons Hus particularly made the greedy and immoral clergy a target of this message. This attack continued to be resented deeply by several hearers. We have seen that Hus was prominent in the exposure of the sham and iniquity of Wilsnack. There were priests whose income dropped drastically as a result of this and it did not dispose them to feel kindly towards their outspoken critic. We have seen that in the university debates Hus did not pull his punches. Not all theologians can easily forgive and forget and there were those who passionately desired his downfall. Many also are likely to have been simply jealous in the face of Hus's popularity and success.

However, strangely enough, Hus himself was not the first

target. We have seen that Stanislav and Stephen Páleč had been right at the forefront of the reform movement and had in fact seemed to be more staunch supporters of Wyclif than Hus himself. We also saw that Stanislav was one of Hus's colleagues in the Wilsnack investigation. Although Stanislav had both recanted and affirmed orthodox Roman dogma on the question of transubstantiation, rumours of the events in Bohemia had reached Rome's ears and both Stanislav and Stephen Páleč were summoned to appear to answer charges on these particular issues. After delaying for a while, the two set out. The whole affair looked ominous. The very fact that Rome had summoned a man who had to all intents and purposes recanted already showed that she was not going to allow rebellion to develop without taking severe measures. On arrival at Bologna, the two were robbed and thrown into prison by Cardinal Baldassare Cossa, one of a group who had recently deserted the Urbanist pope. They were surprised to be blamed for continuing to acknowledge the existing Roman pope. They had been unwittingly caught up in the turmoil of an endeavour to end the schism which we will describe in the next chapter. Yet they were not forgotten by their own friends. On the suggestion of Hus, the rector of the university addressed a complaint to the cardinals assembled at Pisa. It stated that these venerable men, Stanislav, Professor of Theology, and Stephen Páleč, Bachelor of Theology, 'well-beloved sons of the university', had been deprived of their possessions and wrongfully thrust into prison. The letter went on to praise 'the vigorous wisdom, praiseworthy conversation, and solid doctrine' of these men and begged for their release. Apparently they were soon liberated, but without receiving back their possessions. In their hour of trial, their friends had proved loyal to them.[17]

Meanwhile, Archbishop Zbyněk, who had never favoured the more radical party, arrested a young Master of Arts on the charge that he had called Wyclif an 'evangelical doctor'. A form of recantation was insisted upon, and even though this was not public, the Czechs took this as a defeat. Sadly it would seem that a sense of insult to the Czech nation loomed larger in their feeling of indignation than did the underlying theological issue. Their immediate reaction in choosing the condemned man as their key spokesman in a forthcoming debate only alienated the archbishop further. Zbyněk then showed by his choice for the 1408 synod of a preacher who was totally dissimilar from Hus that he was now taking a stance in firm opposition to the reformers. Other synod measures, such as the prohibition of criticism of the clergy in Czech and the restriction of the use of Czech hymns, were in the same vein. At about the same time the reformist clergy, harking back to the forty-five articles of Wyclif which had been condemned, refused to accept such a blanket condemnation but declared rather that they should not be taught in their 'heretical, or erroneous, and offensive' sense, thus implying that they might be taught in a correct way.

There next followed an incident which brought a direct and open confrontation between Hus and his archbishop. A priest, Nicholas called Abraham, had preached in Prague without permission and had been called to account by one of the strongest opponents of church reform. When Abraham retorted that as a priest he was free to preach without special permission, he was accused of heresy. Although Hus did manage to ensure that he was not pronounced guilty of heresy, Abraham was banished from the diocese. It was yet another instance of the silencing of a worthy and zealous priest.

Hus could no longer remain silent. He picked up his pen and asked his archbishop why adulterous and evil priests walked about unmolested 'while humble priests, who uproot the thorns of sin, who fulfil the duties of your administration with proper devotion, are not avaricious, but offer themselves freely for God's sake to the labour of proclaiming the gospel – these are jailed as heretics and suffer exile for the very proclamation of the gospel?'[18] Such words by themselves would hardly have been likely to have endeared him to the now very sensitive and prickly archbishop. Yet what followed was even more direct. 'It rests with Your Paternity to reap the whole harvest of the kingdom of Bohemia, to gather it into the Lord's barn, and in the day of your death to give account from each sheaf,' was a clear-cut evangelical emphasis.[19] This was, of course, the heart of the issue. The stopping of Abraham from preaching had nothing to do with procedural matters, correct form-filling and proper applications to preach. It was, as Hus realized, for other reasons altogether. Hus then closed by urging the archbishop to drive the laggards to work and to remember that God's Word is not bound and the salvation of souls must ever be the pastor's chief concern.

At this point specific charges were brought against Hus himself. They stopped short of accusations of heresy but were serious enough. It was said that in his sermons Hus sinned against charity by rendering the clergy odious to the people in his denunciations. It was further stated that in the presence of a large and mixed congregation of the Bethlehem Chapel, 'contrary to the regulations of the holy church and the teaching of the fathers', he declared that all who claimed money for confession, communion and baptism were heretics. Another charge was that while officiating at the funeral of a man notorious for holding a number of livings at the same time, Hus exclaimed that he would not accept as gift the whole world on condition of dying possessed of so many benefices. He was also alleged to have praised Wyclif in a lavish way and, in a repetition of the first charge, was said persistently to have defamed the clergy.

The initiative was now with the archbishop and Hus was now the one under challenge. Yet it was Hus who seized the opportunity to write a long letter to his superior. It has been criticized, and perhaps rightly so, for its sarcasm. For example, part of the accusation was that Hus was reported to have said things 'before the whole multitude of people of both sexes' and his absurdly hair-splitting rejoinder was to say that he did not say these things before the whole multitude of people in Rome and in Jerusalem. It has also been said that the letter reaches the extreme limit of what is permissible to a priest in writing to an ecclesiastical superior. With this criticism we have less sympathy.

Hus begins by quoting 1 Peter 3:15, 16 as a justification of his lengthy letter and then employs his usual arguments against simony. Turning to the question of whether he had wildly branded all priests as heretics, he retorts with simplicity and honesty that he only labelled such as heretics if they were simoniacs. He realizes that 'many priests whose shoes I am not worthy to take off' are manifestly not greedy but would rather help poor people out of their own means than grab money off them. There is no reason to doubt the genuineness of Hus's answer.[20]

It is interesting, in the light of future developments, that Hus was also accused of wishing to destroy 'laudable custom'. In refutation of this charge he quotes with ease men of the past who support him, but he also makes this far more searching point about custom and tradition in the church as he astutely and tellingly cites a pronouncement from a decree of the past: 'Although the majority suppose that something is allowed because of long usage, the law of death has become valid; they ignore thereby the fact that the crimes are the heavier the longer they keep the soul in bondage.'[21] In this way he defeated his opponents with their own weapons.

The most interesting parts of the letter then follow. These consist of his reply to the charge that he had implied by his comments at a funeral service that a rich pluralist had gone to hell. Evidently there had been some violent parsonic apoplexy at his outspoken words. One wonders whether here Hus is being uncharacteristically evasive and less than open in his reply. He admits saying that he feared lest the man be damned and mentions his desire of diverting 'the multitude of the clergy, who were present at the sermon, from avaricious gathering of pluralities of benefices'.[22] Then, going off on a tangent and arguing from numerous scriptural examples that it had been right for him as the preacher to have said, 'According to my opinion – not anticipating God's judgement – I would not accept the whole world to die with so many and so great benefices', he concludes somewhat lamely that he had not 'denied that Master Peter of pious memory was not a good Christian'.[23] This is rather a come-down! Yet, to be fair to Hus, he may well have been preserving a balance between using the man to draw a clear warning and yet refraining from pronouncing the final verdict on his eternal state. By contrast Hus is much more consistently positive in answering accusations about his praise of Wyclif. It is obvious to the reader that he is far more genuinely hopeful for Wyclif's salvation!

Scriptural quotations follow in profusion as Hus then deals with the complaint that he had preached excessively against the clergy. He is in the position of being able to point to occasion after occasion when Christ himself denounced false teachers in general and the Pharisees in particular. There is an attractive Quaker saying that it is better to light a candle than curse the darkness, but Hus is well able to demonstrate in an irrefutable way that exposure of evil teaching is in fact part of the Lord's own ministry. Hus does not miss the opportunity of showing that Christ himself was defamed and slandered for preaching in this kind of way.

In a vitally important section he argues that the real target of their complaint is not the preacher John Hus, but the Word of God itself. 'They likewise heap shame upon me and ascribe lies to me, saying that I heap shame upon the clergy. However, I preach the sacred Scriptures – not I, but principally the Holy Spirit and indeed Christ the prophet or his apostle thus speak,' he writes.[24] If therefore, he quotes from Isaiah 24:7 or Lamentations 4:13 it is not merely he who speaks but the very voice of God himself. Like the Saviour before him, he refuses to be silenced by numerous objectors to the truth. He effectively cites Christ's own words in reply to the disciples who were alarmed and abashed by the criticism of the Pharisees: 'Leave them alone [that is, to be offended] they are blind leaders, leading the blind.'

Not all Hus wrote can be defended, but the greater part can. The letter seemed to open up an unbridgeable gulf between Hus and Zbyněk. Relationships were not now merely strained; they had disintegrated entirely. But there were complicating factors, and before we look at the last surviving letter from Hus to his archbishop it will be our task to look at these factors, since they played a part in the widening breach not only between Hus and Zbyněk but, as it happens, between Zbyněk and many others in the realm. Yet, in doing this, let us not lose sight of the fact that like all truly great spiritual battles this was one between a lover of God's truth and those who opposed it. Hus was quite right. It was Isaiah, Jeremiah, indeed the very voice of God himself they were seeking to silence, and not merely that of a preacher called John Hus.

# 10.
# The great schism

In a sonnet the poet John Donne asks of God, 'Show me deare Christ, thy spouse, so bright and clear.' In this plea he asks to see the true church. He then wonders whether there is in fact an answer to such a question. Does the church, as it were, come and go? Are there long gaps when she is not present?

> Sleepes she a thousand, then peepes up one yeare?
> Is she selfe truth and errs? now new, now outwore?[1]

It is a question that many men have asked, though few have put it in such a poetic way.

It must be acknowledged that there were not a thousand years of unrelieved darkness and then a sudden, unannounced brilliant shaft of light shedding its ray on Bohemia alone. Always God has had his own people. Christ himself has promised to preserve a church in every age and he surely keeps this promise. Indeed many of the worst Roman doctrines were only just being fully developed immediately before the time of Hus and some were not full grown until many years or even centuries later.[2]

To take but one example at this point, we might point out that among the followers of Hus there arose a strenuous insistence that the laity should not only eat of the sacramental bread but also drink of the sacramental cup. For this they earnestly contended. But many of them also knew and said that the custom of receiving only the bread was of very recent origin. It was seen not only to be error but also to be novelty. The old biblical way had been practised for centuries.

The whole growth in the claims of the papacy is a vital

issue for us to consider. Here is the verdict of one historian writing on the medieval period: 'Obedience to the pope was essential to a man's salvation . . . the nature of his office gave him a quality that was in essence divine. "*Non homo simpliciter sed quasi Deus in terris.*" The popes wrote and spoke as if they had the keys of heaven and hell. The pope could establish a law binding on all Christians merely by his will. "Whatever," Bernard of Parma said, "is done on the authority of the pope, is done on the authority of God Himself."'[3] These were stupendous, some would say outrageous and blasphemous claims, especially when we realize that the sentence in Latin reads, 'He is not merely a man but, as it were, God on earth.'

In 1302 Boniface VIII in *Unam Sanctam* spelled out his claims with no ambiguity and certainly with no self-effacement. The faithful were told that the pope was the head of the church and all Christians had to be subject to him for salvation. He declared, 'If therefore the earthly power err, it shall be judged by the spiritual power; if the lesser spiritual power err, it shall be judged by the higher, competent spiritual power; but if the supreme spiritual power err, it could be judged solely by God, not by man.'[4] According to this claim, the pope was above mere human judgement.

However, there were complications and the complications were truly tremendous. This leads us to say more about the papal schism to which we have frequently alluded but which hitherto has not been dealt with in any detail. In 1377, after the popes had resided for sixty-eight years at Avignon in France, the pope came back to Rome. When he died a year later, his successor Urban VI was elected. The scene was apparently a very stormy one during the election. The following is one report of events: 'Take heed,' the crowd cried to the cardinals, 'take heed, give us a Roman pope or we will turn your heads as red as your hats,' and 'By the bowels of God, you shall make an Italian or a Roman pope or else you shall die.' At this one cardinal is alleged to have promptly said, 'Come, come, my lord, let alone an Italian or a Roman, better I say to elect the devil himself than die!'[5]

This is but one version, for it is indisputable that after the election the whole sacred college assembled and wrote to the cardinals still remaining at Avignon to say that it was a genuine election. They only repudiated all this a few months later when the new pope began to show his true colours of belligerence, coarse rudeness and possible insanity. They then withdrew, stigmatizing Urban as 'Antichrist, devil apostate, tyrant, deceiver, elected by force' and elected a rival pope, Clement VII, who went back to Avignon, declaring that 'A half-crazed mob forced out of us the temporary election of an apostate, a murderer, a heretic stained with every crime there is. He had acknowledged that his election could only be provisional, no more . . .'[6]

To this Catherine of Siena, who loyally supported Urban, made the ready reply: 'You say that he, Urban, is not the true pope, because you named him out of fear, dreading the wrath of the people. That is not true; but even if it were, you would merit death for choosing a pope in the fear of men, and not in the fear of God.' She also wrote to the Italian cardinals in particular reminding them of their adoring of Urban and asking, 'Are you not idolaters and shams for thus adoring him as Jesus Christ on earth?'[7] Of course, Catherine was not implying that a true pope should not be addressed in this way but that the cardinals were wrong to do so if he were not a true pope. It ought also to be emphasized that Clement VII was aptly nicknamed by contemporaries 'the Butcher of Cesena' for his leading role in cruel and violent acts in Italy. He was in fact a thoroughly evil man. It was not out of some noble desire for a righteous and holy man as pope that the cardinals had proceeded to a second election.

With regard to these events the true facts are hard to come by. There were stormy crowd scenes at Urban's election, yet he himself said the crowd was '*vinolentia*' (drunk with wine) rather than '*violentia*' (violent). There would appear to have been strong demands that a Roman pope should be elected, but it is certainly true that the cardinals initially gave no indication that the election was not genuine. Some would argue that much has been exaggerated and they were not under great pressure. At any rate, the local people were gladdened by the choice of Urban and in faraway England, Wyclif, for a brief moment, welcomed his election in terms he must soon have strongly regretted, referring to the new pope as 'an evangelical man from whose works it behoves us to believe that he is the head of the church'. Later Wyclif was speaking far more realistically, as he saw the two popes, each claiming to be the sole head, thundering forth and accusing each other of being the Antichrist. Wyclif then vividly described them as being 'like dogs quarrelling for a bone' or 'like crows resting on their carrion'.[8] His disillusionment with the papacy was complete.

Soon many others were to be disillusioned. This was no schism where a rival pope set himself up with a hundred or so supporters and retired into some remote valley, a forgotten and almost comic figure. Each pope had a vast body of supporters. Some nations supported Urban, others his rival. Some nations were split down the middle. Moreover the schism, despite many efforts to heal it, was continued by the successors of the opposing popes. From 1406 to 1409, during the middle part of the ministry of Hus, the representatives of the two lines were Gregory XII at Rome and Benedict XIII (one of the cardinals present at the original election of Urban) at Avignon. During this lengthy period, when life expectation was comparatively short, many people lived out their whole lives not knowing where to find the true head of the church. The dilemma has been expressed in verse:

> Whom must we take for pope? Whom must we choose?
> Which is the pope when there are two or three?
> Must they that give the power which they use,
> Superiors, equals or inferiors be?
> When one at Rome, one at Avignon was,
> And each a council had which took his part,
> Which for the true communion then must pass,
> Which was the church from which none must depart?[9]

However simple this verse may be, it does express some vital questions. If Rome speaks always with a recognizable voice, how is it possible that for so long many were utterly confused? How did this affect the matter of salvation? On the national level people heard one pope excommunicate the other. On the local level they might be told that the 'holy oil' for baptism was not truly sanctified because it had been blessed by a bishop who supported the wrong party. While some, such as Froissart, may have shrugged the shoulder and said, 'Such matters do not belong to me,' more in tune with the feeling of the age was the popular belief widely current towards the end of the fourth century that, since the commencement of the schism, no one had entered Paradise.[10]

Indeed it was wellnigh impossible in medieval society, constituted as it was, for people not to be influenced in some way. It might be true that only royalty, the intellectuals and clergy engaged in earnest discussion of the deeper issues but at a more mundane level the pockets of few people were untouched. Barbara Tuchman has put it clearly: 'Since papal revenue was cut in half, the financial effect of the schism was catastrophic. To keep each papacy from bankruptcy, simony redoubled, benefices and promotions were sold under pressure, charges for spiritual dispensations of all kinds were increased, as were chancery taxes on every document required from the Curia. Sales of indulgences, seed of the Reformation, became financially important. Instead of reform, abuses multiplied, further undermining faith.'[11]

The monk Dietrich de Vie expressed a widespread feeling about all this in a Latin poem. 'The pope, once the wonder of the world, has fallen,' he wrote. 'Now is the time of Simon Magus . . . Golden was the first age of the papal court; then came the baser age of silver; next the iron age long set its yoke on the stubborn neck. Then came the age of clay. Could aught be worse? Aye, dung, and in dung sits the papal court.'[12] Making amends for his earlier rash affirmation, John Wyclif exclaimed, 'Christ hath begun already to help us graciously, in that he hath cloven the head of Antichrist, and made the two parts fight against each other!'[13] It was true that in his inscrutable wisdom God was working out his purposes even amid all the sordid confusion. Wyclif had shrewdly perceived this.

John Hus himself obviously felt strongly about the confusion caused by the schism. He referred contemptuously to the 'two-headed split'.[14] In the sermon preached at the 1405 synod, after berating the clergy and monks for their degeneration, he asked, 'Who causes the schism of the Saracens but a cleric? Who causes the Greek schism but a cleric? Who the Latin schism but a cleric? And who now partitions the

Roman Empire but a cleric?'[15] The very schism itself was a factor which caused Hus and many others to think deeply and search the Scriptures on the whole question of papal claims and power.

Thus, in face of a widespread desire to see the schism healed, both Gregory XII and Benedict XIII had been elected only after solemnly pledging that they would do their utmost to bring peace to the church and heal the schism. In the sermon after his election Gregory stated, 'To whatever place it is possible that a union can be secured in, I am resolved to go. If destitute of gallies, I will embark in a skiff; and if the journey must be by land, and horses cannot be procured, I would sooner go staff in hand on foot, than fail to keep my word.'[16] Yet it was easier said than done. All efforts to bring them together failed. One would not leave the sea coast, the other would not approach it. Benedict dare not go to Italy. Gregory said he had no ships. It was facetiously said that one was a land animal afraid of the sea, and the other a sea animal afraid of the land.

Frustrated and weary of all this, cardinals from both loyalties called the Council of Pisa in 1409, and after deposing them both, then appointed Alexander V as pope. Not surprisingly, neither of the other two would abdicate or acknowledge the decision of Pisa. Both still had groups of supporters, even though these had drastically dwindled, and so the situation was that now there were three popes, all claiming the sole allegiance of the faithful, all fulminating in blood-curdling terms against those who did not acknowledge their claims, and all claiming to be the sole vicar of Christ on earth.

Before we take our leave of Benedict XIII, who does not come again into our story, we might recall how, stubborn, imperious and unrelenting to the last, he resisted all the decisions of councils, all the entreaties of ambassadors, all the desertions of former supporters, maintaining his position until his dying day with but a handful of followers and yet with full papal dignity. 'Here is the Noah's ark, the true church!' he exclaimed, referring to his residence at Peniscola.

At one point two very courageous or perhaps foolhardy monks set out on behalf of one council to confront him in his lair and to bring charges of schism and heresy against him should he refuse to resign. It is said that, as the monks approached in their black garb, Benedict said to his retainers, 'Let us hear the ravens of the council.' But the monks were equal to this as they replied, 'There is nothing surprising that ravens should come near a dead body!'[17] How they lived to tell the tale it is difficult to imagine! Benedict lived in a very remote spot.

When the Council of Pisa deposed the two rival popes, they immediately sought support in every direction. In fact Wenceslas, whom they particularly wished to win to their side, had been formally informed of their intentions as early as May 1408. (The period from May 1408, when plans were first afoot, up to June 1409, when Alexander V was elected, was very important.) The response of Wenceslas was to advocate a policy of 'neutrality' and to urge that neither of the two existing popes be supported. Wenceslas was playing for more than religious stakes in this venture. It will be recalled that he had been deposed from the office of Holy Roman Emperor, a deposition which he had never accepted in his own mind. He knew full well that Gregory XII had consistently supported the claims of his rival, Ruprecht of the Palatinate.

Since the Pisan authorities had assured Wenceslas of their support for his claims on this question, in return for his support of their actions, Wenceslas was on the verge of abandoning Gregory completely. He did not do so immediately, however. There were still problems at home. The realm had been accused of heresy and Zbyněk had put his own signature to these accusations. Hus was, of course, implicated. The king was furious and Zbyněk fled, taking particular care to ensure that the cathedral treasures were brought to his place of refuge. It was to be a brief act of bravado. The archbishop soon returned to Prague and under pressure even issued a declaration that 'he, through his vicars in spiritual matters and his prelates . . . had diligently made and held a strict examination in the city, diocese, and province of Prague and neither had found, nor could find, any error or heresy'.[18]

Wenceslas himself was for the moment satisfied with this outward and insincere compliance. He had been particularly sensitive to the charges of heresy which had been so frequently bandied about in connection with his kingdom. But it was a declaration that had been made by Zbyněk under duress and it was evident that it was made with bad grace and that it did not quench his own simmering resentments. Nor did it endear Hus to him or restore their former friendship in any real or true sense.

Hus himself in 1408 was busy facing the accusations brought to him and making the long formal reply to Zbyněk which we have examined, and which seems to have been relatively successful. Yet some of his services must have been very dramatic as the spies redoubled their activities, for there was more than one who listened eagerly for any careless word. The inquisitor used to listen in rather a melodramatic guise with his hood drawn over his forehead to prevent recognition. So too did a former priest of the Bethlehem Chapel itself.

On one occasion the attention of Hus was drawn to one of these spies, who was in the congregation taking notes. Hus happened to be preaching that day on the difference between the law of God and the commands of men. He compared them to corn and chaff, asking rhetorically what comparison there could be between the corn of God and the chaff of men. He then urged the people to cling to the laws of God but to spurn the unlawful commands of men. Realizing that this was the crucial point at issue between himself and the archbishop, he paused and cried out to the skulking form in the congregation, 'Man in the cowl, write that down in your notebook and take it to the archbishop.'[19] Here Hus pointed to the archbishop's palace on the opposite bank of the River Vltava. It is not difficult to imagine the hum of excitement spreading through the congregation, the inquisitive craning of necks and significant nods.

Soon Hus was to be drawn into further conflict with his archbishop on a question which in all probability did not particularly excite the reformer. When Wenceslas had commanded the nation to embrace the policy of neutrality towards the popes and therefore withdraw active obedience from Gregory, Archbishop Zbyněk along with Bishop John of Litomyšl continued to support the Urbanist pope. It has been suggested that the former took this line in typical 'soldierly fashion' and as a man who could not lightly break an oath. Others have said more plausibly that since Zbyněk was so unscrupulous in other ways, this explanation is hardly feasible.

All this precipitated much conflict between the king and his archbishop. Hus seemed to be drawn into the quarrel almost wearily and reluctantly. In his last surviving letter to Zbyněk, written at the end of 1408 when the conflict on this issue was imminent and the battle-lines were being drawn up, Hus expressed his disgust with the duplicity of Gregory. 'Nor can I approve my apostolic lord's failure to observe the oath he swore and which is known to almost the entire Christendom,' Hus wrote, referring to Gregory's promise at his election that in order to end the schism he would be willing to resign, if his rival would do the same.[20] In the following year Hus was to note carefully that the gathering at Pisa in fact pronounced Gregory XII to be a heretic. Although Hus often alluded to this in his writings, and although he did support the Pisan authorities, he did this without any great enthusiasm, realizing that this was no lasting solution to such a deep-seated problem.

Meanwhile Hus, despite his successful defence against the earlier charges, was facing renewed hostility because of his frequently expressed love of Wyclif's writings. Clergy who otherwise sympathized with his opposition to simony and pluralism were increasingly infuriated by his stance on this issue. Soon he and his supporters were again given an opportunity to give voice to Wyclifite sentiments. This opportunity occurred when a French delegation came to secure Wenceslas's open and public support for the Pisan authorities and, as was customary on those occasions, a debate was held. At this debate many of the Czechs went to the heart of the matter by categorically denying the church's power to alter the teaching of Christ in any way. The reliance of the Roman church on extra-biblical tradition was thus undermined.

Stormy debates in the university characterized the opening of the year 1409. Several Czechs defiantly defended theses of Wyclifite tendency and also annoyed the Germans by attacking them on other theological issues. The fury of the Germans was exacerbated even more when Jerome of Prague taunted them publicly for their defamation of the Czech nation. Accusing them of being 'heretics in life and morals', he charged them with voicing an 'accusation of heresy against our most holy Czech nation, though there is an ancient saying that no true Czech can be a heretic, as, it is well known, has been true from old time'. Then, after praising Wenceslas 'our most glorious prince' and further lauding the nation in the same lavish way, he added insult to injury by extolling the value of Wyclif's writings and urging the young men 'to get to know the wealth of truth in Wyclif's books'.[21] The fact that he went on to urge them to do this in a discriminating way and reject anything contrary to the faith would hardly have been noticed by his already deeply incensed hearers.

It was not only within the hallowed walls of the university that these issues were being debated. We have evidence from a young student who testifies how the town was seething with rumours at this time and how he heard 'from students and townsmen that Jerome, Hus, Páleč and their companions had been excommunicated'. Apparently even the furrier with whom he was lodging had heard a story about a visit paid by the judges and sheriffs to the university campus. Thus, on returning home, the student was asked by his landlord, 'Have you heard the news?' and was then told that the trio had been excommunicated for saying among other things that the bread is not the body of Christ. It must be understood that this had not actually happened.[22]

Clearly there was distortion and exaggeration. But it is a fact that the student's landlord was eagerly waiting to hear the latest theological titbit from the university. The debate was also quite literally spilling over into the very market-places. We have an eyewitness account of how a friar in a church provocatively excommunicated all who would not surrender Wyclif's books and in this connection specifically named Hus, Jerome and Stanislav. Jerome was not one to take such things lying down and the contemporary narrates how 'After dinner, when Jerome was told about the excommunication, it was the general belief in the market-places even among the layfolk, that Master Jerome would have dragged the friar out of his house and convent if a crowd of laymen and craftsmen, especially the cutlers, had not been present.'[23]

A chronicler in this very year said that 'in general in Prague all the people took the part of Hus'.[24] We can see this was not so. The cutlers and other craftsmen for some reason would seem not to have supported the reform party. (Unless, of course, they were simply a group of men who wished to prevent violence.) But what we can say is that everywhere groups of people seemed to be caught up in urgent conversation, some being only too ready to turn from words to blows. The whole city was astir – the expectant throng in the Bethlehem Chapel, the news-conscious landlord, the gossiping groups in the market-place, and also the ever-excitable king who was trying desperately to keep a firm control of the whole explosive situation.

The French were still present awaiting the king's decision about Pisa and were continuing to plead with him to support their cause and the council's decision. When Wenceslas had almost decided in their favour, great was his dismay and fury to learn that at this juncture the Germans at the university had strongly aligned themselves with Zbyněk in his support of Gregory as pope and were also continuing to champion the cause of Ruprecht as emperor. In face of this, Jerome and others were determined to undermine the position of the Germans at the university and reverse the voting procedure, securing for the native Czechs the majority of three votes rather than for the Germans.

Later an accusation was brought against Jerome by contemporaries that 'when he saw how things were in the university, Jerome, together with Master John Hus, with other noble men of Bohemia, . . . wishing to make a stand, went to the King of Bohemia that now is, telling him how things stood, arguing that these things were a bad example, and were leading to the destruction of the Bohemian language. And he persuaded Master John Hus that in his Bohemian sermons he ought to tell the Bohemian people that they should no longer allow themselves to be thus treated by the Germans.'[25]

There was much acrimony, there were complicating factors of a nationalistic kind and, it must be admitted, there was much unaccountable see-sawing of emotion in Wenceslas himself, who now strangely seemed to turn a complete somersault and make promises to the Germans that he would maintain the old order. A hostile witness testified a year or so later how Hus and Jerome came to the king seeking to convince him on this matter. However, it was not straightforward, if we can trust this account: 'Nevertheless, moved by anger, the king exclaimed: "You are always making trouble for me with your associate, Jerome: and if those whose concern it is will not take care of it, I myself will burn you!"'[26] The whole issue seemed to lie once more in the balance.

# 11.
# A bonfire of subversive literature

Wenceslas was finally to be won over by the Czech group. Several factors contributed to this. Some courtiers were astute enough to wait until the king's anger had subsided and then to proffer their advice. There were also the persistent pleas of the French contingent who adduced the example of the University of Paris which unashamedly gave its own countrymen the greatest powers. But perhaps what ultimately tipped the scales was the counter effect of the persistent resistance of the Germans, who were provocatively making preparations to pack their bags and go to a university under the rule of Wenceslas's rival Ruprecht. Despite the general confusion, the prospect of a drastically reduced university population and the memory of his recent outburst against Hus and Jerome, Wenceslas finally ratified the famous decree of Kutná Hora. When it was published on 18 January 1409 it stated that 'It is not right to give a stranger precedence over a compatriot' and then announced that the voting positions in the university were to be reversed.[1] From henceforth the native Bohemians were to have the majority vote.

At first the Germans resisted, but soon a large exodus was under way. Smarting with bitterness against Czechs and against Hus in particular, over a thousand took their belongings and scholarship to Leipzig and Erfurt. In face of such desertion, reassurance was needed that the right thing had been done. A very skilful defence of the decrees drawn up by a lawyer friend of Hus and replete with biblical quotations was also very important in securing its acceptance. The writer cleverly drew attention to the original design of Charles IV who specifically desired the education of the native population.

Various writers narrate rather melodramatically how Hus, prostrated and ill because of his fierce conflict with the king, received the news of the decree on his sick-bed and seized, with hands that still trembled from fever, the magna carta of the Bohemian nation. When two other visitors arrived still unaware of the news, Hus excitedly informed them and showed them a copy of the document, crying, 'I am nearly dying; if then I die, defend, I beg you, the rights and the freedom of our nation.'[2]

Whether the above account be authentic or not, it is clear that in all this conflict nationalistic aims had become confused with gospel truths in a way that is not scriptural. It may, for example, have been perfectly right for the Germans to have been deprived of their voting superiority, but the claims of Jerome that no Czech was a heretic – and Hus himself said similar things – identified the Bohemian nation far too closely with the truth and success of the gospel. Hus was one who would have to learn lessons on this point and on many other. 'Praise God,' he declaimed in one of his public sermons at this time, 'we have excluded the Germans.'[3] He was referring to the voting question but it was a rash utterance made in the wrong place. The pulpit is not a place for political utterances of this sort and Hus misused it in employing it in this way.

However, in reply to accusations that he had wished to see the Germans expelled from Prague itself, Hus, in some lectures delivered during the crisis, repudiated the accusation and strongly blamed the decision as he advised them to 'annul their foolish and illicit vow, which the devil had inspired'.[4] Even here his language was hardly winsome and conciliatory, but there would seem no reason to doubt his sincerity and we should realize that some of the accusations against him were made by enemies who had a vested interest in seeing his downfall. When an informer stated that Hus had deliberately raised contentions between the Germans and Czechs, his reaction was forthright and evangelical and bears the stamp of truth. 'Christ knows that I love a good German more than a bad Czech, even if he were my brother,' he retorted.[5] This was an utterance that reflected his deepest conviction.

Yet Hus was soon in further bad odour with the Germans

when, in October of this same year, he accepted the arduous and thankless role of rector and consented to preside over the much depleted University of Prague. He threw himself whole-heartedly into the task of reconstructing a badly battered institution, giving the acceptance speech and delivering the customary oration on the anniversary of the death of Charles IV in November. He was also lecturing, promoting students and witnessing the sad return of Stanislav and Stephen Páleč, both subdued and browbeaten men after their spell in prison.

When Alexander was formally appointed pope by the Council of Pisa in June 1409, Wenceslas had publicly adhered to him. Yet Zbyněk continued his allegiance to Gregory, even placing Prague under an interdict which was not observed. Alexander was therefore at one and the same time considering measures against certain students who had refused to surrender copies of Wyclif's books, and also starting proceedings against Zbyněk himself, when, in a sudden flurry of events and series of strange about-turns, Zbyněk suddenly made his peace with him. There was openly expressed relief at the archbishop's decision. Prior to this there had been disturbances and rioting when Zbyněk had fled from Prague, declaring that it was not safe, and attacks had been made on the homes of parish priests, many of whom had had to flee with their concubines. The news of the about-turn was received almost rapturously. The *Te Deum* and mass were celebrated in all the churches in the capital. The big bell of the town hall rang out periodically as citizens were summoned to rejoice. As the city was illuminated by night, trumpeters pealed forth. It was felt that internal strife was now over. In actual fact, it had hardly begun.

Zbyněk was no sooner reconciled with Alexander than he was fully restored both to full favour and to a key position of responsibility. It was said that he bought his way back into favour with the usual gifts. It was clearly far more advantageous for the pope to have the allegiance of a powerful archbishop than a mere preacher. As Zbyněk himself had urged, he was given permission to take action on two fronts. He was instructed to appoint a six-man commission to examine the works of Wyclif and 'if such were found heretical' he was to 'remove them from the eyes of the faithful'.[6] A second and far severer measure was that preaching was to be forbidden everywhere except in cathedral, collegiate and parish churches and those belonging to monasteries. Although the Bethlehem Chapel was not actually mentioned, it was obvious that this was directed at its ministry since it did not belong to any of these exempted categories.

The bull issued to this effect in December 1409 did not reach Bohemia until 9 March 1410 because of the severe wintry conditions. The archbishop immediately appointed to the commission six men of known anti-reformist conviction. It was therefore a foregone conclusion that Wyclif's writings would formally be condemned. At once there was a steady stream of protests. Individual students voiced their disagreement. Many university masters demurred – some presumably because they hated the thought of the loss of valuable literature; some of the higher academics because they were peeved as masters had often been permitted to look into literature forbidden to students in general; some simply because they knew many of the books were on general philosophical themes and censorship seemed irrelevant, and some, like Hus and his friends, out of sheer love of truth. Despite pleas from the university that the books should not be destroyed, on 16 June the decisively negative findings were read out, and the command was issued that specified works of Wyclif should be delivered up to the archbishop within six days.

In open defiance of Zbyněk's speech Hus quickly put together a short treatise in which he quoted profusely from the Fathers to show that books ought to be read for the truths they contain, rather than being burned. However, despite this flurry of literary activity, there is little doubt that it was the decree against preaching that struck most of all at the root of Hus's convictions. He had now with success been seeking for some years to reach large sections of the population in his own ministry at the Bethlehem Chapel. It was in the pulpit of this very chapel that he stood and fervently resisted the decree.

Hus's text on 22 June, the week following Zbyněk's announcement, was from Luke 5:1: '. . . Jesus was standing . . . with the people crowding around him and listening to the word of God.' Hus's intentions were presumably obvious to all as soon as he announced his text, but if any doubts remained these would soon have been dispelled by what followed. Hus firstly pointed out that Christ preached although the Pharisees and scribes constantly opposed him in this. He went on: 'Because our scribes desire the same, commanding that there be no preaching in chapels, even such as had been approved by the apostolic authority; therefore I, wishing to obey God rather than men, and to conform to the acts of Christ rather than to theirs, appeal from this wrongful command first of all to God, to whom belongs the principal authority to grant the power to preach, and further to the apostolic see, which should radiate greater authority than that of the prelates.'[7]

Then three days later, on 25 June, there was a sensational service at the Bethlehem Chapel, which was packed to capacity. Hus read out a properly drawn up document of appeal against the order of Zbyněk. It was addressed to Pope John XXIII (Alexander V having died in the previous month) and was signed by Hus and others. He referred to the privileges of the university being overridden, charged Zbyněk with going beyond Alexander's decree, which did not actually mention the destruction of books, denied the accusation of heresy (referring to Zbyněk's own declaration to this effect in 1408), alluded to the death of Alexander V, which Hus thought of as invalidating the whole procedure and pointed out that many of the works of Wyclif involved were not even theological.

Hus's formal protest then merged into a sermon. He had concluded the protest by pointing out the evil of the other aspect of the decree, namely the prevention of preaching in the Bethlehem Chapel. Now he was to give weight to those words as, in his stirring sermon, he continued to inveigh against the accusations of heresy hurled against the kingdom so regularly, arguing dangerously that such were totally unfounded. 'But I say, and thank God, that I have hitherto seen no Czech being a heretic,' he asserted.[8] Once again the nationalistic element had usurped the gospel proclamation. The assertion was false, as Hus was soon to find out. But it all met with a ready and enthusiastic response.

We have an account of this meeting from a hostile pen, an account which certainly captures the emotional nature of the gathering. '"Behold," cried the angry orator, "the pope who has just died," meaning Alexander V of blessed memory, "wrote that there are many men among us whose hearts are infected with heresy." At these words all the people cried out: "He lies! He lies!"'[9] The writer of the hostile account meant that the people called the late pope a liar. Hus admitted later that the people had cried out, but said that they shouted, 'They lie', referring to the prelates rather than the pope. The difference is really of little account. Either account underlines the surge of emotional rapport with the preacher and the spontaneous feeling of indignation that swept through the chapel.

The account continues: 'Thereupon John Hus added: "Herein is fulfilled the prophecy which James of Taramo wrote, that in the year 1409 one would arise who should persecute the faith and the gospel of Christ; inasmuch as the late pope – I know not whether he is in heaven or hell – ordered on his asses' skins that the archbishop should burn the books of Wyclif. Behold, I have appealed against the decree of the archbishop! Will you stand by me?" Whereupon the people replied: "We do and we will." "It is time then," replied Hus, "that he who will defend the law of God should gird himself with the sword."'[10]

It is very difficult to sort out truth from error in all this. We must remember that the only surviving account of this sermon is the hostile one sent by Zbyněk to Rome. It is not far-fetched that Hus should refer contemptuously to the bull as being written on 'asses' skins'. Nor is it hard to imagine that Hus expressed doubts as to the salvation of the pope. Already his convictions were being clarified on this issue. Whether he appealed to a prophecy or not is doubtful. It would not be typical of him to argue in this vein. It is also unlikely, in face of Hus's known views, that he called for people to resort to violence. However, there can be little doubt about the upsurge of emotion and fervent assent that greeted his appeal in the congregation.

Wenceslas, often a shrewd reader of popular feeling, seems to have approved of Hus's utterance insofar as he urged Zbyněk to take no further steps in haste. Wenceslas was hoping that an expected royal visitor might be accepted as mediator in the dispute. However Zbyněk could delay no longer. 16 July saw the archbishop assembling the various ecclesiastical dignitaries in the court of his palace, which was like a fortified castle. The crowd then saw Zbyněk, hardened and determined in his opposition, lighting up the skyline with lurid flames as he himself personally set fire to the pile of more than two hundred books. To accompany the act the assembled ecclesiastics sang the *Te Deum* and bells tolled from all the towers of 'many-towered Prague' as though for a solemn funeral.

However, Zbyněk's boldness was to evaporate rapidly as he cowered in his archbishop's palace, amazed by the violent reception to all this. Two days later he excommunicated Hus and then hurriedly retired yet again to a castle some distance away. He accurately judged the mood, for a sense of outrage was felt and rapidly shown in all quarters. Some of those who had lost books, of considerable value and laboriously inscribed, were smarting at the financial loss and were triumphant when Wenceslas said that they must be reimbursed. Disturbances were widespread. Three Carmelites were apprehended for preaching against Wyclif and, were it not for timely intervention by a knight, one of them would have drowned when he was unceremoniously pitch-forked into the river. Much more logical and restrained was the plea of Hus who told hearers at the thronged Bethlehem Chapel, 'Fire does not consume truth. It is always a mark of a little mind to vent anger on inanimate and uninjurious objects. The books which are burnt are a loss to the whole nation.'[11]

There was a real element of student protest, which is not surprising, since students had been prominently involved in the refusal to surrender books, in appeals to the pope on this score and in the signing of Hus's recent appeal. Unlike Hus, who maintained a calm and dignified front during this period of upheaval, the students, naturally enough, were less seemly by far. They composed their simple ditties which, though little more than doggerel, were sung lustily in churches and streets by the common people.

How these choruses must have rankled with the

archbishop, as they cruelly lampooned his lack of education! Zbyněk must have frequently been conscious of his lack of theological learning in comparison with Hus, and all the more so since only comparatively recently Hus had pointed out the archbishop's error in some statements he had made with reference to the Lord's Supper. Two of the choruses are as follows:

> Bishop Zbyněk, a b c d,
> Burnt the books but could not read
> What was written in them.
>
> When Bishop Zbyněk burnt the books
> And Canon Zdeněk lit the pyre
> He brought great shame on all the Czechs;
> Woe will it be to all bad parsons.[12]

Yet all this did not remain on the level of mockery and banter. Violence began to spill onto the streets. That Zbyněk was not totally without supporters is brought out by the contemporary chronicler who wrote, 'Henceforth there was great discord among the people. The choirboys who lived on the castle (the Hradcany) waylaid all passers-by who adhered to Hus, and when they saw one they seized him, dragged him into the common room, stripped him, and whipped him unmercifully with birchrods.'[13] Apparently choirboys were not the docile, innocent little creatures that manufacturers of Christmas cards would have us believe.

Zbyněk might have the support of his choirboys, but the allegiance of much of the university body, as distinct from a few of the younger and wilder students, was demonstrated in July when a disputation of some two weeks duration saw speaker after speaker rise and defend works by Wyclif. Hus himself rounded off this defence by preaching, as the introductory part of a sermon, part of a discourse by Wyclif. His clear intentions were to show that Wyclif could be understood in a perfectly orthodox way. He ended by entreating his audience that they should pray for both the dead pope and his successor John XXIII.

There were appeals from nobles and from the town councils of the city of Prague, but support was from the throne downward as both Wenceslas and his queen addressed appeals to the pope and cardinals. The king's missive, manly and open though it was, principally stressed the sufficiency of the University of Prague in assessing the rights and wrongs of the issue. Nationalistic feelings were to the fore. With the queen there were totally different notes. In her first letter to the pope she strongly protested against a decree 'which, contrary to the precept of our Lord Jesus Christ, forbids the preaching of the Word of God, except in monasteries and parish churches' and begged that 'the Bethlehem Chapel, which we consider most useful to us and the inhabitants of our kingdom for hearing the Word of God, may not be deprived of its privilege'. Her letter to the cardinals, returning to the same theme, insisted 'that the Word of God must not be fettered, but should be preached in hamlets, streets, houses, and indeed everywhere where the necessity arises'.[14]

A little later both the king and queen again addressed themselves to Pope John XXIII and the cardinals. Once more it was the queen who went to the heart of the question. To the pope she complained of the legal proceedings at the papal court which had caused disgust in the kingdom, and of the repeated excommunications. She specially interceded for the Bethlehem Chapel 'in which she had frequently heard God's Word', and begged that 'John Hus, her faithful, devoted, beloved chaplain might, because of his many enemies, be relieved from the obligation of appearing in person before the pope'. In her letter to the cardinals the queen likewise pleaded that this preaching centre might stand unmolested 'for the honour of God, for the salvation and quiet of the people, and for her own pleasure'.[15] It is almost inconceivable that one who went so unerringly to the heart of the matter would not have had the heart of the matter in her.

Understandably Hus had support from colleagues and friends. While some of this was encouraging and helpful, other actions were both foolhardy and provocative. Thus we have a picture from an opponent of the reformers of how he saw events. He recounts, 'Jerome signed and posted up in many places a notorious libel against the Lord Zbyněk, Archbishop of Prague, and once, while Hus was preaching, Jerome stuck his head out of a window of the chapel of

Bethlehem and abused Zbyněk of happy memory most gravely before a great crowd of people, and stirred up the people against him.'[16] In the pulpit Hus continued to deal with these matters for the most part in a sane, biblical and proper manner, manifesting true courage and a real sense of divine commission.

There will always be those who only venture to attack a man when his protection is taken away. By now it was clear to all that the archbishop had completely washed his hands of Hus. It was a signal to others to hurl their accusations of heresy at the reformer, who hitherto had not been accused in this way. In a reply to a nobleman, Hus referred to those who denounced him to his correspondent as a heretic, 'although not one of them dares to stand forth publicly as my adversary'. They lacked the courage of their convictions. They attacked from a discreet distance. Hus strongly inferred that the archbishop likewise was less than straightforward in accusing him to the pope. Waxing eloquent in his defence of the preaching of the gospel, Hus caustically observed that 'Truly the prelates have now assumed the spirit of the pagans and the Pharisees prohibiting the preaching of the gospel in chapels and in other appropriate places.'[17] He insisted that in these circumstances God must be obeyed rather than man.

Towards the pastor of Prachatice, which we may recall as the place of Hus's own school-days, Hus showed not a vestige of respect. This man had been pastor since 1381, but did not reside there although he drew the stipend. As a young boy Hus would assuredly have heard of him. Now he had ventured to accuse Hus of heresy. The retort was swift and of a whiplash effect. 'Oh, that you would learn to know yourself,' challenged Hus, after deploring the cowardly accusations of the pastor, 'how perhaps for thirty or more years you have sheared the sheep of Prachatice, but where do you reside, where is your labour, where is the pasturing of the sheep? Do you not remember the Lord's words: "Woe to the shepherds who feed themselves, but the sheep they do not feed!"?'[18] The man, one of those who had participated in the burning of Wyclif's books, should rather have proved them wrong 'reliably from

Scripture', just as he should have accused Hus in a proper biblical manner.[19]

Urged by others to write to Pope John XXIII, Hus complied in September of this year. The letter begins respectfully and submissively enough with 'humble subjection with the kiss of the blessed feet'.[20] But soon there were more truculent tones as Hus criticized John's predecessor, Alexander, for his charging the city of Prague with heresy. All the disturbances and disputes Hus blamed on the false accusations of enemies and in an appeal on behalf of the Bethlehem Chapel he entreated that 'Your Holiness' beneficence shall free the Word of God and annul the sentence of the burning the books, since the sons of Your Holiness are now regarded as heretics'.[21] What would the new pope make of all this?

Who was this new Pope John XXIII? He was Baldassare Cossa, the very same cardinal who had been responsible for the imprisonment of Stanislav and Stephen Páleč. We saw how on that occasion, although he released them from prison, he did not return their possessions. This was typical of him. One who served as secretary to many popes described him as a monster of avarice, ambition, lewdness and cruelty. In stinging rebuke, he thus addressed him: 'You did not enter by the door but by the window. Of you it has been asserted, and with justice, that you broke through the threshold with a golden axe, and silenced the watch-dogs by cramming them with food, in order that they might not bark at you.'[22]

Many satirical poems circulated among the common people at this time. One of them would have been a most fitting description of the atmosphere around John XXIII.

If you want to see the pope,
Remember, it is for ever true:
The poor can never get in,
Only givers are welcomed with praise.
Therefore, the pope, they say,
If we want to grasp it well,
Desires to eat up by himself
Everything that others have.[23]

At the time of his elevation to the papacy John was about forty-three years of age. He was a tall and strongly built man with a prominent nose and chin. He was a man of handsome clear-cut features whose eyes gleamed from beneath bushy eyebrows. Although he had from early years been destined for the church, he had not relished this and had turned to a career in naval warfare – some said, to piracy. Warfare seemed his natural element. When, after turning back to the church, he was appointed papal legate, he was sent by Pope Boniface to Bologna and other cities to extort vast sums of money. He displayed no reluctance for this and indeed butchered many in Bologna, earning for himself the title of '*diavolo cardinale*' ('devilish cardinal'). Nor did he in any way shed his bloodthirsty instincts on becoming pope. It was even alleged by many that he poisoned his predecessor, Alexander V, in order to obtain office, but the evidence relating to this accusation is obscure.

Obviously, ecclesiastical pre-eminence had its lure for him. Yet in the words of a contemporary writer, he was 'great in temporal things, but a zero in spiritual ones'.[24] One of the accusations later brought against him was that he disbelieved in any future life. If the charges of Wyclif were true, then John would not have been the first among the hierarchy of the church to have been a thorough-going unbeliever. Regrettably, there is even more to say. 'Almost all contemporary writers assert that he was tainted with unnatural vice,' comments one writer,[25] and it seems clear that he was immoral, cruel, cynical and unscrupulous. This was the man to whom Hus's appeal was addressed.

# 12.
# Interest spreads beyond Bohemia

For convenience' sake we shall try to summarize the lengthy and complicated papal proceedings against Hus. As recorded earlier, after the burning of the books Zbyněk had excommunicated Hus, in an act which was of doubtful legality, since Alexander V, the pope who was involved in the accusations, had died a month or so earlier, in May 1410. Proceedings were then put into the hands of Cardinal Oddo Colonna, later to become Pope Martin V. We must also mention here the verdict of the masters of Bologna University who, when asked by the pope to pronounce on the burning of Wyclif's books, condemned the action of Zbyněk.

It would seem that Hus and his friends, as yet ignorant of the unscrupulous wiles of papal procedure, attached far too much importance to this decision at Bologna. Thus in a letter to an unknown and friendly priest, who had inquired after his welfare, Hus referred to the passing to and fro of his case among the cardinals and papal hierarchy and described, perhaps with almost excited relief and elation, the embarrassment felt by the cardinal in charge at this favourable decision from Bologna. Hus related how the cardinal was 'very angry that letters were brought into Bohemia concerning the decision of the masters who were then in Bologna, that the books should not have been burned'.[1]

Yet, where it suited the papacy, decisions like this could be tossed aside. Therefore, ignoring the decisions of Bologna and all the pleas from royalty, nobles (Zbyněk irritatedly complained to the pope over the support for Hus of the 'magnates') and commoners in Bohemia, Colonna gave full approval to all the actions of the archbishop, ratifying Hus's excommunication and instructing Zbyněk to continue the proceedings against him 'to aggravation, reaggravation, and the invocation of the secular arm'.[2] This was in August 1410. Hus was summoned to go and face the pope and cardinals. On the reception of the summons, in September of the same year, Zbyněk placed Hus under an aggravated excommunication.

Hus did not go in person but instead sent legal representatives. There was a fruitless appeal against Colonna's irregular proceedings. While this appeal was pending, Colonna issued another excommunication in February 1411 because Hus had not appeared in person. The pope himself took charge of the case for a time, and then, after handing it over to a four-man commission in June 1411, finally passed it back once again to Colonna for his jurisdiction. This was all very involved and all very slow. In fact John XXIII had reasons for acting with some caution and tardiness in all this since he very much needed the political support of Wenceslas in face of the fact that his own rival Gregory XII had refused to lie down and be buried and still commanded a measure of support.

When Hus refused to go to Rome and sent representatives, he gave clear reasons for his refusal. Among these were the following curt and pointed comments: '. . . There is but little of God's truth at the papal court observed there in accordance with God's law.' '. . . I would deprive the people of the Word of God, and while on the way what good could I do? And if I came to the court, what kind of holiness would I acquire there?' 'Finally, I did not appear at the papal court lest I lose my life for nothing. For every place was full of my enemies, both Czech and German, seeking my death. The pope-judge is my enemy, the cardinals likewise are my enemies.'[3]

Hus thought he knew why his own cause fared so badly and in a minor Czech treatise he summed up the situation as he saw it with reference to the refusal to give a proper hearing to his representatives. 'The pope did not allow a hearing, which they demanded at his court exclaiming: "Grant us a hearing, as you should do to a pagan, a Jew, or a heretic, or even to the devil if he came to you and demanded a hearing!" He, however, always turned away his head and transferred the whole case to cardinals. They, then, accepting from my foes beautiful horses, silver goblets, and precious rings, refused to pass judgement. The pope then turned the case over to others, but the same thing happened . . . After that the pope once again assumed charge of that trial, saying that he himself wished to be its judge and that "Everyone else has already profited by that trial except I"'.[4] One of the stages mentioned by Hus was the passing on of the case to four cardinals under the leadership of Zabarella, a man disposed to be more lenient. This was to be but a temporary respite. Nevertheless it was an invaluable breathing-space in which Hus could still do the work God had planned for him.

Rome was now fully involved. But people in other nations were also showing keen interest. While the Germans were obviously surveying events with a hostile gaze, in England considerable interest of a different kind was engendered among the survivors of the Lollards. A supply of books was sent to replace those burned by the archbishop, and Sir John Oldcastle, Lord Cobholm, wrote to one of Wenceslas's courtiers urging him to steadfastness in the faith. However, by far the most interesting document is that addressed to Hus himself by a Lollard, Richard Wyche, a man who was himself to be burned at the stake some thirty years later.

After a lengthy exhortation to steadfastness in face of the wiles of the Antichrist, Wyche concludes by referring both to England and to Bohemia: 'There is one thing in which I rejoice, that in our kingdom and elsewhere God has so greatly strengthened the hearts of some people, that they gladly endure imprisonment, exile, and even death for the Word of God,' and 'Finally, dearest friend, I do not know what to write to you, but I confess that I would desire to pour out my heart, if thereby I could confirm you in the law of the Lord. I salute also from my inmost heart all the faithful lovers of the divine law, and especially your co-worker in the gospel, Jakoubek, praying, that they intercede for me with the Lord in the universal church of Jesus Christ.'[5]

Hus was evidently very heartened by this missive from England. In his reply he described how he read it before a congregation of 'nearly ten thousand people' (possibly a number comprising a series of meetings each of two thousand or more). Apparently the people all desired to have a translation of the letter and Hus obliged them. Thanking them for their help in prayer, Hus then specifically expresses gratitude 'that under Christ's direction Bohemia received from the blessed England through your labours already so much good'.[6] Hints of growing opposition and rejection follow as Hus refers to the tares which appear rapidly to be springing up in their midst.

Yet it is not the opposition that looms large in the letter. Rather it is joy in the spread of the gospel in Prague and indeed throughout the land that dominates as Hus continues to speak of the reception of God's Word: 'Under the direction of our Saviour it is most ardently received by the multitude, the lords, knights, burgers, and the common people . . . Be assured, dearest brother, that the people wish to hear nothing but the sacred Scriptures, especially the gospel and the epistles. Wherever in city or town, in village or castle, a preacher of the holy doctrine appears, the people flock together in crowds, disdaining the incapable clergy.'[7] Without exaggeration this can truly be seen as a revival time.

When God is mightily at work, we may be sure that Satan will not be silent. Hence Hus alludes to the fact that he is denounced as a heretic, censured, attacked but none the less protected and preserved up to this time. Not forgetting to thank the English for the manuscripts, Hus closes his letter on a very optimistic note: 'Our lord king and his entire court, the queen, the lords and the common people favour the Word of Jesus Christ. The church of Christ in Bohemia greets the church of Christ in England, desiring to share in confessing the holy faith in the grace of the Lord Jesus Christ.'[8]

Hus was now a national figure. This is also confirmed by a letter he wrote at about the same time to the Polish king, Wladislaw. It is mainly an exhortation to trust in God and follow 'the peace-loving King Lord Jesus Christ' after a signal victory had been gained.[9] Hus lightly but knowledgeably touches on a particularly proud act of the enemy who had been humbled during the encounter: they had presumptuously sent the Polish king two swords, inferring that his men had no weapons with which to fight. The existence of this letter is but one more testimony to the rise of the peasant's son from Husinec. At home he had the ear of his own royal family. Abroad he corresponded with the highest in the land.

Three letters of Hus written during this same year illustrate how his word carried great weight not only in Prague but in the different church communities throughout Bohemia. The theme of the letter to the people of Louny, a letter written on the same day as his reply to Richard Wyche, is that the Christians at Louny should earnestly seek true unity and should above all else build themselves on the Word of God. Those in the way of Antichrist are 'priests who desire that human prescriptions be more strictly observed than the Word of God'. Hus warns, 'However, I trust God that he will deliver you from these evils, so that you may keep his law rather than the prescriptions of men.' In very strong terms he then describes both the bliss of the obedient in heaven and the awfulness of hell, with 'everlasting fire, darkness, excruciating suffering, and unending burning with the devils'.[10] It would seem here that we have a glimpse of the stark choice and momentous eternal issues with which the evangelist confronted his own congregation. 'If there were more hell in the pulpit, there might be less in the community,' is a saying relevant to any age.

The letter to John Barbatus and the people of Krumlov displays in typical vein Hus's love of Fathers such as Augustine and Gregory as he musters quotation after quotation to prove that the lower authority must yield to the higher and that God must be obeyed rather than men. Yet scriptural argument is by no means laid aside as Hus adroitly utilizes various biblical quotations to reinforce the point made by Isidore, who wrote, 'If anyone in authority states or commands anything beyond the will of God or beyond what is clearly enjoined in the Holy Scriptures, let him be regarded as a false witness of God or as guilty of sacrilege.'[11] Thus with Hus, although tradition can be called on, it is only Scripture that is determinative and supreme. All this means that clerics such as Zbyněk, who forbid preaching, should be ignored or disobeyed.

Displaying his wide and thorough grasp of the Word of God, Hus then triumphantly turns against the users a verse of Scripture frequently employed by his papal opponents. In an endeavour to prove that the cardinal or superior should be obeyed, they often resorted to Deuteronomy 24:8, being careful to quote only the first part of the verse which reads, 'In cases of leprous diseases be very careful to do exactly as the priests, who are Levites, instruct you.' From this they argued that there existed a hierarchy whose word must be loyally and blindly obeyed. Without actually citing it, Hus reminds his correspondents of the latter phrase in the same verse, where God says, 'You must follow carefully what I have commanded them', and makes the simple deduction that such leaders are only to be followed loyally when they themselves loyally follow the Word of God.

But by far the most fascinating of all these letters is that to the people of Plzen, to whom Hus wrote in the autumn of the year. He was replying to a letter from them. The reformer begins by deploring the fact that a unity under God's Word has been shattered by the enemy. Having abandoned the Word of God, they have turned back to 'feastings, games and other wrong doings' and failed to drive away 'ravening wolves'.[12] Very blunt, clear warnings on the need to repent and prepare for Christ's coming, or be damned, round off the first part of the letter. At this juncture Hus had evidently received another communication from this group and therefore proceeds to deal with the specific issues in it. In looking at this we can see vividly outlined the conflicts, disputes and tussles that were taking place throughout the kingdom.

Hus lists no less than four glaring and fatal errors propounded by priests from this particular district and queries whether the people's reaction should be that of timid silence or lame acquiescence. Hus states the issue baldly and boldly. 'If this is so, and no one will oppose these errors, it is a great sign over you that you have greatly fallen away from the truth, especially those of you who are learned and possess understanding. For St John Chrysostom comments on that word of Christ, our Saviour: "Do not fear those who kill the body," that with those words Christ has shown that "not only is he a traitor to truth who speaks the truth hesitatingly, but also he is a traitor to the truth who does not defend it unhesitatingly, as it ought to be defended. For a priest is in duty bound to preach boldly the truth which he has learned from God. Likewise a lay man, that is a non-priest, is in duty bound confidently to defend the truth which he has heard expounded from Scripture by the priest. If he does not do it, he betrays the truth."'[13]

Hus then turns to the four issues and dogmatically refutes the view expressed by the priest in that area that the Scriptures should not be read in the vernacular, asking, 'How is it that you permit priests to forbid people to read the law of God in Czech or German?'[14] Hus is indignant. It is not the reading of the Word of God that should be abandoned, but rather such evil priests. Always with Hus the availability of the Word of God in the language of the people is paramount.

The second point is perhaps the most vital one. Here obviously Hus was dealing with the popular universalism of that day as proclaimed by a priest who had 'preached that no one, even though he sin mortally, is the servant or son of the devil'.[15] He makes short shrift of this assertion, quoting about nine scriptural passages which demolish it, the most important of which are John 8:44, where Christ informs those who vehemently and maliciously oppose him that they belong to their father the devil, and 1 John 3:7–10 where we read, 'He who does what is sinful is of the devil' and that there are 'children of God' and 'children of the devil'.

The third and fourth errors were that it had been said by the same spokesman that the priest could be 'God's father and the creator of God's body' and that 'the worst priest is better than the best layman'.[16] Launching into an uncompromising attack, Hus cleverly links his answer with what he has said on the second point. 'Be assured,' he writes, 'that whoever preaches thus is a servant and son of the devil, and is worse than the least good layman. Likewise, that priest is not the father of God: for if God were the son of that priest and he were the son of the devil, then would God also be a son of the devil!' 'O brave Christians! have you all died that you allow errors to be bandied about and the Word of God to be restricted? Awake and do not let the devil rule over you!' he urges in his stirring climax.[17]

The parrot cry that no Bohemian could be a heretic was clearly not true. In this very letter Hus labels the widely erring priest as 'a disseminator of a great heresy'.[18] Because of circumstances, the battle had in earlier days seemed like a battle with purely nationalistic overtones. It must sometimes have seemed like a never-ending series of contests between the Czechs and the Germans. Yet in reality the gospel never divides in this way. Courageous and sincere servant of Christ as he was, Hus was to find out increasingly that a man's enemies might well be of his own household, his own local church, his own denomination and even his own seemingly evangelical group. It is to his eternal credit that as the ranks began to divide and many to slip away or even go over to the enemy, Hus did not desist in his own quest to please Christ fully and sacrificially.

Indeed there were now those who began to draw away from the reformer who had once stood firmly with him. At the famous dispute held in the university at the beginning of the year, Stephen Páleč, although elected to supervise, had declined to take part, leaving Hus himself to bear much of the burden alone. Páleč now stated in a letter that although the writings of Wyclif had many attractions, he himself thought it most unlikely that any of the Bohemian clergy would venture to suffer death for the truth. He for his part preferred a faith which would allow him to go safely anywhere. Hus and Páleč had once stood shoulder to shoulder. They had seemed bosom companions. It was no longer to be like this. Páleč was obviously subdued and browbeaten by his experience in prison. His earlier fervent advocacy of Wyclif's evangelical views, often in far stronger terms than that of Hus himself, was now to seem like empty rhetoric or youthful hot air.

Meanwhile relations between the king and archbishop took a sudden turn for the worse. Zbyněk had imprisoned a cleric who criticized him and Wenceslas ordered the stoppage of payment to certain clergy and confiscated cathedral treasures. There were further reasons for the king's anger. He was annoyed because by order of the pope Zbyněk had had the sentence against Hus read publicly in all the churches of Prague. Furthermore, he was also irritated by the fact that although he had commanded that those who had lost valuable manuscripts at the burning of the books should be reimbursed, little had been done in this matter. Part of the king's retaliatory measures involved the confiscation of the property of those who had been prominent in this burning escapade.

Retreating to his castle for the umpteenth time, the archbishop proceeded to excommunicate a number of officials and, when this was ignored, had recourse to the extreme step he had taken two years before of putting the town under an interdict. Although religious services should have stopped if this had been obeyed properly, Hus and his friends ignored it and continued to preach as usual. In fact they were drawing up the regulations for a college of students which was to be founded in connection with the Bethlehem Chapel at this very juncture.

Yet Zbyněk did not remain firm for long. The king had forbidden observance of the interdict, which fell flat. It has been suggested that because of his desire to retain the support of Wenceslas, Pope John XXIII himself warned the archbishop against unnecessarily precipitating conflict. So after two weeks the archbishop accepted arbitration proffered by the king. Once again a commission was appointed. The excommunication was to be lifted from Hus; the interdict was to be withdrawn from Prague; the pope was to be approached with a view to securing Hus's release from the necessity of appearing before the Curia; a declaration that there was no heresy in the land was to be promulgated; the sequestrated property was to be restored to the clergy.

Hus was instructed to write to the pope and cardinals. In his letter to the pope he refuted a whole list of charges made against him, namely, that he had denied transubstantiation, that the lords may deprive the clergy of temporal goods, that tithes are not necessary, that indulgences are of no value, that the clergy should be smitten with the sword or that he had caused the Germans to be expelled from the university. It is obvious that Hus never did cease to believe in transubstantiation. It is almost certain from this utterance that his words in the pulpit about taking up the sword were misquoted and there is no reason for believing that he had been the prime cause of the conflict with the Germans.

On the question of the sequestration of church property, it is difficult to exonerate him entirely. In a sermon Hus had rallied to the king's defence in his conflict with Zbyněk, asserting that 'Our King Wenceslas, in forcing the priests to preach and officiate by seizing their revenues, exercises a power given him by God . . . For if the priests followed the example of their Maker, they would not complain much concerning the seizure of their revenues, not to speak of their complete confiscation, for the Author of faith himself patiently underwent the impounding of his garments and did not advise drawing back from the sacrifice of his body.'[19]

Despite the reference to Christ's own self-abnegation and humiliation, this is not a satisfactory approach, especially in connection with Hus's over-ready identification with the policy of the king, who could be very unjust. In another sermon preached at the Bethlehem Chapel, Hus expressed himself explicitly, but also untypically, about the subjection of the clergy to the state: 'All men, even clerics, ought to be subject to Caesar and the princes of this world; this is evident from the words which Christ addressed to Caesar's heathen servant, Pontius Pilate: "Thou couldest have no power against me except it were given thee from above." Lo, power was given to the princes from above, and Christ confirms their estate.'[20] He cites the instance of Solomon deposing the high priest Abiathar as a proof of this argument. Yet it may accurately be said that statements uttered somewhat rashly in this crisis hardly do justice to his final outlook or normal opinion, which gave much glory and sovereignty to the church of Christ herself rather than to the secular state. On the question of indulgences, we shall see that Hus would soon have to regret writing those words.

When Hus writes to the pope about his conflict with Zbyněk, about his refusal to stop preaching and about his reluctance to travel and appear personally, we can have more sympathy with his arguments – that is, until we reach the conclusion when he speaks rather fulsomely of the 'complete accord' which he had with the archbishop due to the intervention of many of the nobility (named in the letter) and 'through the offices of the most serene prince and lord, Lord Wenceslas, King of the Romans and King of Bohemia'.[21] The peace thus negotiated was a hollow and forced one. It was shortly going to be shattered. Hus must have known this. His whole approach at this point is vitiated by his own excessive submission to the powers that be. This was a crutch that God was ultimately to wrest from beneath his arm.

If we are to present a true and accurate picture we must also be critical of his letter to the cardinals. For in a series of arguments which might be true but which are carnal and certainly utterly futile Hus began by reminding the cardinals of his loyalty to their decision at Pisa and Zbyněk's initial opposition. He spoke of the 'abandonment of Gregory XII, when I effectively counselled princes, nobles, and lords and steadfastly preached to the clergy and people, that in the interests of unity and of the holy mother church they should adhere to the sacred college of cardinals'.[22] He then mentioned 'Lord Zbyněk, Archbishop of Prague, at that time an adversary of the sacred college of cardinals'.

Hus was to learn through a very hard school that playing ecclesiastical politics and appealing to such sources were not only of no avail but also, in a sense, dishonouring to God. Reliance on the arm of the flesh was gradually to be seen in its true colours, but as yet Hus did not think biblically on these matters. We recall that when Zbyněk excommunicated Hus after Alexander V had died then Hus and his supporters had contended that the commands of Alexander were now invalid. Once again we are led to wonder whether Hus was still avoiding the real issues and taking refuge in technicalities and the man-made rules of the church rather than in simple reliance on the Word of God.

Moreover at the time of writing Hus could still speak with respect of the power and authority and even the basic goodness of the college of cardinals. 'You stand as the principal luminaries, who should enlighten all parts of the world', at the beginning of the letter, leads to his closing acceptance of their promise 'as the promise of the pillars of the church' to those who adhered to the decrees of Pisa.[23] If this be deemed less than manly and far from biblical let us remember that Hus also wrote here with a sincerity that cannot be questioned: 'The Lord Jesus is my witness that I am innocent of those charges of which my adversaries accuse me. Nevertheless, I am ever ready before the University of Prague, all the prelates and all the people who have heard me and to whom I appeal, to render full account of my faith which I hold in my heart and confess by word and in writing, even if fire were lighted during the hearing.'[24] It is also significant that within a fortnight of this he was again defending Wyclif in the presence of an Englishman, John Stokes, in a speech that was to be remembered against him later.

God was to grant his servant opportunity to prove the truth of these words but before an even bigger congregation and audience than even the splendour of Bohemia or Prague could provide. The fact of the hollowness of the reconciliation between Zbyněk and Hus was speedily to be demonstrated. Smarting under the humiliation of having to write the various letters to Rome, Zbyněk delayed, demurred, sought in vain an audience with the king over a period of some weeks and then, annoyed by the rebuffs and slights and feeling thwarted at every turn, left Prague and died unexpectedly. His death was indeed so unexpected that some suspected poisoning. It was a sad end to a sad life.

An excerpt from a letter which Hus wrote in 1410 to a nobleman, who had heard about the various accusations for heresy, not only reveals the reason for the clash between Hus and his archbishop, but also shows why there was in the end to be a final conflict unto death. The reasons are clear-cut and straightforward: 'Am I bound to obey the archbishop in his command contrary to the command of God? Be it far from me! "For we ought to obey God rather than men," said the apostles, even though the chief priests prohibited them to do so. Am I greater than Christ and his apostles, that I suffer not for the gospel? Be it far from me! For our Saviour says: "The servant is not greater than the lord, nor a disciple than his master."'[25] It is a call to discipleship that Christ constantly issues.

## 13.
## Ring out, wild bells!

Particularly popular in Prague is the Old Town Square where Praguers have so often gathered to demonstrate the fervour of their feelings on some issue of the day. Thousands crowded there on the night of 1 August 1968, to indicate what they thought of the Russian invaders. Dozens of young people were perched on the famous statue of John Hus, who for them was little more than a symbol of national defiance. Yet, strangely enough, in the same square you will find another object which symbolizes the conviction of Hus perhaps even more effectively than does his gigantic statue. It is the Orloj, an ancient clock, whose original mechanism was constructed in 1410, while Hus was still in the city embroiled in conflict.

The clock today is, of course, a much improved version of its earlier counterpart. It is in fact a marvellous combination of art and technology. Let a modern traveller tell the tale: 'In the middle is the clock itself, with a complex dial that indicates not only the time of day but also the movements of the sun, moon and planets. Below the dial is the calendarium, a circle of paintings depicting the Signs of the Zodiac and the Labours of the Months. But it is the device at the top of the Orloj that, just before the hour strikes, causes passers-by to linger in an expectant group in the square below.

'On the hour, two small doors spring open revealing figures of the Twelve Apostles that troop in procession from one side to the other. Meanwhile, alongside the clock-face a skeleton symbolizing Death pulls a bell-rope with one hand and brandishes an hourglass in the other. When the last Apostle has disappeared, a cockerel in a niche above the doorways flaps his wings and crows. Finally, the bell of the Old Town Hall strikes the hour. And generally you will hear a small volley of applause from the spectators down below.'[1] The question for 1412 was above all the question of 'apostolic authority'. Men today applaud statues of the apostles. Who, in 1412, would have merited apostolic applause?

At this very period of Hus's ministry it almost seemed as though every bell in the city was constantly in action. Unerringly they seemed to herald the key moments of the climax of the conflict of this man of God within his own beloved city of Prague. They had been pealing when the works of Wyclif were burned and now, accompanied by the rumble of drums, they were to ring out with inviting appeal to lure people to approach the papal indulgence seller as he plied his wares. We have already observed that with the multiplication of popes there was a multiplication of indulgences. Money had to be obtained somehow or other to offset the loss of revenue from lands adhering to a rival. John XXIII was particularly guilty in encouraging abuse of the practice and especially so in this instance.

Laden with these lucrative commodities, priests and friars left Rome, travelling into the different kingdoms. It was their practice to enter the principal church and take their position before the altar. Upon a floor strewn with rich coverings and under awnings of silk, placed there to keep off the flies from the industrious and hot salesmen, they began their sales patter. 'I have heard them', writes a biographer of this particular pope, 'declare that Saint Peter himself had not greater power to remit sins than themselves.'[2] This independent testimony is particularly interesting.

However, the indulgence under consideration now was almost a panic measure. It all began because of the embarrassment of Pope John XXIII at the lingering influence and power of one of his rivals, Pope Gregory XII, who had secured the support of a very dangerous leader, King Ladislas of Naples. Ladislas had actually driven John from Rome. Proclaiming a crusade against Ladislas, Pope John issued two bulls in the September and December of 1411 excommunicating Ladislas in blood-curdling terms and imploring men 'by the blood shed by the Saviour' either to take up the sword against Ladislas or to provide money for someone else to fight. This was termed 'taking up the cross' in papal terminology. The bull promised remission of sins for which the guilty parties were contrite and which they had confessed. The second bull also denounced Gregory XII as a heretic.

Indulgences had been employed by the church for several centuries. Originally they had been in the hands of the local congregation, then they were administered by the priests, then by the bishops and finally they had been taken over by the pope. In the early days a local congregation might impose a 'satisfaction' on someone whose penitence was being proclaimed publicly. For example, they might feel it right to prove the sincerity of the penitence by calling for fasting, the reciting of 'paternosters' or some other external act. Where there was either a lessening or removal of this imposition this was the beginning of what we call 'indulgences'. For example, because of the poor health of the person, a specified number of visits to church services might be demanded instead of fasting, or the genuineness of the penitence might be accepted and no further satisfaction called for. In the first case the offender had received a 'partial indulgence'; in the second a 'plenary' one.

As the pope gained supreme control, he was, of course, himself seen as having the power to remit part, and indeed the whole, of a sentence. Plenary indulgences were regularly granted to those taking part in a crusade, where it was widely assumed that a crusader killed in such a cause would instantly enter heaven. Obviously this was a much coveted indulgence, applicable not merely to punishments inflicted in this life but also to those of the after-life, and cancelling out the punishment of purgatory. But what about those who stayed at home during a crusade? They could often obtain an indulgence by helping to defray the expenses of those who went. Indulgences were now increasingly being purchased by money. Often people were invited to obtain an indulgence by helping to contribute to some huge building project. This was particularly so in Luther's day, although the people themselves were not always told the full story or given the properly audited accounts. They were not supposed to know exactly who might be profiting!

At first indulgences were employed rarely and only on special occasions. Eventually, as the popes felt more generous, they were used more regularly and certain individuals were able to purchase a plenary indulgence from their confessors at the moment of death. In 1344 large numbers in England shared in this privilege, together with the queen of the realm. According to one authority, 'They were all assured that in the last resort it would suffice for a layman to pronounce the words, "May the Lord absolve you from your guilt and punishment according to the privilege which you say you have received from the supreme pontiff," for the indulgence to have its full effect. It was a saying of Clement VI, the pope of 1344, that "a pontiff should make his subjects happy". He could scarcely have done more to put this basic maxim of government into effect.'[3]

It must be emphasized that indulgences were only supposed to be of use to those who had repented and confessed, and that they were available for relief from temporal pains and not for eternal salvation. The belief was tied up with a belief that the pope had a 'treasury of merit' at his disposal. Pope Clement VI summed it up like this: 'One drop of Christ's blood would have sufficed for the redemption of the whole human race. Out of the abundant superfluity of Christ's sacrifice there has come a treasure which is not to be hidden in a napkin or buried in a field, but to be used. This treasure has been committed by God to his vicars on earth, to St Peter and his successors, to be used for the full or partial remission of the temporal punishment of the sins of the faithful who have repented and confessed.'[4] Also part of this 'treasury of merit' were the good deeds of the Virgin Mary and the particularly virtuous saints. It was seen as an inexhaustible supply. Such was the basis for the theory.

Needless to say, the man in the street found it extremely difficult, if not impossible, to read the small print. Technically indulgences were supposed to remit only temporal punishment. But on countless occasions they were offered as though they supplied forgiveness for guilt as well. Some would argue that the papal bulls on some occasions implied this. In fact Hus asserted that the bull of John XXIII was in error on this account, although his opponent Stephen Páleč denied this, arguing that the fault was merely with the form of absolution used by the indulgence seller rather than with the pope's bull. Once again this is an illustration of the way in which the whole matter was confused. If two skilled and highly trained theologians could disagree over the precise wording and meaning of the bull, how could the man in the pew be expected to detect the subtleties of the qualifying clauses? The fact is that he did not exercise discrimination. He simply believed that the indulgence was an expensive but valid ticket to heaven, with no stop, either brief or lengthy, in the harrowing fires of purgatory. He was extremely relieved at this and was prepared to pay much to purchase one.

Although indulgences had undoubtedly been a weapon in the papal armoury over a considerable period, it has been suggested that they had rarely been employed in Bohemia on any scale. Many had been disturbed in 1393 when Hus, who was not among the objectors, spent his last few coins on the indulgence. With this background and undercurrent of unease in mind, the newly appointed Archbishop of Prague did at least strictly prohibit the taxing of people in the confessional. Therefore they could not be told, while in the confessional, how much, according to their means or ranks, the indulgence would cost them.

In the second of the two bulls of John XXIII two men had been named as being authorized by the pope to promulgate the indulgence. One of these, Wenceslas Tiem, was the one destined to bring it to Bohemia. He arrived in May 1412. He seems to have been as thoroughgoing a rogue as Tetzel himself. Obviously he could not undertake all the work himself and therefore he had to find clerics as unscrupulous as himself who would pay for the privilege of hawking and selling the indulgence in various areas and then try to line their own pockets by getting as much as they could from the people. It was generally the greedy, the immoral and the drunkards among the clergy who rushed to buy this privilege. In addition to all this, the indulgence seller had also speedily bought over King Wenceslas, who was going to share in the proceeds of the sale. Wenceslas Tiem was also well received by the archbishop and the masters of the university.

But there was one man at the university who did not

welcome what was happening. This was John Hus. He did not stand entirely alone but he found that supporter after supporter fell away as he sought to set in motion discussion at the university. Undeterred and almost single-handed, he promoted an extended critique of the whole issue on 17 June. The title of the debate was very significant. It was on 'Whether it was permissible and expedient according to the law of Jesus Christ, whether it was to the glory of God, and the salvation of Christian people, that the bulls of the pope concerning the raising the cross against Ladislas, King of Apulia, and his accomplices be commended to the faithful in Christ.'[5] The glory of God, the truth of God's Word and the salvation of souls were, as ever, to the forefront of Hus's thinking. It has been suggested that Hus foresaw the momentousness of the issue far earlier than did Luther in similar circumstances.

Stephen Páleč, who had recently been awarded his doctor's degree and made Dean of the Theological Faculty, had even tried to stop the debate taking place. For Hus and the man he described as the 'friend of his youth' it was the definitive parting of the ways. Hus specifically said that it was 'the sale of indulgences and the erection of the cross [i.e. the crusade] against Christians which first separated me from that doctor . . . to him I said at last and have never conversed with him since: "Páleč is a friend, truth is a friend; and both being friends, it is holy to prefer the truth."'[6] This was a rift which was to go on widening up to the time of Hus's death. Páleč immediately showed why this was inevitable by ordering that there should be no more debate on the bull. Those who will not defend the truth invariably end up by seeking to stifle open discussion of the truth. Among his contemporaries within the university teaching staff Hus now became more and more an isolated figure and ultimately a deeply hated one.

Nor was King Wenceslas at all pleased with the stand of Hus. We have seen that he intended to make a considerable amount of money himself in the transaction. Moreover, he was understandably extremely sensitive over the whole issue of the charges of heresy within the kingdom. He had done his utmost to pressurize Zbyněk into reassuring the papacy that all was well. And here again were his leading theologians once more at loggerheads with real acrimony, rather than a spirit of light-hearted debate prevailing. How Wenceslas must have wished that Hus was far more of a theological pacifist and less of a trouble-maker! During the whole debate Hus, aware of his much diminished support among the hierarchy, used the argument of Elijah standing alone for truth in face of the huge number of the prophets of Baal. But Elijahs have rarely been popular among the kings of the day and from this juncture it would seem that Hus lost much standing with Wenceslas.

Hus strenuously debated, assiduously wrote and fervently preached against this particular indulgence. We shall not stop to examine the specific occasions when he said certain things. Over the period his statements are consistent and it is with his viewpoint that we are chiefly concerned. The basis of his attack was five-pronged. He attacked the way remission of sins was abused, the warlike aspects of the whole transaction, the manner of the sale, the disparagement of the Bible that was evidenced in papal procedure and the criminal cowardice of certain theologians.

In the wording of the absolution given by the indulgence seller, if not in the text of the bull itself, it was clearly stated that to those who were contrite and who had paid the proper fee there was granted the full remission of all sin including punishment and guilt. If this was not the precise wording in the bull itself, the intention of the bull was nevertheless clear and in tune with what the seller declared in absolution. Those listening to Hus preach at this time would have heard him assert in the spirit of indignant criticism that the sellers extended their palms and said, 'Whoever places money here, his sins will be forgiven.'[7]

In reply to such a claim Hus insisted that only God Almighty has the right to remit sins. Priests can only assure the penitent that their absolution is complete if their penitence is sincere and if they are resolved to walk in the way of obedience. Indeed Hus is on record as querying whether confession to a priest was essential, adducing as proof the acceptance by God of the penitent tax-collector in the parable of Christ in Luke 18:9–14. He pointed out that the penitent was accepted although he confessed to God alone. The parable is, of course, a striking summary of justification by faith. His question as to what John XXIII would do if a man killed the indulgence sellers, robbed them of their money and then became penitent without offering restitution, is both humorous and relevant. Nor is it far-fetched. In Luther's day an incident such as this did take place though the seller was beaten up, not killed. One hopes that the assailant did not get the idea from Hus! However, Hus did stress that true penitence always led to obedience and, wherever possible, restitution. He taught plainly, as did Luther, that the truly penitent man does not desire to escape all his obligations in this life. To flee the wrath to come is right; to shirk cross-bearing now is wrong.

On the aspect of the warlike nature of the crusade Hus found much to say. He was obviously not a pacifist, as we have seen from his letter to the King of Poland. War might be waged for certain just causes, in his view, but he condemned those who waged it for greed. War should be conducted with moderation. Hus used clear scriptural argument as he wrote, 'Now, war is permitted neither to the popes, nor to the bishops, nor to priests, particularly for temporal reasons. If, in fact, the disciples of Jesus Christ were not allowed to have recourse to the sword to defend him who was the chief of the church, against those who wanted to seize him; and if St Peter himself was severely reproved for doing so, much more will it not be permissible to a bishop to engage in war for a temporal domination and earthly riches?' he wrote.[8] Astutely he took the issue back to the original Peter and alluded to the incident in John 18:10, 11, where the Lord Jesus Christ rebuked Peter for taking up the sword to defend him. Hus also mentioned Christ's rebuke of the blood-thirsty attitude of James and John to the Samaritans, as recorded in Luke 9:51–56.

On the text frequently used to justify the pope's position, 'Here are two swords' (Luke 22:38), Hus argued that the pope did not have authority in both spheres but that one sword belonged to the secular rulers and the other was the spiritual sword to be wielded by the priesthood. He also reminded his contemporaries that Christ said that his kingdom was not of this world, and very tellingly quoted Ambrose, who said, 'Behold, my arms are my tears: they constitute the defensive weapons of a priest; and I cannot resist by other forces.'[9]

The third area where Hus challenged the papal claims was in the way the indulgence was hawked about. What perturbed him most of all was that remission of sins was granted in the pope's own name. Biblically the response of Hus was to call attention once more to an incident involving the original Peter, who could not himself forgive a man's sin but could only point him to the one who alone could forgive (Acts 8:20–24). Hus also affirmed that the free grace of Christ really was free. It must not be tied to the payment of money for a crusade before it became properly effective. Like Luther after him, he also wondered why a pope who had such powers did not free all people out of sheer love. John XXIII must have felt the power of the thrust that 'Many popes who have issued the fullest indulgences have been damned themselves.'[10]

The fourth area of debate in all this controversy was the question of authority. It has already been seen that at every turn Hus supplied either scriptural proof or scriptural refutation. When he described the types of restitution that the priest might fittingly recommend to the truly penitent person his counsel was on scriptural lines. The advice was not to be arbitrary or trivial. Among other things he asserted that we are no more to fear unrighteous papal excommunications than the apostles were to be terrified by the evil ban of the synagogue. Again Hus had firm biblical basis for saying this, as John 16:2–4 confirms.

In keeping with this biblical emphasis, Hus also pointed out the recent origin of the type of indulgences that were being hawked about: 'No saint in Scripture has granted indulgences for the absolution of the penalty of the trespass during a certain number of years and days: our doctors have never dared to name any of the Fathers as having instituted and published indulgences; because, in fact, they are ignorant of their origin: and if these indulgences, which are represented as so salutary to mankind, have slumbered, as it were for the space of a thousand years and more, the reason most probably is, that covetousness had not at that period, as at present, reached its highest point.'[11]

Although Hus revered the Fathers and, interestingly

enough, supported the point we have made earlier that much of the worst Roman dogma was of comparatively recent origin – indulgences were unknown for a thousand years – his first source of authority was Scripture. Therefore, when he read of that strange clause in the bull, whereby the descendants of Ladislas were damned to the third generation, his rejoinder was to the effect that God in Ezekiel 18 had declared that the son shall not have to bear the iniquity of the father. Invariably it was to Scripture that he turned in order to refute error.

Although we have noted how many former theological colleagues abruptly forsook Hus at this juncture, it is also worth recording Hus's perceptive comment that some obeyed the bull out of ignorance, some out of opportunism and some out of fear. In the latter category were the theologians, 'who say one thing about the bull in private and another in public . . . for they fear the loss of their benefices, of men's worldly honour, and of their earthly life'.[12] This in one sense is one of the saddest comments of all. Indeed differences between theologians are rarely, if ever, solely in the intellectual realm. This was in fact the nub of Hus's complaint against Stephen Páleč. Hus summed it up like this: 'On the publication of the bull of crusade and indulgences, he presented me with a paper, in his own handwriting, stating the palpable errors of the bull. I keep this paper still in my hands, as evidence of what I say. It was on his consultation with another colleague, that he changed his course and went back.'[13]

Hus brought a similar charge against the scholars, asking them why they did not stand firmly by Scripture and why, when entreated in the convocation of the university to pronounce on this matter, they had replied that they did not wish to pronounce on papal bulls. 'But in corners you have written differently,' was the thrust of Hus's sad and indignant rejoinder. After again mentioning the volte-face of Stephen Páleč, Hus then referred to yet another theologian who had proclaimed that he would rather die than support the bull but who, on hearing of Páleč's defection and also of threatening noises from the king, himself then neatly swerved back into line.[14]

If the cockerel on the Orloj clock had been crowing then,

it would have had to herald many desertions. Páleč was hardening in his opposition. He continued his campaign of slander and hatred against his erstwhile friend. Firstly, he attributed to Hus some strong words about Pope John XXIII being the Antichrist which had in fact been uttered by Hus's friend Jakoubek, as Páleč well knew. Secondly, he sought to bring Hus in further bad odour with the king by stressing the fact that defiance of the crusading bull was no less than defiance of the king's own decree. That the king, never placid or docile, was near to boiling point can easily be seen. Páleč was aware of this.

Yet by contrast Hus furnished the courageous leadership which the situation required. Things that he had said had obviously put the authorities on edge, but they knew that he was not a spokesman who could lightly be ignored. Consequently he was summoned to the palace of the archbishop and the representatives of the pope questioned him as to his willingness to obey the apostolic mandate. How relieved they were to hear that he would always be willing to submit to such mandates – until he then proceeded to enlighten them as to the meaning he attached to these words, a meaning totally different from the one which they attached!

'Lords, understand me,' began Hus and then went on to explain, 'I said that I heartily aspire to fulfil the apostolic mandates and to obey them in everything; but I call apostolic mandates the teaching of Christ's apostles. In as far as the mandates of the Roman pontiff are in harmony with the apostolic mandates and teaching . . . to that degree I am most willing to obey them. But should I find any of them opposed, those will I not obey, even if the fire to burn my body were placed before my eyes.'[15]

It is hardly likely the dignified papal emissaries were amused by being misled in this way by a mere preacher. Nor were they likely to appreciate the irony. But unlike the wild pranks and jests of some of his supporters, it was a gentle but pointed display of wit that went to the root of the matter. How fitting that the figures of the apostles should now look down on the square where part of this conflict was enacted! There is indeed an element of rich symbolism in their presence as we think of Hus firmly grounding himself on the apostolic word in his opposition to the evil, soul-damning devices of Satan.

# 14.
# Hus leaves a riot-torn town

The whole atmosphere in Prague was now tense. Like a tinder-box, the slightest thing would be likely to set it ablaze. 'Prague at this time gave special opportunities for men with a talent for street agitation,' is a very apposite comment of a modern historian.[1] The very size of the city must be taken into account. By the end of the century it had the highest population for any city in central Europe. In the New Town there was a concentration of manual workers and it has been calculated that there was a high degree of poverty and a degree of unemployment partly due to the influx of peasant immigration. Apart from students with lectures to skip, there were people with time on their hands and a grudge in their hearts as they contrasted their own poverty-stricken plight with an over-endowed church and the fat, sleek, simoniacal benefice holders of some of the larger churches. Already there were signs of the belligerence of many. Chests intended for the indulgence money had been smeared with mud. At St Vitus Cathedral, where one of the chests was sited, it received a pronouncement addressed sardonically to the disciples of the evil demons Asmodeus, Belial and Mammon. The large iron chests began to look less secure and impressive than they had done when they had first been installed, amid pomp and ceremony.

Hus was obviously not without support. Unfortunately for him, some of the support he received was damaging rather than helpful. Here we must mention again Jerome of Prague, Hus's close friend, who had intellectual brilliance, striking debating powers, the gift of kindling wild enthusiasm in others, and many aristocratic friends, including King Wenceslas himself, but little wisdom, tact or sense of proportion. While the voice of Hus was for balance and moderation, that of Jerome was for extremism and even violence.

On 17 June at the disputation which was held in the university, although Hus had opened up a discussion on indulgences, it was Jerome, in a long harangue, who swept the youthful audience off their feet as, in a torrent of eloquence, he brushed aside the sympathetic rector's plea for caution and issued a clarion call for action. Jerome was very much a 'reformation without tarrying for any' kind of man. The students lapped it all up and in an old chronicle we read this account of the climax of the meeting: '. . . And when the disputation was ended many more of the students followed Jerome than Hus, for the speech of Jerome had pleased then more.'[2] There were not enough fireworks with Hus on this occasion.

What would the students, who were so eager to follow the fiery orator Jerome, have learned? They would have quite definitely learned how the Christian should not conduct theological debate and engage in spiritual warfare. It is related that on one occasion during sharp contention with a monk, Jerome, irritated at being so strongly opposed, went so far as to fling his opponent into the Vltava river. Apparently the monk reached the bank. 'But,' naively comments the chronicler, 'he found, when he touched the land, that he had lost the thread of his argument, and was unable to pursue the discussion.'[3] This sums it all up. Jerome seemed to have this effect on people.

Such stories seem almost endless. To be sure, many were narrated by opponents, but frequently Jerome himself more or less admitted that there was some substance in a particular charge. Thus it was alleged that 'The same Jerome publicly boxed the ears of Beneš of Boleslav, a preacher of the order of the friars minor, in the street and in the presence of many. And drawing a knife, he would have struck him with it, and probably have killed him or wounded him fatally had he not been stopped by a certain master Zdislav of Zvířetice.' Jerome's defence on this occasion was to admit that there was an incident but that, when insulted, he merely struck the friar 'lightly on the mouth with the back of his hand'![4]

He was also accused of inducing a friar to leave a monastery in Prague and thereby to commit apostasy. 'With him and other armed men he came in to the prior and ordered the friar to put off his monastic habit, and there Jerome clad him in secular clothes,' ran the accusation.[5] Although Jerome denied the part which spoke of armed men, thus casting doubt on the spectacle of paramilitary forces roaming the street, he did once more admit the accuracy of part of the account. He confirmed that, moved by pity, because the prior did not provide the friar with even the bare necessities, he encouraged the friar to leave. This the friar then did freely. Shortly after this the friar was accidentally drowned while bathing. The opponents of reform not unnaturally saw this as an act of God's judgement for what they branded as apostasy.

One great humanist of the day, who was almost spellbound under the fiery eloquence of Jerome, described the eloquent Bohemian as a 'second Cato'. Another observer also added that 'He was a far greater scholar than Hus.' Indeed this is probably so. Jerome had been on a constant tour of almost every university in the then known world. The former writer also said, 'I only fear that all nature's gifts have been bestowed to work his ruin.'[6] Well might Hus himself have thought that Jerome was rather conspiring his friend's ruin. Yet in face of this Jerome's constant deference to Hus in his saner moments and his ready recognition of the other's truly greater qualities of leadership are all the more impressive. Unfortunately this deference was not going to be exercised sufficiently over this period, as we shall see.

On top of all this, the mob in general soon had a golden opportunity to display their dubious talents. Opponents alleged that once again Jerome was behind the planning of an escapade that brought nothing but shame and discredit on the reform movement. This is probably true and it is certainly well established that one of Wenceslas's own favourite courtiers, the very one to whom Lord Cobholm, the Wyclifite from England, had sent his plea to stand firm in the faith, was also a leading instigator. It is interesting that a contemporary described the crowd as 'Wyclifites', yet the participants hardly brought honour to the name of Wyclif.

Without Hus or others knowing, a student in the guise of a prostitute led a wild mob, with a large student element (students have always loved a protest march) in a grotesque procession through the streets. Many brandished sticks and even swords. The student had round his neck and arms silver bells which constantly rang. In front of him the large sheet of paper, to which leaders were attached, was supposed to represent the papal bull declaring the indulgence.

All the patter of sales talk delighted the large crowd who followed to the famous Charles Square. The 'bulls' were put under an improvised gallows and, to tumultuous applause from the crowd, they were ceremoniously burned. This part was clearly intended as a parody of the burning of Wyclif's works some two years previously. Many strands were now being drawn together. The reaction of Wenceslas, who may have been away when it all took place, was to command that no satirical songs be sung about the indulgence. Sales were rapidly going down.

Yet, much as we deplore the violence of the 'supporters' of Hus we must make it clear that there was and had been violence from the papal side. We have already looked at some of this. Violence begets violence. Obviously resentments lay burning. There were scores to be settled. A particularly ugly scene lay ahead. In some ways it was the culmination of all the unrest. As part of the student protest and undercurrent of wildness that Jerome and others had engendered, three young men, Martin, John and Stafcon, protested vehemently against the sale of indulgences in the services at three different churches. This was all part of a pattern which cannot be justified. For example, we know that the sellers had constantly been abused. None of this was the proper way to settle the dispute.

However, much could be put down to foolhardy, youthful enthusiasm and, when the three young men were arrested, Hus met the councillors and pleaded for leniency towards them. We give the account from a contemporary hand since it does splendidly capture the courage of Hus: 'Then Master John Hus with many other masters and students went to the town hall begging the councillors that they would allow him [Hus] to appear before them, for that he wished to talk with them; and thus they allowed him with some other masters to appear before them. The other masters remained before the town hall with their students, of whom there might be about two thousand. Meanwhile, Master Hus spoke to the councillors, begging them to do no harm to the three because of the indulgences, and saying that he was himself the cause of the opposition to the indulgences. If therefore, anything was to be done to them for this, let it rather be done to him, for he was the first cause of it.'[7] Hus was reassured and the people sent home.

But, alas! the promises were empty promises, for the chronicler continued, 'And when almost all the people had dispersed, the councillors ordered the judge and the executioners to lead the young men aside and behead them.'[8] After a pious woman had thrown three linen cloths over the bodies, with much lamentation and outcry, they were solemnly carried to the Bethlehem Chapel and laid there as an anthem was intoned. It was clearly seen that they were martyrs to the cause of reform. Lords and ladies as well as students voiced their grief.

Wenceslas the king, weary of the rioting and tumult, is reported to have said, 'Even if there were a thousand such, let them suffer the same fate as the others! And if there are not enough justices and officers here in the kingdom, I will have them brought from other areas.'[9] Hus, who was present when this was imputed to Wenceslas, insisted that it was slanderous and that the king did not order the execution. Nevertheless it was true, as Hus was reminded, that Wenceslas had voiced annoyance at contradiction of the papal bulls and that such interruptions in services were anathema to him.

Perhaps it was because of the explosive situation and the known anger of Wenceslas that Hus himself made no immediate reference to the men the following Sunday. For his moderation he was accused of cowardice by one rich cleric. However, later Hus clearly praised the men for defending the truth and identified himself with the popular view which saw the men as martyrs to the cause of reform when he wrote, '. . . Simple laymen and priests, taught by God's grace, teach very many by the example of a good life and, gainsaying publicly Antichrist's lying words, perish with the sword. This is seen in the cases of the laymen, John, Martin and Stafcon, who resisted Antichrist's lying disciples, and perished together by the sword.'[10]

Moreover the above must not be seen as an isolated incident, for Hus immediately added, 'And others, exposing their necks for the truth, have been martyred, being seized, imprisoned, and murdered and yet did not deny Christ's truth – priests, and also laymen and women.'[11] Obviously there had been a pattern of violence against those who loved the Word of God. It is all the more sad that some had in actual fact provoked this.

Looking both at the recent incident and the earlier assault by the choirboys, Hus turned his thoughts to praise as he wrote, 'But the good Lord gave to faithful priests his Holy Spirit so that they preached courageously against those liars, and likewise to faithful laymen, that they boldly risked their lives. Three of them, Martin, John and Stafcon, sacrificed their lives for God, for they were beheaded in Prague for opposing the lying sermons. Others were torn, scourged, and beaten by the choirboys in a Prague church; still others were condemned, dishonoured, and imprisoned. Glory to thee, O dear Christ, that thou still grantest thy faithful such gifts to confess thy truth!'[12]

Other sad incidents continued to occur. Spoiling for a fight, Jerome carried the campaign of physical violence against the preachers of indulgences to the provinces. Again we hear of him entering a parsonage 'accompanied by many armed accomplices and with wrathful countenance and angry heart he burst out with these or some such words: "Get out, you liars, with your lies. For your master the pope is a liar, a heretic, and a usurer, and has no power to grant indulgences."'[13] He is then supposed to have driven the two preachers of the indulgence out of the churchyard to the outer parts of the town.

On 29 September 1412 Jerome, who seemed at this time ubiquitous, or certainly so wherever there was any affray, witnessed a dispute between a friar who was displaying relics and a citizen who plainly declared the relics to be a fraud and for good measure trampled them and a shrine underfoot. Jubilantly joining in the brawl and grabbing a sword from a peasant standing nearby, Jerome then proceeded to wield it so menacingly that he captured three friars, two of whom he handed over to the magistrate and one he kept in his own house for a few days. In the embellished story of hostile witnesses Jerome was said to have tortured the friar, and to have unsuccessfully attempted to drown him. Although he denied all this latter part, Jerome did admit capturing three men and keeping one in captivity for a while. He was undoubtedly a character!

After the tragic episode of the procession, Wenceslas urged his theologians to come to accord. There were various meetings and endeavours to secure peace. Hus on one occasion refused to surrender a text of a speech he had made on the subject, saying that he had taught nothing in secret. In determined opposition Páleč and others were renewing their condemnation of the articles of Wyclif and adding seven new ones specially designed to combat any criticism of the authority of the Roman church, of the role of custom or tradition in the church, or the pope's power to call a crusade or authorize an indulgence. In a complaint against Hus addressed to the king, they typically and pathetically said, 'We believe simply as our fathers believed and as Christendom for hundreds of years have held and believed, that the pope can grant full remission of all sins . . .'[14] Soon after this, in a foolhardy gesture, Hus avowed his willingness to produce the text as required and defend it to the death by fire. If any failed to prove him wrong they should suffer the same sentence.

Hus also retaliated by defending Wyclif publicly and especially his view that those who cease preaching or hearing the Word of God on account of an unjust excommunication are themselves excommunicated by God. He also advocated that there could be preaching without episcopal permission and proceeded later to defend other theses of Wyclif in what has been described as a 'quixotic manner', insofar as he omitted or introduced phrases which quite changed their meaning. Both Stanislav and Stephen Páleč now assailed him in public ignoring the distinctions that he had carefully made. Páleč also said that anyone defying the pope's orders should die.

As yet Hus was unharmed in person but, in July 1412, he was put under major excommunication for non-appearance before the papal court. There were two forms of excommunication, the greater and the lesser. The lesser meant that the offender could not receive the sacraments. In the greater, all intercourse with fellow Christians was forbidden. The language of these excommunications can only be described as vile. 'Let him,' so Clement VI declared, in the bull condemning the Emperor Lewis the Bavarian in 1346, 'be damned in his going out and coming in! The Lord strike him with madness and blindness and mental insanity. May the heavens empty upon him their thunderbolts, and the wrath of the Omnipotent burn itself into him in the present and future world.'[15] Apparently there was another side to the pope who wanted to make people happy!

In Hus's case it meant that people were neither to eat or drink with him, to offer him shelter or to converse with him. Wherever he himself took refuge, all church services should stop and not be resumed until three days after his departure. Should he die there should be no proper burial. If it did happen that he was buried, his body should be dug up. All this was done with the usual crude and devilish ceremonial. Hus mentions in a letter that stones were thrown at his door. Tapers were lighted, seen to be burning and then suddenly extinguished and thrown upon the ground. But among the crowds – and there were many there discussing and protesting – none could have failed to notice the pealing of the bells, as they chimed, gonged, clanged and rung out the excommunication of the doomed man. Perhaps the bells were impressive, but perhaps they were also a symbol of the noisy, empty ritualism that Hus was so fervently attacking.

In fact, if Hus's preaching during this crisis had been heeded, it is likely that there would have been a few less bells sounding forth. Had he not declared, 'Did Paul grant indulgences? Certainly not! Nor did he beg from the churches in order to cast large bells or build enormous churches, but he begged for the sake of priests who preached the Lord's word. He did not grant indulgences such as now the mendicants sell, but declared, according to Scripture, what God wished to grant . . .'? And on a later occasion did he not write, 'They gape at the pictures, the vestments, chalices and other marvellous furnishings of the churches. Their ears are filled with the sound of bells, organs, and small bells, by frivolous singing which incites to dance rather than to piety'?[16]

But indubitably the preaching had been heeded. Included in the papal instructions was a command to pull down the Bethlehem Chapel. So great a threat is true gospel preaching to the Roman church! Realizing that he would get justice from no other source, Hus now appealed directly to Christ. He drafted a lengthy document and we quote from one small section where, after citing appeals to God from certain messianic psalms, he wrote, 'Supporting myself with this most holy and most helpful example of the Redeemer, I appeal to God from the grave oppression, the unjust sentence, and the pretended excommunication of the pontiff, the scribes, the Pharisees, and the judges seated in the seat of Moses. To him I commit my cause, following in the footsteps of the Saviour Jesus Christ . . .'[17]

In the document Hus recounted how his representatives had been unfairly treated for almost two years and not even given a hearing, and how all the pronouncements of Prague in his favour had been studiously ignored. He also referred to his public reconciliation with Zbyněk. He then pointed out that the Old and New Testament demanded that the judges visit the place where the alleged crime had been committed and investigate properly on the spot. Moreover, this must not be done merely in the presence of witnesses who were enemies, but in a fair manner.

The die was indeed now cast. There was to be a brief interlude before the final dénouement, but in the closing words of his appeal, Hus made the cleavage between Rome and Christ apparent to all who would see for themselves: 'I, John Hus of Husinec, master of arts and *formatus* bachelor of sacred theology of the University of Prague, and an appointed priest and preacher of the chapel called Bethlehem, make this appeal to Jesus Christ, the most just Judge, who knows, protects, and judges, declares and rewards without fail the just cause of every man.'[18]

Meanwhile there were those who were delighted by the command to pull down the Bethlehem Chapel. Sunday service was not always the quiet, serene, peaceful pastime that many have come to expect. Hus narrates, 'A beginning of it was made by the Germans when, led by Bernard Chotek, clad in armour, with crossbows, halberts, and swords, they attacked Bethlehem while I was preaching.

The Lord God, however, confused their way so that they did not know what to do, as is known to many people.'[19] They then made another attempt which was foiled by faithful Czechs and which prompted this outburst from Hus: 'Consider the German audacity: they would not dare to pull down a neighbour's oven or a stable without the king's permission, and they would dare to attempt to destroy God's church! But the Lord God did not grant them the power . . .'[20]

Yet what should his reaction be to the excommunication and the interdict in particular? Would not the people be deprived of all kinds of religious services if he stayed? The king was in favour of his leaving. He simply longed for respite. It would seem that his colleagues at the Bethlehem Chapel advised his temporary absence. Yet it is evident that Hus was torn and given contrary advice by many. In the end he did leave in the month of October though he did not at this stage go far away and it would seem that when he came back to preach the interdict was applied. However, when he came back to do some quiet work at the Bethlehem Chapel a blind eye was turned.

Hus was in a considerable dilemma, indeed in spiritual anguish over the rightness of the decision and the whole matter continued to torment him for some time afterwards. 'I have pondered in my mind that evangelical word of our Saviour in John 10: "A good shepherd lays down his life for his sheep. But the hireling and he who is not a shepherd, whose own the sheep are not, sees the wolf coming and leaves the sheep and flees; and the wolf snatches them and scatters them." On the other hand, I have pondered the other passage in Matthew 10: "When they persecute you in one town, flee to the next." This then is the precept or permission of Christ: which of the two opposites to choose I know not,' he wrote.[21]

Wisely he looked back at what saints of old had done and the advice of Augustine to a contemporary's question proved helpful. Augustine had concluded, 'Everyone, therefore, who flees in such a way that the flight does not deprive the church of the necessary ministry, does that which the Lord prescribed or permitted. But he who flees in such a way that Christ's flock is deprived of that by which it lives spiritually, is that hireling who, seeing the wolf coming, flees, for he has no care for the sheep.'[22] Apparently Augustine in the above letter gave the example of Athanasius who had fled, lived to fight another day and indeed had fought most courageously for the Lord.

Yet the fact that he had left Prague continued to trouble Hus's conscience. In a letter to a preacher written in the following year, Hus urged him to stand firm, as he drew on the image of the faithful watchman in Ezekiel 3, and then somewhat plaintively added, 'I suppose that I sinned when I gave up preaching at the king's will; therefore I do not wish further thus to sin.'[23] What would trouble him particularly would be his role only a little while before his departure in defending the thesis of Wyclif that the man under an unjust excommunication who ceased to preach is thereby excommunicated by God. However, another phrase in a letter from exile sums up the situation much more accurately as he wrote, 'However, as concerning the fleeing from the truth, I trust the Lord that he will grant me to die in that truth.'[24] These were prophetic words.

# 15.
# A theology of grace opposed by traditions of men

A prominent feature in Prague is the River Vltava. The fact that Prague has such a striking and impressive site is very much due to the fact that it stands on the bank of this deeply incised river. Bedřich Smetana sought to portray something of the moods of this river in the most famous of all of his tone poems in the *Ma Vlast* suite. It is simply called 'Vltava' or 'Moldau'. With brilliant orchestration the composer suggests with flutes in the opening bars the first source of the river in the forest-clad mountains of Southern Bohemia, and then with clarinets the second source. The river is on the move. It has begun its 250-mile journey over rapids and gorges. It swirls in the St John's rapids and then broadens as it approaches the capital, through which it flows in serene majesty. It is now a quarter of a mile wide, though its waters are shallow. Then the Vyšehrad appears. The river pays homage and disappears into the distance as it flows triumphantly into the Elbe, and at last disappears from view.

Words can hardly capture in any adequate way the variety and power of the music but one man has made the attempt, seeking with some success to convey the composer's feelings and achievement, as he writes, 'He brought the great river into his room, remembered every emotion he had felt from the first time he had seen it, the countless times he had gazed at it, the changing character of what began as a lively, sparkling stream, hopping and leaping gaily over a million rocks and stones, gaining in speed and broadening, running deep through green glades, coursing with seeming pride through ravines, meandering across the grasslands, thundering over falls, and flowing with majesty into the great city; tumbling with deep-throated authority down its weirs, passing beneath its spanning bridges, winding off into evening sunlight.'[1]

Although the music was designed purely as a picture of natural beauty and grandeur, it also happens to be a peculiarly fitting symbol of the life of Hus, with the slow beginnings, the contrary impulses, the resolution of conflict, the tumultuous episodes, the sudden plunges, the joyful intervals, the twists and turns of events and then the serene, even flow of a clear-minded and humble-minded Christian man facing his martyrdom with calm and great dignity and passing into an unfading sunlight which is not of this creation.

Of course, the Roman Catholic opponents of Hus would not agree with the way we have used this symbolism. In fact two of his principal antagonists used symbolism drawn from this very river to attack his growing departure from Roman Catholic orthodoxy. In seeking to express their conviction that, although some parts of Christendom may err in particular matters, yet the Roman church may never do so, they spoke of the River Vltava, which is ever the same although its water ever changes. Such, in their view, is the Roman church, which remains unaltered and firm in adherence to truth even though on the human level it may appear to change as particular cardinals come and go.[2] One of these writers was Hus's erstwhile teacher, companion and supporter, Stanislav. An argument of tremendous importance was now taking place among the Czechs who had once stood so firmly together. Disagreement over the fundamental truths of the gospel lay at the heart of this controversy.

Therefore, before we look at the activities of Hus in general during the period of exile which was to last about two years, we must try to survey and sum up in particular the debate which continued between Hus and Stanislav and Stephen Páleč, who alone wrote no less than four works against Hus. We have indicated that Hus did for some months linger near to Prague. He probably did this because significant discussions were afoot. Wenceslas was still keen to secure agreement between the contending parties and free his kingdom from the suspicion of heresy. In February of 1413 the opponents of Hus produced their important work, the *Consilium*, as a basis for agreement. It was a non-starter from the outset but, since it clearly shows the cleavage in doctrine between the two parties, it is worth summarizing.

The writers first of all assert that the clergy have always held with the Roman church belief in the seven sacraments and in the ceremonies, indulgences, offices and censures of the church, together with veneration of relics. 'Of that Roman church the pope is the head and the cardinals the body. They are the manifest and true successors of the prince of the apostles, Peter, and of the other apostles of Christ,' is their unambiguous and uncompromising claim.[3] Only in this body is there full and complete authority to be found and there are no other legitimate successors to the apostles than this Roman church. Therefore, the document continues, it is manifestly sinful to set aside the church's judgement with regard to the forty-five articles of Wyclif.

In their second point, after describing the opposition of Hus and others, they go right to the heart of the conflict as they write, 'Certain of the clergy of the kingdom of Bohemia, however, little considering the pope and the cardinals, and refusing to consent [that the pope is the head and the cardinals the body of the church], desire to have the Holy Scriptures as the judge in such matters; which Scriptures they interpret and are wont to interpret according to their own understanding – an interpretation not current among the learned of the church . . .'[4]

The third point of issue (the document was referred to as the 'three truths') was that inferiors were failing to show obedience to the Roman church 'in all things whatsoever, where they do not prohibit anything purely good or prescribe anything purely evil . . .'[5] As a result, great disrespect was constantly being shown towards ecclesiastical superiors. On this last point, in his reply Hus could show how the very writers of the document had failed to obey Rome in several recent and glaring instances. For example, when in 1400 Pope Boniface IX had deprived Wenceslas of his office of Roman Emperor, they had not concurred. Furthermore, in 1406 they had adamantly refused papal directives to receive a certain individual as a member of the theological faculty. But, of course, the real point at issue was the second one. What was the true source of authority? Was it the infallible Word of God alone? Or was it Scripture as interpreted by the tradition of the church?

Hus had earlier defined the Roman church as comprised

of 'all Christians who hold the faith of Christ which was taught in Rome by the holy apostles Peter and Paul', which is a very different definition from that of his opponents.[6] For Hus scriptural teaching was the final rule in the church. That Hus venerated, abundantly used and frequently learned from the writings of the Fathers cannot be doubted. Again and again we have seen evidence of this, and we have quoted but a tiny fragment of the available material. But what he declared in the aftermath of the indulgence controversy remained his paramount and unyielding conviction. He wrote, 'Accordingly, I humbly accord faith, i.e. trust, to the Holy Scriptures, desiring to hold, believe, and assert whatever is contained in them as long as I have breath in me.'[7]

The battle raged to and fro. Both the opponents of Hus were convinced of the authority of custom or tradition, Stanislav even referring to 'the scripture of the canon law'. Language grew more and more heated. Because Hus objected to the title 'most holy' as applied to the pope, an enraged Páleč jeered that Hus calls shoemakers and tailors (his adherents), saints, rather than the most holy pope. He called Hus a *baccalarius deformatus* instead of *formatus* (that is, Hus was deformed in his learning rather than truly educated), and derisively referred to him as 'Husko' or 'little Hus'. For his part Hus, with a resounding, almost monotonous intensity, referred repeatedly to Páleč as the *'fictor'* or the liar. 'What is the purpose of this quacking, my good story-teller?' Hus demanded of Páleč.[8]

No punches were pulled. 'Páleč calls us Wyclifites, as if we have deviated from the entire faith of Christendom. Stanislav calls us infidels, perfidious, insane and accursed clergy,' wrote Hus to a close friend.[9] The about-turn, lack of moral courage and evident lying saddened him. He recalled how both of them, after their unpleasant experience at Bologna, had testified against the evil lives of the cardinals whom they now supported. To Master Christian, Hus could say, 'You know how Páleč formerly spoke in your house,' and he could sadly recall how Stanislav told lies about the completion of the eucharistic treatise. 'How, then, can I believe them that they are loath to act contrary to their conscience?' he not unnaturally asked.[10] In his view they were 'two renegades from the truth'.[11] Ultimately he was to say of Páleč in a striking phrase that 'he turned and walked backward like a crab'.[12]

It was heated. It makes unpleasant reading. But it was not just a personality clash. As Hus saw their retreat from Scripture and their evasive and dishonest method of exegesis, he unerringly pounced on the basic unbelief of Páleč, who had described Scripture as 'an inanimate thing, not itself capable of speaking', bluntly challenging him as follows: 'Do you not know, good *Fictor*, that sacred Scripture is a book of life, itself passing judgement?' It is 'truth dictated to men by the Holy Spirit', by which Scripture and Christ 'both I and the *Fictor* shall be judged in the Day of Judgement'.[13]

Here is the nub of the issue. Hus knew and experienced the Scripture as a living Word breathed out and conveyed by the Holy Spirit. His opponents were strangers to the experience so vital for saving faith. Indeed there were many points where Páleč seemed close to the universalism of the parish priest so strongly combatted by Hus. No wonder that Páleč vehemently objected to the assumption of the term 'evangelical clergy' by Hus and his party. In Páleč's view it 'is not evangelical but rather diabolical clergy' that they should be called.[14] Amid all this flurry of words Hus could legitimately and rightly say, 'I will confess the evangelical truth as long as God permits, for I trust in that Witness whom no multitude of witnesses can divert from the truth, nor the Roman curia can terrify, nor any gift can suborn, nor any power can conquer.'[15] These words come from Hus's reply to Stanislav and they state the age-old eternal conflict. Hus was the true believer opposed by the modernists and the ritualists of his day.

Hus's standpoint was consistent during these last years. Right at the end of his life he affirmed in an answer to two of his opponents the authority of the Bible and said this: 'Finally I rest with the conviction that every word of Christ is true; and what I do not understand, I commit to his grace in the hope that I shall understand it after my death.'[16] Everywhere in his writings the Scripture was his standard. He constantly revealed a tremendous grasp of the Bible and some of his letters are almost a maze of biblical quotations.[17] Urging his own people in Prague to follow the divinely inspired wisdom of the prophet Jeremiah, who said, 'Stand by the roads, and hear and ask for the ancient paths, which is the good way; and walk in it, and you will find refreshment for your souls,' he defined at the same time what he meant by this: 'That way is the gospel of God Almighty, the apostolic epistles, the Old Testament, as well as the lives of the saints which are found in the law of God.'[18]

Some fine biblical exposition forms the basis of his work *On Simony*, in which he asserts on almost the first page that the 'Holy Scriptures' are to be his rule.[19] True to this promise, he expounds incident after incident from the pages of the Bible and asserts the superiority of truth to all custom. In this connection he quotes with approval one of the early Fathers called Cyprian who said, 'Custom without truth is an old error; accordingly, abandoning the error, let us follow the truth.'[20]

This, too, is Hus's standpoint in his work on *The Church*. As well as insisting that the canonical Scriptures are infallible, cannot be broken and must therefore be the test of all other writings, he declares with reference to statements of the pope (called bulls), 'For to Holy Scripture exception may not be taken, nor may it be gainsaid; but it is proper at times to take exception to bulls and gainsay them when they either commend the unworthy or put them in authority, or savour of avarice, or honour the unrighteous or oppress the innocent, or implicitly contradict the commands of counsels of God.'[21] The words are unambiguous. Hus stood on Scripture alone as his final authority.

The contrast is all the more marked when, in one letter to a monk, on the theme of whether such should own property, amid the abundant quotations, there is not one from Scripture. 'A monk owning a farthing is not worth a farthing,' is one of the quotations from Bernard which Hus supplies.[22] This letter, so strongly owning the Fathers rather than Scripture, is hardly worth a farthing! Happily it is most untypical. Indeed in one of his most important letters Hus firmly condemned his opponents' reliance on traditions. Hus could even close a strongly worded letter to the prior Stephen, a fierce assailant of Hus, and to the group of monks associated with him, with this challenge:

'Would it not suffice you to condemn the man's opinions, and to wait for his condemnation by the judgement of God or of the Scriptures?'[23] It is by the Scriptures that the judgement of God will be displayed.

In the end Hus was brought to a very strange and important decision in all his conflict with Stanislav and Stephen Páleč. Wenceslas had in fact appointed committees which were very strongly weighted in Hus's favour. In fact his two opponents, feeling that the tide was going against them and refusing to yield to Hus's arguments, both left Bohemia for exile. Was Hus then to be left in sole charge of the field? Was he again to be saved by the intervention behind the scenes and the bullying prods and hints of the king? Many of his own friends at this time were writing to him and urging him to accept a compromise solution which would please the king but which would nevertheless still say that the pope was the head of the Roman church and the cardinals the body.

In a long reply to his friend Christian of Prachatice, which is full of denunciation of the pope and his decrees, and then in a further final letter, Hus hardly tried to placate the influential king. In the former letter, after sarcastically referring to 'the indulgences "of the pocket and purse"', Hus exclaimed, 'Oh, if the disciples of the Antichrist were content to hold that the holy Roman church consists of all the faithful, saintly Christians, militant in the faith of Christ, whom Peter, Bishop of Rome, and above all Bishop Christ taught! Even – were it possible – if Rome with the pope and the cardinals were overthrown as Sodom was, that holy church would still remain.'[24]

In the so-called *Responsio Finalis* (Final Reply) which followed soon afterwards, rejecting any compromise formula, which might please the king but which would have pressed remorselessly on his own conscience and constituted a betrayal of the truth, Hus wrote, 'One must not sin in order to avoid death . . . He who speaks the truth will have his head broken. He who fears death loses the joy of life. Truth conquers all things.[25] The same letter also mentions Páleč's accusation that they had departed from the entire faith of Christendom. It was a strong charge. Was this true?

It is a simple fact that in their respective positions both

Hus and Páleč had a long line of predecessors. In 1199 Pope Innocent III wrote to the people of Metz, an area which had a bad record for heresy. Apparently there were far too many Bible-reading groups. Often the priest, who knew far less than these lay folk, was frightened to confront them lest his ignorance should be exposed. Exasperated by these lay groups, the pope therefore issued this warning: 'For the Scriptures are of such profundity that not only the simple and the illiterate but even the learned ones cannot attain to a knowledge of it, so that it is enjoined in the Law of God that every beast that touches the holy mountain shall be thrust through with a dart . . . , since in the church the doctors are charged with the preaching therefore no one may usurp this office.'[26] It was a worry when lay folk, according to an inquisitor's account, were able to recite long sections of the Gospels of Matthew and Luke. They 'could repeat them without a halt and with hardly a word wrong here or there'.[27]

There had been such Bible-reading groups in Bohemia for many years. Some of the Waldenses, after being driven out from their Piedmontese valleys, found refuge within the fortress-like walls of the Bohemian mountains. One account tells us that Peter Waldo, the founder of the group, finally settled in these regions. Such groups derided the clerical tonsure, believed that prayer should be in the vernacular rather than Latin, ridiculed the legends of the saints, denied purgatory, found no place for lights in churches and holy water, but venerated above all else the light that came from the holy Word.[28]

Such Bible-reading groups were obviously viewed with alarm and disapproval by the authorities. The terrible ignorance of the clergy during much of this period is acknowledged by many writers. One of the most interesting admissions is that of the well-known Roman Catholic historian Philip Hughes who writes, 'The evidence seems to be conclusive that the average priest was not able really to preach to his parishioners.'[29] It is very revealing to learn in this connection that very few clergy had books and in one area, out of sixty wills of clergymen which are available for scrutiny, only two of them show that the priest possessed even a Bible.[30] And, of course, there is no proof that even those who had a Bible actually read it.

The reason for all this is clear. In that age, as in many eras, the Roman Catholic church, far from encouraging reading of the Scriptures, actively opposed it wherever she could. In 1229 a council of the Roman Catholic Church in Valencia actually placed the Bible on the list of forbidden books. 'We prohibit also the permitting of the laity to have the books of the Old and New Testament,' is the beginning of their blasphemous decree.[31] There were also various decrees against unauthorized preaching of the Bible. At all costs people must be prevented from getting a grasp of its contents. We recall that a little while before Hus's birth such a decree had been issued jointly by the pope and Charles IV. Rome was worried lest any reading the Bible should begin to query her own claims.

The rapid success of the gospel in Bohemia may be traced in part to the fact that some people had had access to a translation of the Scriptures in the Bohemian language. Apparently there had been a translation made by a monk about the year 1382. However, it is interesting to note how Cochleius, a vehement opponent of the Hussites, viewed this. He wrote, 'Furriers, shoemakers, tailors, and that class of mechanics, by their frequent attendance on sermons, and their zealous reading of *the Scriptures that had been translated for them into the vernacular tongue,* were led to open discussion with the priests before the people. And not men only, but women also, reached such a measure of audacity and impudence as to venture to dispute in regard to the doctrines of the Scripture, and maintain themselves against the priests.'[32] This Roman Catholic writer could hardly express strongly enough his disgust and disapprobation that people could read the Scriptures in their own language and make up their own minds.

Moreover those who did know the Scriptures often only knew them in a distorted way. A life of a Franciscan monk, Salimbene, who lived from 1221 to 1288, shows that he did know quite a lot of Scriptures. Yet he did not know them accurately. Nor did he seem to live by them. On one occasion he corrects a widespread misquotation of his day when he points out that Paul did not say, as many affirmed, that we are to live 'though not chastely, yet cautiously'! However, in his own reference to 1 Timothy 3, the passage in question, he, too, omits the fact that Paul mentions that the bishop is a married man.[33] Hus shared this error.

In this particular era a very popular book was St Bonaventura's *Hundred Meditations on the Life of Christ*. This contained a good twenty per cent of legend and romance and there was no indication of what was Scripture and what was not. In particular the Virgin Mary was often introduced as speaking, although there was no biblical warrant for what she said. It was against this kind of method in preaching that Wyclif and his poor preachers protested. They insisted that the Scriptures themselves must be preached in their true context. In their strong accusations were they exaggerating the faults of their day?

A brief glance at Chaucer shows that they were not. Chaucer's clerk, Nicholas, happens to remind the carpenter of Noah's flood. As he does this, he is sure that the latter will remember the least biblical feature of the story. And so it happens. Obviously in the miracle plays (often a substitute for preaching) and in the type of preaching of the day, with the emphasis on humorous, dramatic or racy stories, it was the legendary aspects that came to the fore. Regrettably, the hearers themselves would be unable to distinguish fact from fancy if they had no access to or knowledge of the Scriptures.

Therefore with regard to the miracle play the carpenter in Chaucer alludes to the refusal of Noah's wife to board the ark until she has drunk one more pot of ale with her jolly gossips on the shore. As she stands drinking, she says, according to the miracle play,

> Here is a bottle of Malmsey good and strong
> It will rejoice both heart and tongue.
> Though Noah think us never so long,
> Here will we drink alike.[34]

In keeping with all this, Noah is seen as a harrassed, henpecked husband and when, in despair, the sons hustle Noah's wife onto the ark, she greets Noah's welcome by hitting him on the head. In the interest of humour and dramatic characterization fidelity to Scripture and indeed reverence for its sacred quality are totally rejected. This is a far from dated issue.

In the *Canterbury Tales* the great English poet puts into the mouth of a friar these words:

> I went this morning to your church for mass
> And preached according to my simple wit;
> It wasn't all on texts from Holy Writ,
> For that's too hard for you as I suppose,
> And I prefer to paraphrase or glose.[35]

As the particular tale in which this character appears shows, 'to paraphrase or glose' means 'make the Scripture mean what you like'. In his reported sermon the friar is preaching furiously on purgatory and urging the congregation to buy their friends' souls out of the fiery flames. He himself is going to pocket the money. Admittedly this tale about the friar is told by an enemy and rival, but in the light of historical information we possess, we see that it aptly reflects the situation of Chaucer's day. Indeed, out of the seven professional religious people whom Chaucer portrays in his 'Prologue', six are rogues and only one is seen as a genuine follower of Christ. He is the poor parson. He did teach the Word. No less an authority than Matthew Spinka, along with others, would see this man as a Lollard, a follower of Wyclif.[36]

Let us listen to V. H. H. Green, a contemporary writer with few evangelical sympathies, who nevertheless puts this particular issue clearly and succinctly. He writes, 'Heretics like Wyclif and Hus, seeming to place the authority of the Bible above that of the Church, stressed its literal meaning. The ecclesiastical authorities, alarmed by the protest, condemned attempted translations into the vernacular (such as Wyclif and his associates, John Purvey and Nicholas Hereford, had made at the end of the fourteenth century) and were hostile to interpretations of the Scriptures which challenged orthodox teaching. Thus, while the Bible remained the basis upon which medieval culture had been reared, for all but the trained theologian it was little more than a mosaic of quotations and a catena of stories. Comprehensive knowledge of its contents was the reserve of a small class of ecclesiastics and used by them in part to uphold their authority and curb any threats to it.'[37]

This was one of the major reasons why Hus was so relentlessly pursued by the Roman Catholic authorities. Evangelicals hold Scripture as the supreme and God-given form of inerrant and infallible verbal revelation. Hus was clearly among the evangelicals. His opponents recognized this without difficulty. His writings and preaching confirm it abundantly. God was going to give him a final breathing-space in order to continue his witness in both these spheres.

# 16.
# An oasis period

It could almost be said that the exile of Hus was an oasis period before the final dénouement. By this we do not mean that it was a holiday period. Far from it! It was a period of strenuous activity in many directions. Particularly active throughout was Hus's pen. A brief comment from a letter of 1408, put alongside a remark made in one of the letters written in exile, may help us to see part of God's purpose in setting his servant aside and removing him from Prague University and the Bethlehem Chapel pulpit with all their incessant demands. We give first the earlier passage.

'I would write more, but the duty of preaching the gospel does not permit.' 'Finally, I beseech you, dearly beloved, pray for those who proclaim God's truth with his grace; also pray for me, that I may write and preach more against the malice of the Antichrist, and that when need is the greatest, God may place me in the battle-array to defend his truth.'[1] Hus desired to be in the forefront of the conflict where the heat of the battle was raging.

Both before and immediately after leaving Prague the time was for Hus one of prolific literary activity, an activity which earlier duties had prevented him from performing. More scholarly works than this book list and discuss separately the various written works, of which an increasing number were in the Czech language. We shall not seek to do this in full detail. Suffice it to say that his great work on *The Church* and the fiery tract *On Simony* were written at this time, along with replies to Stephen Páleč and Stanislav and more practical and devotional works on the Ten Commandments and the Lord's prayer. Since there were other tracts and booklets it can be seen what a prolific period this was. Presumably Hus was rapidly putting into print the kernel of the preaching, lecturing and debating of the previous years.

Always the evangelist is present. In these writings Hus had not forsaken his main role. This is particularly seen in the ejaculatory prayer that suddenly confronts the reader during some involved theological argument. Thus in *On Simony* we may suddenly be faced with the writer's confession: 'O loving Servant, dear Master of all the world! We, thy priests, have fallen away from following thee; we neglect thy service; we strive excessively for power . . .'; or with the author's burning passion for souls: 'May God grant that all may be soundly converted, to the salvation of their souls as well as to diligence for the salvation of the souls of others!'[2]

Readers of *The Church,* after perusing a chapter entitled 'Christ the head of the elect' are led to this prayerful conclusion: 'Almighty Lord, who art the way, the truth, and the life, thou knowest how few in this present time walk in thee, how few imitate thee as their head, in humility, poverty, chastity, diligence and patience. Open is the way of Satan; many walk therein. Help thy weak flock, that it may not forsake thee, but follow thee unto the end in the narrow way.'[3]

Nor must the letters be forgotten as we consider the impact of his writings. The numerous letters to the Praguers and to friendly individuals were heeded, saved and treasured that they might still be read today. We select just three more letters to illustrate the wide range of his influence. A further letter to the Polish king summoned the recipient to act for the truth against evil clergy. Another letter to the nobility in Prague, beseeching them to preserve the preaching, and reminding many of them that they had supported such preaching in their own chapels, was not without effect. Further afield a professor of theology in Vienna University received a very direct rebuke informing him that he was a 'professor not of sacred theology but of infamous villainy'![4] This was because of his unscrupulous and lying charges of heresy. Even these strictures, it must be recognized, were part of an evangelistic call to repentance.

In connection with this flow of books and pamphlets we must also mention Hus's continued allegiance to much of the teaching and to the person of Wyclif. Just before leaving Prague, Hus had again spoken in support of the English reformer in the presence of the Englishman John

Stokes. Hus pointed out that Wyclif had been hated by many, and particularly by the higher clergy, because he was far too straightforward and challenging for their liking. Let us listen to Hus on this subject. In a treatise against Stokes he declared, 'I am drawn to him [Wyclif] by the reputation he enjoys with the good, not the bad priests at the University of Oxford, and generally with the people, although not with bad, covetous, pomp-loving, dissipated prelates and priests. I am attracted by his writings, in which he expends every effort to conduct all men back to the law of Christ, and especially the clergy, inviting them to let go pomp and dominion of the world, and live, with the apostles, according to the law of Christ. I am attracted by the love he has for the law of Christ, maintaining the truth, and holding that not one jot or tittle of it could fail.'[5]

In both *On Simony* and *The Church* Hus borrowed from Wyclif quite considerably, though, in stating this, we are not impugning Hus's own originality, which in these works was considerable. Even where he did use Wyclif, he was always very selective. Thus in *The Church* he does not make use of the image of the ark and the seamless robe of Christ in describing the unity of the church, as Wyclif did. Nor did he make reference to Solomon and his temple, like the English reformer. Moreover, strong though Hus's language was on many occasions, it was rarely as strong as that of his forerunner, who employed many a biting phrase against his enemies. Yet for Hus, Wyclif was ever the *Doctor evangelicus.*

Some have asked whether he was wise in this support for Wyclif, especially since at certain points he only agreed with Wyclif when large qualifications had been made and on some issues, such as the doctrine of the Lord's Supper, there was no basic agreement at all. For example, one modern scholar in a careful monograph had summed up the findings on their relationship in this way: 'Accordingly, it is important to distinguish between Hus's allegiance to Wyclif as an individual and his doctrinal adherence to Wyclif's teachings. It was in the first respect that Wyclif's influence upon Hus was so profound; in the matter of doctrine their divergences are as striking as their affinities.'[6]

One can see the cogency of this argument. Leff, Spinka

and many others have painstakingly pointed out how repeatedly Hus only goes so far in his agreement with Wyclif and then qualifies quite considerably or quietly states a view which is not compatible with the more radical conclusion of the Englishman. But the fact remains that Hus constantly affirmed his kinship with Wyclif. Presumably he believed that the verities which held them together were very much greater than the divergences in doctrine which separated them. Very striking in this respect is the refusal of Hus to affirm the damnation of Wyclif despite strong Roman Catholic conviction on this point. Thus he affirmed that he wished his soul to be where Wyclif's was, since he had no private revelation that the latter was damned and for his own part he always hoped for the best.

Here we must briefly pause to note how inaccurate V. H. H. Green is when he writes that Hus 'never accepted Wyclif's theory of remanence or his doctrine of predestination'.[7] With regard to the latter point, Margaret Aston would seem to be nearer the truth when she asserts, 'The essence of the case against Hus at Constance was derived from his work *De Ecclesia,* in which he had adapted and developed Wyclif's writing on this question, as well as adopting the Englishman's definition. "The holy catholic, that is, universal church is the body of all the predestined, past, present and future." The emphasis was upon the invisible more than the visible church.'[8]

After all the divergences have been pointed out, what an older biographer said still remains true of Hus: 'To his last dying breath no word escaped his mouth in the least discrediting Wyclif.'[9] The same Council of Constance which burned Hus ordered that Wyclif's body be dug up and burned and cast in the river Swift. In very familiar and moving words one writer put it like this: 'They burned his bones to ashes and cast them into the Swift. This brook hath conveyed his ashes into the Avon, the Avon into the Severn, the Severn thence into the sea, and thus the ashes of Wyclif are the emblem of his doctrine which now is dispersed the world over.'[10] We may rejoice that in Bohemia his books had been so eagerly read.

Yet it must be realized that the books of Wyclif had been eagerly read almost solely by a select band of students at

Prague University. Now, as Hus continued to write in his native language, books and pamphlets were eagerly read by people from less exalted stations and often in remote country areas. When Hus's circumstances are taken into account, this output is truly amazing. For although he was relatively free from the personal clashes with his opponents (but not, of course, from the labour of engaging in theological warfare in print) his situation was far from idyllic. To be sure, on leaving Prague, he had readily found shelter. Indeed the sequence of residences in itself testifies to the effectiveness of his ministry among the higher classes. From October 1412 until March 1413, at a time when he wanted to be near Prague, he stayed with Henry Skopek of Duba, who owned a castle nearby and who in all likelihood was the moving force behind Hus's appeal to the land court in order to get the official support of the government for his cause, a venture in which he succeeded.

From the spring of 1413 Hus sought refuge in the country and was for a time given shelter in Kozi Castle where much writing was done. The ruins still remain. It was, despite the grandiose appellation of 'castle', rather a modest building, surrounded to be sure by a wall and moat, but having for its living quarters only one room in the tower. This was occupied by Hus himself and the whole family, who welcomed him into their midst. There, amid the constant movement and conversation of people, many of his finest works were written. Where there is a will and the moving of God's Spirit, there is certainly a way.

After a period at the end of 1414 under the protection of Lady Anna of Mochov, who was willing enough but not powerful enough to ensure his safety, he went to stay with Henry Lefl of Lazan at Krakovec, at a castle in west-central Bohemia. Since his host had obtained indulgences a few years before for all who came to one of his chapels to pray, it is not hard to imagine the lively discussion that might occur to stop the flow of literary activity! His host who, as a member of the royal council, had been put in charge of the Hussite dispute, nevertheless became a very firm friend of Hus, who gained his respect despite their seeming incompatibility. The day before his death, Hus sent a message to him: 'Lord Henry Lefl, live a good life with your wife.

I thank you for your benefactions. May God be your reward!'[11]

Because of this series of moves Hus found himself in many new areas with new and perhaps unique opportunities, for in no way had he forsaken his prime calling. His message that 'Day by day the truth of the gospel is being spread ever wider . . . I desire to live for those who suffer violence and need the preaching of the Word of God, in order that thus the malice of Antichrist may be revealed, so that the godly can escape it. On that account I preach elsewhere and minister as priest to others . . .' would leave his friends in Prague under no illusion that his zeal was diminished in this respect.[12]

Hus had simply exchanged one pulpit for many others. This was a time of great open-air preaching. Hus spoke at weddings, at funerals, in castles, in forests, by the hedgerows and from pulpits of all shapes and sizes. In the country areas where he ministered vast numbers thronged, many of whom were to form staunch and God-fearing evangelical groups after his death. New areas were indeed being opened up for the gospel. In these months he secured a place in the affections of countless country people which he was never to lose. It has been pointed out that, when, after Hus's death, 452 of the lower gentry of Bohemia and Moravia signed a document of protest, a quarter of those signing came from the areas covered by his final burst of preaching activity.

In one of his works he referred to the preaching journeys. 'I preach in cities, castles, fields and forests,' he writes.[13] Hus was very sure of his divine commission, as this excerpt from a sermon makes plain: 'At first I preached in cities and streets, but now I preach among the hedges, outside the castle called Kozi, and in the byways of towns and villages. For Christ says: "Go into the byways and hedges," understand thereby among the hedges – "and constrain them to enter so that my house be filled." He says "constrain", that is by the threat of eternal pains; and "to enter", that is, that they come "that my house may be filled", that is, by the number of the elect to everlasting bliss.'[14]

Like all true preachers of the Word of God, Hus was frequently filled with a deep sense of unworthiness as he sought to proclaim 'the unsearchable riches of Christ'. In one letter he requested his fellow preachers to pray for him, asking that he might have 'lively speech' and say what he ought to say. However, after asking in this way that he may be endowed similarly to Paul, he modestly added, 'Nevertheless, in beseeching you thus, I do not say that the spirit be given me in such measure as was given to the apostle, for I am not a fit person for it; but that, if possible, at least as to a puppy the broken pieces fallen from the table of my masters be not denied me . . .'[15] It would seem that Hus was here alluding to the incident recorded in Mark 7: 24–30.

Again to the Praguers he wrote, 'Pray for me to God that he may deign to grant me prosperity and success in the preaching of his Word in all places where it will appear necessary – in cities, towns, villages, castles, fields and forests, wherever I can be of help, so that the Word of God would not be stifled in me.'[16] Nevertheless as well as feelings of unworthiness and need there were experiences of real joy as Hus reflected on the way that God had undoubtedly used him over the years. Therefore he could write to his congregation, recalling his twelve years of ministry among them and say, 'It was my greatest consolation in this labour when I learned of your diligence in hearing the Word of God and observed the true and sincere penitence of many of you.'[17] There may have been regrettable nationalistic outbursts and ephemeral emotional responses but there had also been many genuine and lasting conversions.

Moreover, God was raising up other labourers. In one letter punning again on his own name, Hus put it beautifully: 'In place of one preacher . . . He gave them twelve and more. That same Truth in place of one faint-hearted goose, gave Prague many eagles and falcons, who have keen sight, soar high by grace, and skilfully catch birds for the King, Lord Jesus.'[18] After Hus's death, there were other faithful men, such as Jakoubek of Stříbro, who carried on the work. The followers of Hus were called the evangelical clergy – *clerus evangelicus.*[19] Even the fact that opponents were still seeking to have the Bethlehem Chapel pulled down – and Hus makes frequent sorrowful allusions to this – could not prevent God working in his own way to raise a succession of preachers.

Because he was a true pastor, Hus still had an overwhelming concern for the welfare of his congregation at Prague. Understandably there was at first a slight note of anxiety as he realized the pressures to compromise and fall away from the faith. But although the call for perseverance and cross-bearing rings out steadily throughout these letters so frequently that it is almost invidious to quote from them, yet, as he realized that many were indeed standing firm for the faith, a more relaxed note began to prevail.

However, at no time, not even in the days immediately after the exile, was the atmosphere that of gloom. Always Hus was full of confidence in the power and ultimate success of the Word of God. His letters are full of Christ, Christ's words, Christ's character, Christ's trial and crucifixion and Christ's triumph and return. Here is one example from a letter to his friends in Prague, sent on Christmas Day 1413. The letter is from start to finish an exultant hymn of praise.

> 'A loving brother is born to us, a wise master, a safe leader, a just judge, in order that there may be glory to God in the highest, etc.
>
> 'Rejoice, you wicked, because the God-priest was born, who grants to every penitent absolution from all sins, that there may be glory to God in the highest, etc.
>
> 'Rejoice, because today the bread of angels, namely God, became food for men, to refresh the hungry with his glorious body, that they may have peace on earth.
>
> 'Rejoice, that the immortal God is born, so that mortal men may live in eternity.
>
> 'Rejoice, because the rich Lord of the universe lies in a manger as poor, that he may enrich us needy ones.'[20]

Many letters to the Praguers are little more than evangelistic tracts. It is not hard to believe that he meant every word when he wrote to them 'that your salvation was, is now, and shall remain my desire until my death'.[21] In the process of excusing himself to a group of monks because of his refusal to respond to the citation of Rome, Hus informed them that if by his 'appearing and death I could serve some to salvation, I would willingly appear with the aid of the Lord Jesus Christ'.[22] Therefore, writing to a priest, Hus spoke in detail of the faith and hope and the salvation through predestinating love that Christ provides, in a letter fittingly and typically beginning: 'Salvation from the Lord Jesus Christ'.[23] 'If you are not a missionary, you are a mission field,' is an apt saying. Hus was a man burning with a sense of mission to the lost.

The other aspect of this evangelistic concern was Hus's acceptance of the centrality of Christ and his atoning death. In his appeal from the pope's condemnation, Hus had spoken of 'Jesus Christ, the true God and true man, who, surrounded in distress by pontiffs, scribes, and Pharisees, priests, unjust judges, and witnesses, wished by his most cruel and shameful death to redeem from eternal damnation those who have been chosen to be the sons of God before the foundation of the world'.[24] This kind of declaration was the nub of his faith. Therefore in letters he speaks frequently, fervently and lengthily of Christ's sufferings and imaginatively pictures him as Physician, King, Merchant and the All-Powerful One and declares that he alone brings 'deliverance from eternal torments'.[25]

Hus's fervour for the Saviour is equally displayed in the following excerpt from *The Church*. Christ 'is the bishop, who baptizes and takes away the sins of the world (John 1:29). He is the one who joins in marriage so that no man may put asunder: "What God has joined together, let not man put asunder" (Matthew 19:6). He is the one who makes us priests: "He made us a kingdom and priests" (Revelation 1:6). He performs the sacrament of the eucharist, saying: "This is my body" (Luke 22:19). This is he who confirms his faithful ones: "I will give you a mouth of wisdom which all your adversaries will not be able to withstand or gainsay" (Luke 21:15). He it is who feeds his sheep by his word and example and by the food of his body. All these things, however, he does on his part indefectibly, because he is a holy priest, guileless, undefiled, separated from sinners and made higher than the heavens. He is the bishop holding supreme guardianship over his flock, because he sleeps not nor is he, that watches over Israel, weary. He is the pontiff who in advance makes the way easy for us to the heavenly country. He is the pope [*papa*] because he is the wonderful Prince of Peace, the Father of the future age.'[26]

Hus never despaired of seeing a soul saved. This is one reason why, in face of the fury of many of his contemporaries, he would not in any way affirm that Wyclif, so roundly condemned by the Roman Catholic Church, was damned. Hus constantly expressed the hope that Wyclif would be in heaven. For as Hus himself put it, 'I lean more toward hope, trusting the mercy of God than to despair, looking in the direction of eternal damnation, from which the omnipotent God in mercy deliver us, and we praise God for his most gracious mercy, because in the hour of death he is so merciful to forgive.'[27] It was not that Hus did not believe in eternal punishment. He did believe this doctrine; but he also believed in eternal redemption because he had experienced it himself.

# 17.
# Gradual but incomplete enlightenment

Throughout his correspondence and in most of his writings Hus is gloriously and often consistently evangelical. But honesty compels us to admit that he is not always so. That Hus should have some hangover of Roman Catholic belief is not surprising. Luther himself still believed in purgatory when he protested with his famous theses. Only in the ensuing debates and conflict with Rome did Luther go back to the Bible more and more. Indeed it can be argued that in some realms Luther never shed his wrong beliefs on the sacraments and the church. Furthermore, it must never be forgotten that while Luther had years in which to change and modify his views according to the Scriptures, Hus was cut off in his prime and at a time when his views were changing rapidly all the while.

Like all others who begin to study the Scriptures in earnest, Hus was guided to shed his beliefs gradually and, if we are to give a rounded portrait, we must look at some areas where Hus did not emerge into full scriptural light and conviction. We have already seen how he too readily followed the general tendency of his own and previous eras to spiritualize the Scriptures somewhat excessively. In itself this is a small issue, and in his mature output such unwarranted spiritualizing is a very rare occurrence. For example, alongside page after page of solid scriptural exposition in *On Simony* there is only one passage where he resorts to such vagaries, speaking of the dove-sellers cast out in the Lord's cleansing of the temple as 'those who, by the laying on of hands, sell the Holy Spirit for a consideration'.[1]

Yet more importantly we must admit that Hus never formally relinquished certain false Roman Catholic teachings.

We have already seen that, despite some kinder notes, he was very much tied to the medieval view of women and we recall how in his intemperate remarks about Bohemians who could not speak their language properly, he advocated the beating of women. In the light of his maturer views and attitudes this does seem a very strange note and one which we must assume that he ultimately abandoned.

There is no doubt that Hus was changing in many ways. For example, right at the end of his life he was considering the biblical teaching in the Gospels and Paul's epistles on the Lord's Supper and asserting, against Roman Catholic teaching on communion in one kind, that both the bread and wine ought to be received. Yet to some degree we must agree with the verdict of Matthew Spinka, who wrote, 'There were elements implicit in Hus's teaching which the Reformation made explicit . . . Hus was doubtless quite unconscious of the ultimate conclusions which must be in course of time inevitably drawn from his principles.'[2]

Of course, as we quote some of his weaknesses, we trust that what has already been said about his fervour for the Bible, evangelism and countless scriptural doctrines will not be forgotten. We underline yet again that he was a pioneer. It is so easy with the advantage of hindsight to feel a wrong and quite false sense of superiority. As Bernard, master of the episcopal school at Chartres from 1114 to 1119, so discerningly put it, 'We are as dwarfs mounted on the shoulders of giants, so that although we perceive many more things than they, it is not because our vision is more piercing or our stature higher, but because we are carried and elevated higher to their gigantic size.'[3] If we, in our day in evangelicalism, see more clearly on certain points than did Hus, it is because we stand on the shoulders of men like Hus and Luther, and not that we ourselves are men of gigantic size.

Somewhat surprisingly, it is evident from his great work on *The Church* and from his letters that he never finally and totally abandoned belief in purgatory. This is particularly strange because he so strongly saw the key issues in the indulgence controversy. In one earlier letter he misapplied 1 Corinthians 3:12–15 in a typical Roman Catholic way, taking it to refer to the 'fire of purgatory'. We are thus reminded that he was no infallible expositor of Scripture. Yet even in this letter he does assert, 'He who is wholly turned to Christ will escape the fire of purgatory.'[4]

Yet when we consider the following excerpt from his writings we are legitimately entitled to feel that, like Luther, Hus was moving in a biblical direction even if he did not finally arrive there – at least as far as his published writings are concerned. The context of the passage is that, while he is affirming belief in purgatory, he is expressing his own conviction that prayers for the dead were not a very effectual aid. 'Because', he wrote, 'the matter is not spoken of in the whole Scripture, except in the second book of Maccabees, which is not reckoned by the Jews in the canon of the Old Testament. Neither the prophets, nor Jesus Christ, nor his apostles, nor the saints that followed them, ever taught explicitly that we should pray for the dead; but they have said that he that lived a holy life should be saved. For myself, I believe that this practice has been introduced first of all by the avarice of the priests, who take little trouble to exhort the people as the prophets, Christ, and his apostles did, to an holy life; but who take particular pains to persuade them to make rich offerings, in the hope of blessedness and a speedy deliverance from purgatory.'[5] This is by no means an inept comment. He also said, 'It is safer to live well, than to expect release after death by the aid of others.'[6]

Perhaps the greatest divergence from true evangelicalism is to be found in his beliefs about the Virgin Mary. On the one hand he held her to be above the apostles, patriarchs and angelic choirs. Professing belief in her resurrection and ascension to heaven, he affirmed that next to Christ 'she is our foremost helper'.[7] In some sense she contributes to our salvation. Yet on the other hand, in *The Church*, although he does seem to say in one place that she is higher in dignity than Peter, this is in fact one of only two references to her in the whole massive work.[8] His letters occasionally contain allusions to her but, on the whole, they are remarkably low-key ones. Together with other saints, Hus sees her as able to help the Christian. During the trial and death of Christ she accomplished more than all the apostles, presumably because she stayed loyally at the cross while they fled.[9] There are inconsistencies here, but it must also be admitted freely that there is a disappointing failure fully to grasp scriptural truth.

Yet, although we are right in acknowledging that in these respects Hus did have a regrettable hangover from Roman Catholic belief, the depth and range in his changed viewpoint cannot be emphasized too strongly. Conflict drove him to study the issues more deeply and conspired together with study of the Word of God and the guidance of the Holy Spirit to bring about radical changes. It was a big step from his earlier whole-hearted acceptance of all the paraphernalia of indulgences to his costly and almost solitary denunciation of Wenceslas Tiem. We have seen in this the thoroughgoing, wide-ranging and effectively biblical nature of his critique of the practice. There was really little left for Luther to say!

It was a big step from his early belief in relics to his major contribution to the clear-cut findings of the Wilsnack commission and the belligerent statement that bogus relics were to be found everywhere. Once again we must emphasize that the critique was scriptural and fundamental. It did not skate on the surface and merely pin-point external abuses. In the same vein we find him, in a letter from exile, speaking with irony of the fantastic claims of Rome, and all their claims to perform many 'wonders, that is, the miracles done at a distance – for the distance from Roman curia to Prague is two hundred miles – miracles such as even Simon Magus or apostle Peter did not perform!'[10] As a good biblical theologian Hus was properly suspicious of those who, to substantiate their teaching, claimed to perform even greater miracles than those in the time of the apostles. He knew that such miracles were likely to be satanic and such teaching false. He realized that false prophets are not those who speak directly against Christ, but those who come in his name and yet subtly distort the message. As he put it in one of the earliest of his letters from exile, speaking of the Saviour's warning, 'He taught them . . . to regard as false Christs those who assert that they are Christ's principal disciples, while in reality they are his chief foes.'[11]

It was a big step from his earlier advocacy of pomp and ceremonial to his expression of disapproval of the worship of a wooden cross and to his quoting of Chrysostom with approval on the subject of confessions. The latter said, 'I do not bid you present yourselves in public, or accuse yourselves before others; I only wish you to obey the prophet where he says, Lay your way open before the Lord, confess your sins to the true judge, declare your faults, not with the tongue, but the conscience, and then hope to obtain mercy.'[12]

It was a big step from his early enthusiasm for all aspects of saint worship to strong statements like the following: 'This immoderate worship of the saints – a true invention of hypocrisy – is an inexhaustible source of superstitions, to the prejudice of true holiness. The virtues of the dead, whose example is far distant, are cried up, whilst contempt is inculcated for the holiness of the living, whose example would be much more efficacious.' Moreover, he pungently added, 'Men are generous towards the saints who are in heaven, because they are far removed above the attacks of their cruelty, and are to be feared, sitting near God; but they are cruel towards the saints on the earth, because they are interested in crushing virtue . . . '[13] No doubt Hus was thinking here of the attacks upon his own followers.

Most important of all, it was a big step from his early letter to the pope, which he began with 'my humble subjection with the kiss of the blessed feet', to his frequent linking of the papacy with the Antichrist at the end of his life.[14] He would obey the pope if the latter commanded what was in the Bible. But what if the pope's decrees were opposed to the Word of God? Hus gave his answer: 'But should I find them opposed, those will I not obey, even if the fire to burn my body were placed before my eyes.'[15] In the event these last words proved ominously prophetic.

The clash over indulgences could have been foreseen. But the issue went much deeper than just that of indulgences. In *On Simony* he expressed the view that the papal office should consist of true preaching of the Word and administering the sacraments aright, and that the pope is not worthy simply by virtue of his office. He also pointed out that popes contradict each other and that any pope who forbids preaching by his decrees (bulls) is in error. However, in *The Church* his attack is much more thoroughgoing. It was from this work that many of the main accusations made against him at Constance were taken.[16]

It is impossible to summarize all the arguments against the papacy which Hus uses. We merely allude to some. One of the key points is in his interpretation of Matthew 16 and the phrase: 'You are Peter, and on this rock I will build my church' (v. 18). Hus writes, 'Christ is therefore the foundation by whom primarily and in whom primarily the holy catholic church is founded, and faith is the foundation with which it is founded – that faith which works through love, which Peter set forth when he said: "Thou art the Christ, the Son of the living God."'[17] He also quotes Augustine in support. By the phrase in Matthew 16, according to Augustine, Jesus meant to tell Peter, 'I will build thee upon myself, not myself upon thee.'[18]

From this basis Hus moves on to say not only that popes may err, but that they may be the very manifestation of Antichrist. To support this position he quotes from Matthew 24:15 and 2 Thessalonians 2:3, 4. The latter reads, 'Don't let anyone deceive you in any way, for that day will not come until the rebellion occurs and the man of lawlessness is revealed, the man doomed to destruction. He opposes and exalts himself over everything that is called God or is worshipped, and even sets himself up in God's temple, proclaiming himself to be God.' After all this, it is hardly surprising to find Hus saying that the church can exist quite easily without the pope. When in letters he wrote of the need to preach against the prostitute or of 'Satan incarnate with twelve of his proudest devils' it was impossible to mistake or ignore his meaning.[19] In similar vein he pictured the pope sitting, laughing on a war-horse, in marked contrast to the humble Saviour riding on an ass. 'God forbid that Christ's faith be extinct in Christ's simple believers and that the papal grace be absent in infants because of the three beasts who contend about the papal dignity out of arrogance and avarice!' he provocatively exclaimed.[20] He also wondered why one of the three claimants 'called most holy father' did not 'out of the fulness of power constrain the others with their adherents to submit to his jurisdiction'.[21]

Throughout his writings we find scattered hints of his changed views on the church which were now rapidly taking shape. The whole issue of government by remote control was challenged. In *On Simony* he discussed the matter of the pope appointing people to benefices and said, 'For even a simpleton can understand that a pope does not know whether a man whom he has never seen, and who may live a hundred or two hundred miles away, is of good character; nor does he know whether he is acceptable to the people over whom he is to be appointed bishop or priest . . .'[22]

Another point which Hus later raised was the tardiness of the council's actions towards him. After describing in some detail his own long waits, the various appeals, the passing to and fro of papers, he said, 'In the meantime I was weighed down still more by ecclesiastical proceedings.'[23] The medieval papacy has been likened to Charles Dickens' Circumlocution Office in *Bleak House* – swathed in its own red tape. It was a mass of committees, and committees have been described as groups of people who keep minutes and waste hours. Unfortunately in this case, the councils and their committees committed greater crimes than mere time-wasting.

However, the kernel of Hus's position is that there is only one Head of the church who is infallible and this is Jesus Christ. He says, 'When, therefore, my appeal from one pope to his successor did not profit me and to appeal from the pope to a council involves long waiting and because it is of uncertain advantage to beg for grace in the matter of a grievance and censure, therefore I appealed finally to the Head of the church, Jesus Christ.'[24]

To argue that Hus was moving to a biblical understanding that there are only two aspects of the church in the New Testament, the total and the local, is not going beyond the evidence. A strong and vigorous doctrine of the local church emerges constantly in the pages of *The Church*. The two basic passages in Matthew chapters 16 and 18, where Christ himself speaks of the church, are frequently dealt with. Right at the beginning he emphasizes that 'church' means 'congregation'.[25] Many have been saved in Asia and Ethiopia 'who did not expressly recognize Peter'.[26] He speaks at length of the 'particular churches' of the New Testament.[27] With reference to his own excommunication sent all the way from Rome, Hus specifically expounds Matthew 18 and points out that in the New Testament discipline was a local matter between brethren.[28]

Following Jerome, Hus explains to his reader that also in New Testament times the bishop and presbyter were the same person, in other words a known local figure. He envisages a church waging war without the cardinals and expresses the wish that God's 'church should be ruled again as she was ruled by his own indestructible law, by giving bishops and priests who, by evangelizing and prayer and the exemplification of good lives, would diligently feed Christ's sheep'.[29] Quoting his favourite author, Augustine, Hus also stresses that the minister should be someone who has in a sense proved himself: 'To the episcopal dignity, no one should be elected who has not learned to administer a lower office; for the command of the boat should not be entrusted to a man who cannot wield an oar . . .'[30] As Hus himself goes on to explain, this would mean a man who is humble and God-fearing. Such a one was Hus himself.

However exalted a doctrine of the church Hus had, it must not be forgotten that it was because of his belief in the high calling of the Christian that he spoke highly of the body of believers. Sometimes Hus uses language about conversion which is different in terminology from that of the modern evangelical but it can easily be seen that the emphasis is the same. Hus affirms, 'No conduct of any man may be neutral.'[31] In other words, we are either for Christ or against him. In searching language he repeatedly analyses the difference between the church of Christ and the church of Judas and points out that mere verbal profession will not suffice.[32] In a long and moving passage he shows how the genuine faith of Peter was characterized by humility and bore fruit in love.[33] In a reference to the necessity for Paul's sharp rebuke of Peter, Hus makes it clear that he does not suggest that the Christian cannot sin. Yet, when his fault is pointed out, the true Christian is, like Peter, ready to repent.

In his view, faith is a gift of God and 'God, who gave the first faith, will give to his soldier clearer faith'.[34] It is not the empty faith of demons but is faith formed in love. 'This faith is the foundation of the other virtues which the church of Christ practises.'[35] Furthermore, faith means that we not only trust for the past cleansing; we also trust for future provision. Hence a poor parish priest is exhorted by Hus to do right, seek first God's kingdom and to 'trust in his holy mercy that he will not leave you naked'.[36] Although he does not use the term 'justification by faith', Hus constantly writes with the tone and idiom of a justified man. One of his favourite quotations is Luke 17:10, where Christ says, 'So you also, when you have done everything you were told to do, should say, "We are unworthy servants; we have only done our duty."' He wrote, 'There remains still another hole through which monks commit simony: for they issue letters of participation in their good deeds, such as fasts, prayers, masses, austerities and other good works. But they are mistaken when they write, declaring, "We make thee a participant . . ." For to make anyone a participant in good works which would benefit his soul to salvation, belongs to God alone.'[37] Ridiculing the whole concept of works of supererogation, Hus wondered why the monks only shared the benefits of these with the rich.

Very strongly emphasized throughout the early pages of his most famous work, *The Church,* is the doctrine of predestination. After quoting from Augustine he writes, 'From this statement it appears that the holy universal church is one, the church which is the totality of the predestinate, including all, from the first righteous man to the last one to be saved in the future. And it includes all who are to be saved who make up the number, in respect to the filling up of which number all the saints slain under the altar had the divine assurance that they should wait for a time until the number should be filled up of their fellow servants and brethren (Revelation 6:9–11). For the omniscient God, who has given to all things their weight, measure and number, has foredetermined how many shall ultimately be saved.'[38]

Because this is so significant a doctrine in the plan of salvation and is always prominent in any true emphasis on God's grace, we will give two more illustrations. Later in this particular treatise Hus quotes from an old writer, Gregory, on the parable of the drag-net to this effect: 'But we who are bad when we are caught are thoroughly changed in the element of goodness.' Hus immediately adds the comment: 'In this he finds a sign that the wicked who are predestinate are permanently and thoroughly changed into what is good.' There is no falling away from grace. He then further speaks about the man at the wedding reception without a proper wedding garment, and explains it in this way: 'They lack the marriage garment, which is predestinating love.'[39]

Moreover he insists that the gates of hell will not prevail against the church because of God's predestination. Let us hear it in his own words: 'For seeing that Christ is the rock of that church and also the foundation on whom she is builded in respect to predestination, she cannot finally be overthrown by the gates of hell, that is, by the power and assaults of tyrants who persecute her or the assaults of wicked spirits. For mightier is Christ the King of heaven, the Bridegroom of the church, than the prince of this world. Therefore, in order to show his power and foreknowledge and the predestination wherewith he builds, protects, foreknows, and predestinates his church, and to give persevering hope to his church, he added, "And the gates of hell shall not prevail against it".'[40] Hus sees this as a great doctrine of hope.

# 18.
# Hus travels to face his accusers

We have now reached the time when Hus was to make his final departure from his own country. In view of the fact that he had many people to contact in Prague, it is likely that he made a final secret return to the city. His last journey out of the town must have brought back a flood of memories. Did he recall how he had first arrived as an unknown student from a poor peasant background? Did he recall the peace of those early years and the excitement of all the new pleasures and sensations? There would be one object in particular which would almost certainly remind him of some of the fierce contests and sharp comments that had characterized his ministry as he was increasingly led into opposition to the unfaithful clergy.

Hus would have had to make his final trip across the famous Charles Bridge which spans the Vltava river. It is a justly famous sight even today. In 1342 the bridge was destroyed by floods and, since a temporary wooden structure proved insufficient, especially with all the increased traffic to a city which was proving a magnet for many, in 1357 Charles IV undertook the building of the present bridge utilizing the skills of Matthew of Arras and both Peter Parler and his son John. Because of the constant interruptions due to storms and floods the work was only finally completed in 1503.

Even today the piers of the bridge need the protection of huge ramps of tree trunks to prevent damage by ice which flows down the river in winter. But now the bridge stands on its fifteen arches, broad enough for three carriages to drive abreast and defended at both ends by massive Gothic gate-towers with pointed roofs. When it was completed it was soon heard of abroad, chiefly because it was one of the greatest undertakings of its kind. Only the bridge spanning the Danube at Regensberg was longer. The Charles Bridge was 660 yards long.

Such a landmark cannot be missed or ignored. Hus could not avoid alluding to it. Two of his comments which make mention of it take us to the heart of one aspect of his controversy with Rome. Between 1376 and 1412 the five archbishops of Prague, instead of being elected by the local chapter, had been appointed by the papacy with much exchange of money and bribery. Expressing his conviction that a simpler, more honest course was the only God-honouring one, Hus trenchantly declared, '. . . But the Prague bridge is more likely to fall down than a candidate for the Prague bishopric should secure it by such a holy course!'[1] Hus was thinking of the solidity of the structure. And in one of the most aggressive and abrasive of all his utterances Hus was alleged to have exclaimed 'that it would be easier to find a stag with golden antlers on the bridge of Prague than a worthy priest'.[2] However, this was a hostile report.

Yet the bridge today forcibly reminds us of the ongoing nature of this conflict, for one can certainly find many other equally strange objects on the bridge. Over the years there have been erected at regular intervals no less than thirty statues of so-called Christian saints on its parapets. One of these, the first to be erected, is of particular interest to a student of Hus's life and reveals how the battle of Hus is an unending battle and how disturbed his Roman Catholic opponents were by his great influence. Because after his death Hus had become a national hero for Czechs of all faiths and of no faith, the Roman Catholic authorities planned to oust him from the nation's affection by substituting their own cult-figure.

John of Nepomuk was the person selected. He was a priest, who was tortured and killed by Wenceslas the king during Hus's lifetime. After his death his body was unceremoniously tossed into the river Vltava. This much is fact. It was then claimed that he had been tortured for refusing to divulge the queen's secrets passed on under the seal of the confessional – this is unfounded and false – and it was further said that, after his corpse had disappeared for several days, it suddenly emerged aureoled with five stars – which is plainly legendary and absurd. All this was concocted so that he might become the patron saint of the people and draw their attention from John Hus. Therefore the very presence of this image and the fact that every year thousands of pilgrims from all over Bohemia come to pray at the foot of the statue, which is transformed into a small chapel for the occasion, shows that the issue of the identity of the true faith is still a very live one.

Hus obviously died before this legend took shape, yet it is interesting to recall that he was in effect accused of showing disrespect to John of Nepomuk. It was reported by an enemy how on the occasion of the drowning, an event which took place when Hus was a young student, there had been a discussion in the house of Wenceslas, a cup-maker, to the effect that Prague might be placed under interdict. It was alleged that Hus had then protested that there was no reason why all the religious services should be stopped for the death of one man, for such would have been the consequences of an interdict. In fact, the skill of the informer seems aptly displayed in all this, for Hus appears actually to have said simply that neither because of the imprisonment or murder of himself or anyone else should the whole kingdom of Bohemia be deprived of the spiritual ministry. He was in no way condoning the murder or treating it as a light thing. We may legitimately deduce how strongly he would have opposed the creation of this absurd and evil legend. Hus was more interested in the maintenance of a true ministry of the Word than the concocting of false saints.

The young student of those days had now become a mature man of God, an outstanding theologian, a fervent preacher and evangelist both deeply loved and vehemently hated, as all true evangelists should be. His ministry had been powerfully effective in Prague and throughout much of rural Bohemia, but now he was to have an even greater audience. John Hus, son of the peasant from Husinec, was to testify to his faith before the representatives and dignitaries of all Christendom. For, with Christendom still divided in allegiance between three popes, and the character of the most recently appointed one, Pope John XXIII, bringing scandal to the name of the church, and with the troubles in Bohemia having repercussions in other countries, Sigismund, the Holy Roman Emperor, saw the possibility of earning for himself a real niche in history as bringer of peace to a troubled church, and succeeded in persuading Pope John XXIII to call a council.

For much of what follows concerning the account of the journey, the arrest, imprisonment, trial and martyrdom of Hus, we shall be deeply indebted to the lengthy account by Peter of Mladoňovice, a man described by Spinka as 'the most reliable of the eye-witnesses of the trial'.[3] Hus himself described Peter in the closing words of a letter addressed to the members of the University of Prague and written just over a week before his death: 'I commend Peter of Mladoňovice to you, my most faithful and most constant comforter and supporter.'[4]

Of course, it cannot be denied that Peter was a thoroughly involved and committed man. The final paragraph of his narrative leaves us in no doubt on this score. He writes, 'Thus I have therefore described clearly and in detail the sequence of the death and agony of the celebrated Master John Hus, the eminent preacher of the evangelical truth, so that in the course of time his memory might be vividly recollected.' Yet he adds, 'My principle has been . . . to speak of . . . what I have clearly learned from what I myself have seen and heard. He who knows all things is my witness that I lie not.'[5]

Apparently the work of Peter was so highly regarded that the final chapters which describe the death of Hus were regularly read on 6 July, a day which had become a national holiday, for more than two hundred years after the events took place. Luther persuaded publishers of his day to produce both a Latin and German version. The work also circulated among the Calvinists in a French version of 1554 and it gripped the minds and emotions of generation after generation of English readers through the successive editions of Foxe's *Book of Martyrs.* Peter himself died on 7 February 1451.

Peter's *Account of the Trial and Condemnation of Master John Hus in Constance* begins with the recording of Sigismund's proclamation of the council and his sending of 'certain noble lords of Bohemia . . . to conduct Master John of Husinec, *formatus* bachelor of sacred theology, to that council'. It continues, 'They were to assure him of a safe-conduct, in order that he should come to Constance to the said general council for the clearing of his own evil reputation as well as that of the Bohemian kingdom. The king was also willing to send him a special safe-conduct in order that, having come to Constance, he might return to Bohemia. He also solemnly promised to be ready to take him under his and the Holy Empire's protection and defence.'[6]

Then follows the wording of the safe-conduct. Hus was not only to be given a safe journey, but he was also to be helped in the speed of his travels, 'horses, baggage' being provided, and he was to be freed from the payment of any toll or tax at the various bridges, passes and harbours. It has been argued that Sigismund, who was certainly no natural friend of Hus, had been persuaded to give these assurances because his negotiator had secured a much desired concession from his brother, Wenceslas. Wenceslas had, as we have seen, been the Holy Roman Emperor but had been deposed. Sigismund, elected three years previously, had not yet been crowned. Moreover Wenceslas had until this present point demanded that in his own lifetime Sigismund should forego this right. However, in exchange for Wenceslas' agreement to Sigismund's coronation, more favourable terms had been negotiated for Hus.

Hitherto Hus had refused to go to Rome. Yet as Peter narrates, 'Master John Hus, seeing and hearing so many and so great promises and forms of assurance, wrote to the king that he would without fail come to the said council.'[7] However, it is unlikely that Hus had been suddenly and completely overwhelmed by a mood of naive and blind optimism. Other facts make this plain. His letter to Sigismund himself contained this realistic note: 'I have taught nothing in secret, but in public, for my ministry was attended mostly by masters, bachelors, priests, barons, knights, and many others; I thus desire to be heard, examined, and to preach not in secret, but at a public hearing, and to reply with the aid of the Spirit of God to all who should wish to accuse me. I will not, I hope, be afraid to confess the Lord Christ, and, if need be, to suffer death for his most true law.'[8] Another letter to a priest called Martin came to the recipient with the plea that it should only be opened on the death of the sender. It reads very much like the last testament of a friend. And a letter to his parishioners contained this paragraph: 'You may perhaps not see me in Prague before I die; if, however, the Almighty God should be pleased to bring me back to you, we shall meet each other more joyfully. Furthermore, we shall, of course, meet one another in the heavenly joy.'[9]

Therefore, although Hus started on the journey with a measure of optimism, it must have been a guarded optimism. There were many reasons for this. The first and simplest one was that he had already discovered how unfairly his representatives had been treated by the papacy. Their case had not been heard. They had been thrown into prison and cruelly treated. There had in fact been no semblance of justice in Rome's dealings with them. Secondly, he knew that for some years his comments about the Roman cardinals and the pope had been increasingly and devastatingly critical. The papacy itself had been aware of this, had fulminated against Hus in its increasingly harsh excommunications and had during his exile sought to bring pressure on the Bohemian hierarchy to deal with him more severely.

In the third place Hus was not without some insight into the treacherous nature of Sigismund. One of the very lords who had negotiated the safe-conduct on the king's behalf had also quietly indicated to Hus in the hearing of a close friend that he would be condemned. 'I suppose he knew the king's intention,' commented Hus, in a letter dealing with this.[10] Yet it would seem that Hus did not take his warning seriously enough. A fourth factor was that Hus well knew that not only were a group of Bohemian clergy inimical to his safety travelling to Constance but that one, Michael de Causis, had long been resident at Rome, seeking to procure his downfall. This unsavoury character had persuaded the king to loan him some money for restoring certain gold-mines and then when the project had failed had absconded with the money. Men of this calibre found a safe haven at Rome.

Fifthly, there were the pleas or attitudes of friends, many of whom either urged him not to go or, like the impulsive and generous-spirited Jerome, spoke in such a way as to leave no doubt in Hus's mind as to their conviction about the outcome. 'Dear Master,' said Jerome, 'be firm; maintain intrepidly what thou hast written and preached against the pride, avarice, and other vices of the churchmen, with arguments drawn from the Holy Scriptures. Should this task become too severe for thee, – should I learn that thou hast fallen into any peril, – I shall fly at once to thy assistance.'[11]

As a sixth reason there was the obvious fact that many of the German and French and English leaders were hostile to Hus. This was particularly true of the Germans who had left Bohemia during a reform of the voting system at the university and of the Englishmen who had crossed swords with him over the matter of Wyclif. Furthermore, a very revealing letter from Gerson, a Frenchman, and one of the leading theologians of the day, was addressed to Bohemia and to the archbishop. As Gerson was to be an important figure at the council it gives an indication of the likely reception Hus would find for his views.

'Up to the present day,' wrote Gerson, 'various methods have been tried to extirpate heresies from the field of the church, as with so many different scythes. First, they were torn out with the scythe of miracles, by which God testified to the catholic truth, in the time of the apostles. Next they were extirpated by learned doctors, with force of argument and discussion, by the scythe of holy councils . . . Last of all, when the malady became desperate, it was found necessary to have recourse to the axe of the secular arm to cut down heresies, together with their authors, and cast them into the flames.'[12] Gerson went on to point out that in this way ruin was prevented from spreading. In his day, he argued, there were no longer miracles for confirmation of the gospel but there were the splendid and orthodox doctors of the University of Paris – of which he was a member! If people did not heed such authorities, then stronger measures should be taken. Waxing warm in the advocacy of his theme, he urged, 'If, therefore, present remedies are useless, it only remains to put the axe of the secular arm to the root of this unfruitful and accursed tree.' In his view, the salvation of souls depended on such swift and strong action.

Why, then, did Hus go to Constance? The reason was

simple but it must be affirmed clearly. It was a deliberate act. He felt that it was God's time. He could have saved his life, but he wanted to go in order to preach the gospel and testify to the truth. He hoped there would be an opportunity to do this. He was under no sense of external compulsion. At his trial Hus declared that he could have remained in Bohemia, protected in many a strong castle. Immediately one Czech lord murmured his assent. Up to this point Hus's 'hour' had not yet come, or, to adopt the image of one of his own supporters, it was not yet time for the goose to be cooked.[13]

Before he finally left, Hus felt it necessary to affirm publicly in Bohemia what he was doing and also, acting on the advice of a skilled legal friend, to seek to establish his own innocence. Thus he wrote out public notices in Latin, Czech and German, inviting any who wished to accuse him of any error or heresy to stand up and be counted. A letter to Wenceslas and his queen also makes the same point, confirming the fact that no one had stood forth in answer to his other challenges. Amazingly he even obtained a letter from an official responsible for enquiring into heresies which plainly asserted that no error had been found in his teaching. Furthermore, the Archbishop of Prague said before witnesses that 'he knew of no error or heresy against the said Master John Hus, but only that the pope had excommunicated him; and from that excommunication let the said Master John Hus extricate and clear himself as best he could'.[14]

When Hus sought through a representative to ask the same questions of an assembled synod of all the clergy and prelates of Bohemia, his representative was not admitted in person. In all this Hus had strenuously sought to act openly and persuade his adversaries to do likewise, but without success. Once Hus had discovered a truth he was prepared to speak out on it. Openness was one of his great characteristics, and he inspired it in others – even to the point of death. It is so important a trait in his character that we must pause to give further confirmation of the point.

As he rode with his little group of friends to Constance there is one significant phrase in a letter to those left behind.

'You should know that I never rode with donned hood, but openly with uncovered face,' he writes.[15] That we sin by our silences is stressed by him in his work *On Simony*. In *The Church* he points out that the clergy sin by the non-performance of pastoral duties. By such omission the sheep can be killed. Quoting Ezekiel 3, Hus states that the watchman must speak out and warn. Silence in the face of heresy and evil means complicity in guilt.[16] There is much truth in the saying, 'The cruellest lies are often told in silence.' This is one accusation that the opponents of Hus could not bring against him. He certainly was not silent. Is it far-fetched to say that his very demeanour reflected his openness and integrity?

How significant it is that Hus's representative was not admitted in person by the synod of clergy! Hus called on his fellow clergy to defend the truth and was ignored by many of them. Yet Hus had also constantly called on laymen to defend the truth and had been widely heeded. One opponent, Stephen of Dola, bitterly complained that 'Laity, butchers, shoemakers, tailors, and humble mechanics rise up proudly and contemn authority.'[17] They had listened to Hus exhorting them to have the spiritual discernment to recognize a wolf when they saw one, to refuse to give money for his upkeep or support to his ministry, and had acted on his advice. As he left Bohemia, Hus would feel that his message to all Christians had not been without effect when he wrote, 'Therefore, O faithful Christian, search the truth, hear truth, learn truth, love truth, speak the truth, hold the truth till death.'[18] Further confirmation of all this is to be found in the fact that the two knights, Wenceslas of Duba and John of Chlum, who were to travel as his protectors, were described by Hus himself as more than physical protectors, for they were 'heralds of the truth, or, to speak more truly, defenders of the truth'.[19]

Meanwhile, because Hus was in truth a man who, unlike so many of his critics, lived in apostolic poverty, money had to be raised to enable him to undertake the journey to Constance. It has been suggested that many nobles, and possibly the king and queen, contributed to his expenses. Travel in this period could be a very expensive pastime. It could also be exceedingly hazardous. We hear of one man in 1402 being taken through a certain pass in an ox-wagon 'half-dead with cold, while his eyes were blindfolded so that he could not see the dangers of the pass'. Perhaps there were road-hogs then, too! Another warned of the travel prospects as a time 'when you shall have feeble bread, wine and stinking water'.[20] He also warned of the danger of robbers. Indeed one man, writing later from Constance, at an admittedly unsettled time, reported on 'the dangers of the roads'.[21]

Despite all such factors and the additional fears attached to Hus's journey in particular, it was in fact more a triumphal procession than a sombre death march. The fact that much of the route was through Germany made this all the more surprising. His greetings to council men and elders in various German towns were received in a friendly fashion. Various pastors also held discussions with him in a reasonable and kindly manner.

At Nuremberg merchants had announced his coming and it is no exaggeration to say that the whole town was agog, standing in the streets awaiting his arrival. When the local pastor sent a note asking to converse, Hus readily agreed, only stipulating when some local leaders wished for a private talk that this should not be so. 'To them I said: "I preach in public and desire that all who wish may hear me",' Hus wrote to his friends in Bohemia.[22] Everywhere it was the same story – a desire for openness and integrity.

Only one man in Nuremberg seemed displeased. Ever a keen tract distributor, Hus gave away to all the innkeepers a copy of his exposition on the Ten Commandments and remarked how well he was received by them and their wives. Against his expectations he had to declare, 'I confess, therefore, that there exists here against me no greater enmity than among the inhabitants of the kingdom of Bohemia.'[23] Sometimes the discussions continued till the dusk and John of Chlum earned himself the nickname of the 'Biberach doctor', so eloquently did he argue with all and sundry *en route* and so particularly at the small village of Biberach. Hus often playfully referred to him in this way.

Although Hus was treated 'well and honourably in all cities', there were also more ominous signs. One high-ranking cleric preceded them on the route. In a letter to his friends in Bohemia Hus informed them about this, adding that this cleric 'spread the rumour that they were bringing me chained in a wagon, and that people should beware of me because I was a mind reader! Consequently, whenever we approached any city crowds ran out to meet me as if to a show.'[24] Hus, keen evangelist as he was, seized this opportunity by preaching the truth to the gaping sightseers.

Another ominous note was that Hus as yet did not officially possess the safe-conduct from Sigismund. Indeed at Nuremberg one of the knights, Wenceslas of Duba, had left the party to fetch this but the others went on ahead instead of waiting so that they could enter Constance in the entourage and under the protection of Sigismund. All this resulted in Hus's entering the city without the official document and only receiving it two days after his arrival. However, in the event this probably made little difference to the final outcome.

Obviously the journey was costly for many and Hus himself comments on the fact that many of the Czechs, having spent all their money, were in financial difficulties. Some of his last moments of freedom were enjoyed on horseback and he remarked that his 'horse Rabštýn indeed excels them all in strength and high spirit'.[25] The horse and its rider were well matched. They very much needed to be. Yet it is a fine glimpse that we have of Hus in one of his last moments of physical freedom. We recall a stanza from the great Hussite chorale 'Ye who are warriors of God':

Long the Czechs have said
And have their proverb –
That under a good lord
There is good riding.[26]

# 19.
# The mad merry-go-round of Constance

I who but late was seated on a throne,
  Must now in bitterness lament my fall;
In my high place of power I ruled alone
  My feet the kiss of homage had from all.
Now to the lowest deep of shame I'm hurled,
  A victim to the penalty of crime,
The laughing-stock and scandal of the world,
  Gazed at in scorn – the wonder of my time.
Once every land its gold laid at my feet,
  Now wealth delights not, not a friend remains;
From me, cast down so low from my high seat,
  Let those be warned whom glory false sustains.[1]

In this way a chronicle of the time sought to imagine how Pope John XXIII would feel after his deposition by the Council of Constance. For the man who had been involved in deposing two other popes only a few years before at the Council of Pisa was himself now about to be deposed. The council was to be a momentous defeat and terrible humiliation for him.

John was to be deposed for a variety of charges. Mention has already been made of the charges of poisoning of his predecessor, of disbelief in the future life, of sodomy and of many acts of cruelty and violence. Yet John XXIII must not be seen in isolation or as an untypical figure. An ancient scribe saw the issue clearly. 'What judgement', he asked, after copying out the charges brought against John, 'ought we to pass on the cardinals who elected John, after having sworn to choose the best among them, unless indeed the best among them was one who now stood convicted of being a ravisher, incendiary, traitor, homicide, an incestuous fornicator, guilty of crimes more flagrant still?'[2] Moreover, it was by the cardinals who had elected John that John Hus was to be tried!

One writer, who takes a far more favourable view of John, points out that several charges were dropped, including that of poisoning his predecessor. Although he admits that the forty-four that remained constituted a black record, he reasons that John did not contest them simply because he knew that he would not have a fair trial. In face of what we shall see of Hus's strenuous contending for truth at his own manifestly unfair trial, this is a very weak argument. The sceptical historian Gibbon found that this whole episode of the deposition gave him an opportunity that he could not miss as, alluding to the council's summary dealings with the popes, he wrote in his ironical vein: 'Of the three popes, John XXIII was the first victim; he fled, and was brought back a prisoner; the most scandalous charges were suppressed; the vicar of Christ was only accused of piracy, murder, rape, sodomy and incest.'[3]

Pope John XXIII had initially been very reluctant to call the council. No doubt he had realized his own precarious position. However, his dependence on Sigismund for help against his adversary Ladislas had compelled him to agree to the council. Imagine his anger when, just before the council, Ladislas ceased hostilities and the reason for his original decision had gone. Nevertheless John felt compelled to travel to the council and hoped that he might swing decisions in his favour by packing the assembly with Italian supporters and even possibly bribing the emperor and others to support him.

That John's fears had by no means subsided is made clear by a report of his approach to Constance itself. Apparently when he was crossing over the Arlberg, his carriage was overturned, and as he lay in the snow beneath it, he petulantly exclaimed to the lords and courtiers hastening to his aid, 'Here I lie, in the devil's name.' Later as he drew still nearer and looked across the landscape he declared with true prophetic insight, albeit of the Caiaphas type, 'That's how they catch foxes,' as he thought of his own imminent fall.[4] 'Fat fowls,' sneered Dietrich of Niem, 'because they will not walk to the market of their own accord, have to be carried. We are content you have come.'[5]

Obviously his forebodings were indeed well founded, but on his immediate entry there was an elaborate procession with nine white horses, the ninth one carrying 'the true and holy sacrament, covered with a red cloth'. But what was probably far more to the pope's liking was the fact that the burghers of Constance brought him a present: 'The first was a silver gilt goblet, that weighed five silver marks, then four kegs of Italian wine, four large casks of Alsatian wine, eight casks of wine of the country, and forty measures of oats.'[6] The pope duly expressed his thanks. John was also thankful that the other leading participant, Sigismund, the Holy Roman Emperor and King of Hungary, brother of the hapless Wenceslas, had not yet arrived. This gave John a breathing-space for intrigue and bribery.

Sigismund was undoubtedly a more complex figure than John XXIII. A warrior of undeniable courage, he had yet known terrible setbacks and his pride had been badly crushed. In 1396 he had commanded a force of some 100,000 men drawn from all parts of Europe against the Turks. Although it had been their proud boast that if the sky should fall they would uphold it on their lances, they had not only been routed but wellnigh annihilated. Yet the mind of Sigismund was ever full of grandiose schemes for the conclusion of treaties with other great powers that they might together join battle once more with the Turks. In this area he had undoubted insight. The Turks were soon to be the major threat in Europe. But even a writer who seeks to present Sigismund in a favourable light adds, with reference to this issue, 'But his complete inability to meet even the expenses of his own court, a standing jest among his contemporaries, was sufficient comment on the likelihood of these plans seeing fulfilment.'[7]

As might be expected of the son of Charles IV, Sigismund was well educated and fluent in four languages. He had his father's love of learning and pithy speech and the same desire to help poor scholars. He would sometimes say that he could make a thousand knights in a single day, but he could not make one scholar in a thousand years. His fondness for proverbs and apophthegms comes out in the many sayings attributed to him: 'The flatterer is worse than the crow, for the crow picks out the eyes of the dead, but the flatterer the eyes of the living.' 'I kill my enemy by sparing his life.' 'A donkey has a better time than a prince, for his master at least leaves him alone when he is eating.' 'No prince deserves to reign who cannot shut his eyes and ears.'[8] Such sayings indicated considerable native shrewdness and wit. Yet Sigismund, for all this, refused to think deeply and honestly when he was faced with new biblical insight and unfortunately followed out his own precept wrongly by shutting his eyes and ears at the wrong time. Moreover, at the crucial moment, he signally failed to kill his enemy by sparing his life. Fine though it had all sounded, it had been but empty talk.

Such a man, nevertheless, might seem born to rule. There was an appearance of grandeur and chivalry in his manner. He loved occasions of state and revelled in the pomp and circumstance of Constance, which furnished him opportunity to indulge his showmanship at all levels, for it was said that, when it suited him, he would doff his bonnet to an oyster-woman or bandy a jest with her husband. No doubt they would be suitably impressed. Sigismund stood imposingly with his active, supple, well-proportioned frame and long tawny beard. He was 'tall, with bright eyes, broad forehead, pleasantly rosy cheeks, and a long thick beard', according to a contemporary description.[9] He was fond of fishing and hunting, danced with vigour and joy, participated actively and successfully in jousting bouts and loved to be in the saddle. Constance seemed made for him.

Unfortunately he loved to be in more places than the saddle. The attraction of another's marriage bed was too great for him to resist. 'He was witty in conversation, given to wine and women, and thousands of love intrigues are laid to his charge,' is the testimony of the same contemporary witness.[10] 'Never', says an early report of him, 'was a man less wont to keep his marriage vows.'[11] For all this he was staunchly orthodox. It is recounted how he once sent his butler down into Saint Patrick's Hole in Ireland, where the future could supposedly be seen in dreams. There the butler observed a crowd of young women in purgatory, waiting for Sigismund with a bed of fire. When informed of this, the king's immediate reply was 'We must shift that bed to heaven.' Therefore, selling thirteen towns to the King of Poland to raise the money, he built a church.[12] Such a story shows the extent of false belief at this time and gives further proof of the vital nature of the underlying issues in the indulgence controversy in Prague.

Without in any way seeking to impugn the sincerity of Sigismund's desire for the unification of the church at an external level (the only level he would understand) and his evident devotion to Rome, one feels that Constance was in many ways a welcome diversion for the emperor. However, he was not totally blind to the outward faults of the church which he served with such loyalty and wholeheartedness. What he allowed for himself he did not fully approve of among the priests for, confirming the strictures of Hus and many others, he made many a bitter jest about the greed and licence of the clergy, declaring that the difference between the married priest of the Greek church and the celibate of the Latin was that the former had but one wife while the latter had ten. And, although he honoured relics very much as his father Charles IV had done, he realized to some extent the possibility of deception. When buying the skeleton of Saint Elizabeth of Marburg he insisted that his agent be present at the opening of the grave since he did not want to be put off with a 'bit of a dead cobbler'.[13]

The whole affair of Hus seemed commonplace, trivial and even irritatingly simple to Sigismund, who was heard to remark soon after arriving at Constance that 'The case of John Hus and other minor problems ought not to interfere with the reform of the church and the Roman Empire, which was the principal object for which the council had been convened.'[14] Cerretano, the papal notary who painstakingly recorded this in his *Journal*, little realized that he was recording one of the most unintentionally ironic statements in history.

After the pope arrived there was some considerable delay before the emperor came. This was typical of the era. One modern scholar has written, 'The only audible expression of time was the sound of bells in the church tower ringing out the canonical hours. Even so, the measurement of time was often only approximate, for the devices by which it could be regulated, sundial, hour-glass, water-clock, candles, were bound to be inexact by modern standards. Church synods, royal councils and the like were never timed to open at a particular hour or even day and, if men came from a distance, it might be a matter of weeks or even months before the business got under way.'[15]

Indeed many men were travelling from all directions. The various princes and their contingents were arriving at intervals. On one particular day an illustrious Polish prince came with his 200 horses and 4 wagons, another lord from Poland brought 120 horses and 3 wagons, while the Hungarian lord, Pipo, had 150 horses and 3 wagons. Others followed these, before the day was out, and many more horses required to be fed and stabled. Such was the daily pattern over a long period.

One man has attempted to compute the numbers of people who came. His final estimate was over 72,000 people. We do not give all the details, but mention that he has in his list Pope John XXIII with 600 men, 5 patriarchs with 118 men, 33 cardinals with 3,056 men, a whole host of archbishops, bishops, scholars, doctors of theology with their retainers, 5,300 simple priests, 'over 1,400 merchants, shopkeepers, furriers, smiths, shoemakers, innkeepers, and handworkers', 1,700 trumpeters, 700 prostitutes, 39 dukes, 32 princely lords and counts, 141 counts, 71 barons, more than 1,500 knights and 'embassies from 83 kings of Asia, Africa and Europe, with full powers'.[16]

Whether there is any measure of exaggeration in the above computation or not, it was undoubtedly one of the largest and most famous gatherings of all time. Scholars of far-reaching fame jostled shoulders with squires and washerwomen 'who washed and mended the clothes of the Roman lords in private and public'.[17] Students came to look for prebends or simply for the fun of the thing, many being quite happy to earn a day's keep by grooming horses or cleaning out the stables. As we know, there were plenty of horses, so there was ample work.

Everywhere there was movement, colour and action. The trumpeters mentioned in the above lists were not unemployed. Their instruments blared forth at regular intervals, announcing events as diverse as the flight of a panic-stricken pope and the arrival of a present for the king in the shape of a huge beast that looked like a buffalo. Processions wound their resplendent way through the town. Whenever the pope gave his blessing white cloths of the best damask were hung from all the bay windows while walls were covered with cloths of gold. In the vivid phrase of one historian you would everywhere find 'bishops going by in parti-coloured jackets, with sleeves like wings, stopping short at the waist to show off their shapely shanks and shiny shoes'.[18]

Lake Constance, called in German the Bodensee, is shared by three countries. Most of its shoreline is German. It is in a central position and easy of access. It was in the circle of Swabia and under the imperial authority. The town situated on the borders of the lake probably contained about five or six thousand inhabitants at this time. The lake has a moderating influence on the climate and nearby Mainau Island has had a long gardening tradition. Today tulips, narcissi and hyacinths bloom in April and May, while rare varieties of irises and lilies flourish through July, with dahlias coming to flower in September and there are also hothouses of orchids, palms, lemon and orange trees.[19]

Modern travel guides speak enticingly of the scenery and entertainments, but the Constance of the year 1414 was not without its own particular travel guide. Ulrich Richental, citizen of Constance, was public relations officer, traffic director, food manager, recorder of unconsidered trifles, status-seeker and fervent patriot all rolled into one. One scholar has described him as 'Richental, that very entertaining, though very mendacious chronicler of the Council'.[20] He was thus giving his verdict on Richental's *Chronicle of the Council of Constance,* memoirs which were written down for the most part some time after the events took place. Certainly with regard to the things that really matter, such as the trial of Hus, Richental would seem to be wildly wrong. But Richental was not interested in the things that really matter. He was a pompous official, a loyal churchman, a public notary with some knowledge of Latin and an absorption in the greatness, as he saw it, of his own beloved Constance, which he was prepared to defend before all comers. He was sufficiently well known for Sigismund to visit him at his country house just outside Constance on an afternoon in June 1416. He died in 1437.

Therefore, with the proviso that in the really important doctrinal matters Richental is either an ignoramus or simply not interested, we can learn much from his account. He tells us that he was present when the king came looking for a suitable site and describes the various inspections and investigations. We learn from him how the boats brought their loads of hay and their wares, and how he once watched twenty-five arrive in an hour. He gives all the prices of the foodstuff. 'A quarter of onions was 2s. or 20 pence, a quarter of turnips 8d. or 10d., a big head of cabbage 2d. and smaller one a penny,' he narrates, adding that pork, beef, lamb, wild boar's meat, roe venison and stag venison were all available along with thrush, blackbird, badger, otter and beaver.[21] Then after cataloguing a long list of the types of fish which were on display, he tells us, 'There were also frogs and snails for sale, which the Italians bought.' All tastes were catered for.

There are in his pages some fascinating little glimpses of the type of scene that would greet the visitor's eye. He recounts, 'At that time also the bakers arrived in Constance, who baked pasties filled with chicken or fish or egg or whatever anyone likes. They baked rings and pretzels also and had small barrows with one wheel, like those on which dirt and stones are taken up in gardens and carried out. On these wheelbarrows they set small ovens, in which they baked their pasties and other such things. The wheelbarrows with the ovens, which were always hot, they pushed through the city, calling what they had for sale.'[22]

Of course, not everyone felt that everything was so cheap, so plentiful or so appetizing. On arrival, Hus wrote to his friends in Bohemia stating, 'Food is very expensive: a bed costs half a florin a week.'[23] Although he added that horses were cheap, he also said that many of his Czech friends, having spent their money *en route,* were now in want. A poet who went to Constance acidly remarked that the best fare was reserved for clerical stomachs, that meat was scarce, that cabbage might be howled for, and that wine was sour as sloes. Deputies from the University of Vienna also complained of the high prices.

Not all appreciated Constance as did Richental. Indeed our local dignitary was not unaware of murmuring in the background. He records complaints about the price of lodgings, explaining that the pope and king sorted it all out to everyone's satisfaction. He also mentions unruly behaviour among the king's retainers, who, he assures us, were properly dealt with. His theme is, as he himself puts it, that 'in all these matters burghers and foreigners acted with such friendliness towards one another that no complaint or grievance of any kind and no outbreak occurred'.[24] All this he attributed to the providence of God.

In fact we know from hints in Richental and statements elsewhere that there was conflict between the local tradespeople and the hoards of 'interlopers' who descended on the city. There were quite understandably the 'regulars', who resented intruders and claimed a monopoly of trading rights. To meet this problem and to secure proper rights for the visitors and decide rents, early in the morning, on three days of the week, a rota of fifteen papal auditors of various nationalities sat at St Stephen's Church, accompanied by their beadles and providing work for ninety scribes. Afterwards the winning parties were usually seen to be taking away their proctors and writers in order to drink their health in good French wine.

Richental obviously had an eye for detail. Empty protocol fascinated him. Processions sent him into an ectasy of delight. Pomp and circumstance were his meat and drink. Thus we learn from him of King Sigismund receiving the golden rose from the pope and afterwards going on to a balcony with the donor and displaying the same to an enthusiastic crowd. Soon after this Richental, who undoubtedly is a humorist, without any sense of humour soberly relates, 'Before they sat down at table, a doctor of theology preached them a sermon of great length. At the banquet, the pope sat at a table apart, having no one with him. They brought him of each dish enough to satisfy ten men.'[25] Presumably the long grace merited the lengthy meal.

It is Richental who tells us that 700 prostitutes had recourse to the place. Others confirm this fact. Another commentator observed that they lived thirty in a room, that they put up in bathrooms and sheds and those who could find no better lodgings were content with the wine-butts which lay in the streets. Comments Richental, with his informative but unspiritual banality, as he describes the general activities, 'Especially into the Aichorn they went every day. In that wood, there were taverns that sold all manner of wines, whatever were wanted. And roast fowls, sausage, meat, and broiled fish were to be found there and whatever else was wanted, and gay women who belonged to the establishments.'[26] In the next sentence our chronicler states, 'The spiritual lords wandered in any gardens they chose, and no one opposed them, and they did no harm. So the lords passed away their time.'[27] The comment of Benedict de Pileo is yet another confirmation of the seamy side beneath the glitter when he wrote, 'So great is the host of most dainty dames and damsels who surpass the snow in the delicacy of their colouring that you might rightly say of Constance as Ovid declared of Rome, that Venus herself reigns in this city.'[28]

All kinds of activities drew excited crowds, according to Richental. The regular generosity of one archbishop drew hoards of poor people clamouring regularly each week for broth and meat. The king and pope standing on a balcony and throwing down candles drew a crowd of people in 'a great scramble, one falling over another and loud laughter'.[29] The calendar of events must rarely have had a blank space. 'The princes, knights, and squires held many tilts and tourneys and danced afterwards with the ladies. This pleasant life went on with love and friendship everywhere,' records our indefatigable advertising agent.[30]

It is perhaps worth describing the English contribution as Richental gives it. In January 1417 the English bishops invited the town councillors of Constance to a house. 'They gave them a sumptuous banquet – three courses, one after another, with eight dishes to each course. All dishes were served but once, and four at each course were on platters of gold or silver. During the banquet, there were shows and pantomimes by players in rich and costly raiment. They played Our Lady holding her Son, God Our Lord, and Joseph standing beside her and the three holy kings bringing their tribute. They had prepared a shining gold star that went before the kings on a fine iron wire. They played also King Herod sending after the three kings and slaying their children. All the players wore most costly garments and broad gold and silver girdles and played their parts with great diligence and modesty.'[31]

So much for the representatives from the land of John Wyclif. By the time this was performed Hus would be dead. Yet everywhere his influence was to linger. His earlier strictures against lavish and empty funeral rites are amply justified as Richental's sychophantic description of the funeral of a wealthy cardinal shows. Hus had spoken fervently against the danger of dancing and empty pastimes with all the accompanying immorality. Letters from Constance mention the greed of the cardinals, the falsehood in the leadership, the danger for those 'who engaged in many tournaments', the widespread evil of this 'very sinful council'.[32]

'O, had you seen that council,' wrote Hus to his Bohemian friends, 'which calls itself the most holy, and that cannot err, you would surely have seen the greatest abomination! For I have heard it commonly said by the Swabians that Constance or Kostnice, their city, would not for thirty years rid itself of the sins which that council has committed in their city.'[33] In confirmation of Hus's scathing picture we can add to the testimonies we have already supplied that of one historian who has put it like this: 'Wherever the pope has made his abode – until quite recent times – the morality of that city has always enjoyed an evil reputation. Hugh of St Cher, one of the few really learned and virtuous cardinals under Innocent IV, made a memorable farewell speech to the citizens when the papal court was on the point of leaving Lyons: "We found three or four houses of ill-fame when we came thither [seven years ago], and now at our departure we leave the whole city one continuous brothel."'[34] He adds that exactly the same complaint was made about Constance while the council was there. Obviously the rottenness was from the top downwards.

Not surprisingly, Hus for his part had little or no opportunity to sample any of the lavish fare, even had he so desired. His allowance had been far different. But he did have time to meet the equivalent of the King Herod of his day – Sigismund, a man of fair speech and fine promises, but whose word, as Hus was finally to affirm, was worth nothing. It was particularly good, indeed essential for Hus that in these bewildering, even agonizing days, he had the word of another upon which to depend.

# 20.
# Hus is arrested; a pope flees

'Then on the Saturday after the Feast of All Saints, November 3, Master John Hus arrived at Constance and was lodged in the street of St Paul with a good widow named Fida,' reports Peter of Mladoňovice, the faithful follower of Hus.[1] The next day two of the lords, John of Chlum and Henry of Lacembok, went to John XXIII saying that they had brought John Hus to the city under the safe-conduct of King Sigismund. The pope promised that Hus would be unmolested and reassured them that Hus would be safe in Constance, even if he had murdered the pope's own brother.

For a while Hus enjoyed some liberty. The excommunication was suspended so that the city might not be subject to the interdict on his account. Hus conversed with some who came to him and celebrated mass in his own rooms. He was, however, requested not to attend certain services in the churches of the city and about a week after his arrival, as Richental narrates, he was forbidden by the Bishop of Constance to hold these services any more in his own rooms. He was now more or less confined to his lodgings.

One wonders how many exaggerated or totally false stories were circulating about Hus as we recall the deliberate spreading of the rumour that he was a 'mind-reader'. We know how one writer later gave two inconsistent and untrue accounts of Hus trying to escape from the city. In one instance he was supposed to have been found in a wagon and in the other, after being discovered in a wagon, he is supposed to have dashed into the crowd. We have a letter to Prague from one of Hus's close friends which touches on yet another fabrication. The correspondent, convinced that the authorities feared the prospect of Hus's public preaching, refers to their various prohibitions and the common report that Hus was going to preach in a church in Constance the Sunday following and had offered a ducat to every person present. These particular rumour-mongers obviously saw everything in terms of bribes and money!

The day after his arrival Hus wrote to his friends in Bohemia. He was obviously observing events around him. 'The cardinals are numerous; they ride mules, but they are greedy,' he told them, but he was also clearly reassured by the visit of the two lords to the pope and mentions this, adding that the pope said 'that he wished to do nothing by violence'.[2] During this period he would also appear to have prepared two discourses, the first of which is basically a confession of faith. While he clearly professes the supreme authority of Scripture there are still unbiblical features in his belief, but they do not loom large.

However, soon after Hus's arrival the storm clouds began to gather. Stephen Páleč had also arrived and immediately joined forces with Michael de Causis, the restorer of goldmines, who had long been zealously and vindictively seeking Hus's condemnation. In Peter's vivid phrase, these opponents 'scurried around among all the principal cardinals, archbishops, bishops, and other prelates'.[3] They particularly laid stress on the heretical nature of Hus's *The Church,* from which they selected articles. Hus himself was not unaware of all this. A letter written on 6 November, three days after his arrival, alludes to their activity which he sees as incited by the indulgence seller whom he had so firmly opposed in Prague. Hus comments, 'The Pope does not want to quash the proceedings and said: "What can I do? After all, your countrymen are doing it."'[4] When it suited John XXIII he could appear to be a very helpless individual.

By this date Hus was compelled to declare that he would soon be in want of necessities should the council be at all protracted. Knowing the love and generosity of so many friends, he felt able to add, 'Therefore, ask whomever you know of my friends for a contribution, but at first ask conditionally. Greet all the friends, both men and women, and urge them to pray God for me, for I need it.'[5] He was also concerned about his friends who were suffering want, having already spent all their money. Hus felt pity towards them but had no means of helping.

Meanwhile, on 16 November, Sigismund still not having arrived, the sessions of the council were officially opened by the pope. One of the cardinals, who kept a diary and who was later involved in the various cross-examinations of Hus, thus described this event: 'The Pope presided and said Mass and preached a sermon, the text of which was "Love truth".'[6] A more hypocritical beginning could scarcely be conceived.

On 28 November, some three weeks after his arrival, Hus's freedom was brought to an end. His two Czech enemies with a group of higher officials came to his lodgings, saying they had come to summon him on behalf of the cardinals and pope. Despite angry blustering by Lord John of Chlum who mentioned the king's safe-conduct, Hus himself indicated his willingness to accompany them, although stating that he did in fact come to stand before the whole council and not merely before the cardinals. At this point, the widow Fida, with whom Hus had been lodging, said her farewell to him with tears, as she obviously expected the worst. Perhaps in his relationships with women Hus's bark was worse than his bite. Indeed a little later John of Chlum sought to cheer up Hus with such swaps of gossip as 'All your friends, especially Christian of Prachatice, are most attentive to the good widow'.[7] That they could expect Hus to receive such news favourably indicates some change of viewpoint or 'softening' in the reformer.

The next incident is interesting. After exchanging a few remarks with the cardinals Hus had an interview with a Minorite friar, a skilled theologian, who feigned to be a simple soul asking questions. We see here not only the subtlety of the devil's tactics but Hus's theological acumen and also both his aggression and humour. Making a clumsy *faux pas,* this 'simple and unlearned monk' almost immediately went on to inquire 'among other things about the hypostatic union or of the nature of the union of the divine and human in Christ'. Perceiving his deceit, Hus retorted that his questioner was not '*simplex*' (simple) but '*duplex*' (double-faced).[8] Then on discovering that his questioner was reputed to be the 'subtlest theologian' in all Lombardy, Hus exclaimed, 'Oh, if only I had known it, I should have otherwise punctured him through with Scripture!'[9] While we may, sometimes wrongly, take a delight in this kind of approach, it would seem that God had a hard path in store for his servant in order that something of his own self-confident air might be punctured. It must be conceded that there was a somewhat excessively swashbuckling and sabre-rattling aspect to Hus.

Meanwhile at four in the afternoon, as the cardinals gathered to discuss what to do with Hus, his two Czech pursuers were actually prancing about in the dining hall with unconcealed and cruel glee and gloating over his fate. Soon they were clashing with two of Hus's friends, as bitter words were exchanged. One of the friends was indeed Peter, who found himself angrily telling Stephen Páleč, 'That's the way with Master Hus if you give him an ocean or two of the Holy Scriptures; he will not be annoyed by reading them, but will rejoice, for they may very well be in his favour.'[10] It certainly was true that Hus was marvellously at home in Holy Scripture.

As it grew late, Lord John was informed that he could go but Hus must stay. This was too much for the loyal knight, who exploded vehemently in the presence of the pope, reminding him of the safe-conduct and of his own earlier promises. Pointing to the cardinals, the pope here affirmed that they could witness that he never ordered Hus's arrest. Although it is clear that certain cardinals who had earlier been in charge of Hus's case were determined on his arrest, it is damning to note that the papal notary Cerretano clearly writes that the arrest was 'by order of our Lord Pope'.[11] John XXIII was consistent in little other than his lying. Peter himself was conscious from his own information that the pope was lying and indeed says so. However, Lord John had now to leave, and Hus stayed in the papal palace in custody of the armed guards. Later that same night he was taken to another house and guarded there for eight days.

The next move was to the Dominican monastery near the lake. Peter's account of this move and its consequences is sufficiently moving to be included in detail. 'There he was thrust into a murky and dark dungeon in the immediate vicinity of a latrine. There he lay or sat from the said time when he had been incarcerated, that is, from the Feast of St Nicholas the Confessor until Palm Sunday. When he had lain in that prison for several weeks, he fell ill of high fever and constipation of the bowels, so that his life was despaired of. Pope John XXIII sent his own physicians to the prison and they gave him an enema.'[12]

Hus lay in this stinking, foul hole from 6 December 1414 until the early part of January, when he was moved to a slightly better spot in the building, where he was to remain until 24 March 1415. It is revealing that his first word in a letter to Lord John at this period is the simple plea: 'Acquire for me a Bible . . .'[13] However, we must not assume that his friends were in any way indifferent or inactive – far from it. In the days after his arrest Lord John seemed everywhere, brandishing the safe-conduct to all and sundry, putting up posters of fervent protest all over the town, and urging the release of Hus in passionate and heartfelt tones.

At the height of Hus's illness, when he was capable of little effort in any direction, a team of top-ranking Roman theologians, including at least four cardinals, visited him to confront him with his adherence to the doctrines of Wyclif. In his usual manner, Hus pointed out that he had never adhered to all of Wyclif's teachings, and made various qualifications. When he asked for an advocate, the reply was that none could be given to a man suspected of heresy. It would also appear that at this time it was proving very hard to get certain people to witness against Hus. Some wished to be back safely and speedily in their beds at Prague! Nevertheless there were sufficient former acquaintances or colleagues of Hus willing to testify against him to form considerable opposition.

Of course, during this time Lord John could legitimately argue that as Sigismund was still not present at Constance the king himself would be incensed at the breach of safe-conduct. This was really the gist of his forthright and manly appeals of 15 and 24 December. He stressed that 'the detention and arrest of the said Master John Hus were carried out entirely against the will of the above-mentioned my lord, King of the Romans, that were done in contempt of his safe-conduct and of the imperial protection, because the said my lord was at the time far distant from Constance'.[14]

Indeed, it would appear that the king was genuinely

incensed when the news reached him, as he sent messengers to demand that Hus be released from prison. If necessary the doors were to be broken down, he urged. Yet Hus was still in prison when on Christmas Eve Sigismund at last arrived with his queen. There was a nine-hour service to celebrate his arrival after he had been received with due ceremonial.

At about this very time, Hus, with the arrival of Sigismund uppermost in his thoughts, wrote as follows to Lord John: 'I only hear that your lordship is here and is with the lord king. Accordingly, I beseech you to pray his royal majesty – both for my sake and for the cause of the Almighty God, who so magnificently endowed him with his gifts, as well as for the sake of manifesting justice and truth to the honour of God and the welfare of the church – to liberate me from captivity, that I may prepare myself for and come to a public hearing. You should know that I have been very ill and was given an enema, but am already convalescing.'[15]

What would the king do now that he had arrived? By the third of January Hus could write again to his friends in Constance from his Dominican prison, 'I marvel that the lord king has forgotten me and sends me no word.'[16] In fact two days before this the king had given the council permission to deal with Hus as they felt right. Since the council proceeded to deal with him as though it were but a continuation of the excommunication of some years earlier the fate of Hus was indeed sealed. This was just what his legal adviser had wished to avoid.

Yet in prison Hus was by no means twiddling his thumbs and wasting time. Ever the caring evangelist, he was writing 'certain very beautiful little treatises at the request of some of his jailers'.[17] As he had rapidly won the sympathy and affection of the widow Fida, so it would appear he also quickly won round the jailers and their wives. He wrote on the Lord's prayer, the Ten Commandments and marriage, as well as other things. At the end of these writings can be read the names of Robert, James and Gregory – the names of the men for whom they were written.

There were also late-night sessions of writing on more theological themes, as Stephen Páleč had been hounding him with various questions, and Hus worked into the night hours composing a reply, as a letter indicates. In a vivid phrase, Hus described Páleč as 'the ringleader of them all, a veritable pointer dog'.[18] 'During the days of my life I have not found a harsher consoler in illness than Páleč,' he also wrote.[19] Yet in all this Hus was also beginning to look beyond second causes to the direct hand of God. This is shown in a letter which he wrote a couple of weeks later. Writing of the activity of God, Hus says, 'He has mercifully visited me with a grave illness and again healed me. He has permitted my very determined enemies to attack me, men to whom I had done much good and whom I had loved sincerely.'[20] To receive wounds in the house of a friend is one of the deepest of all afflictions. What a contrast to the attitude of Hus when Páleč was in prison! Hus was learning that the rod was nevertheless in the Father's hand.

What Hus said about his illness indicates that he would have been prepared in mind and heart for a letter from his friend and constant supporter, John of Chlum, sent on 4 January. He would be pleased to hear assurance from John that King Sigismund had spoken to the council about Hus and secured for him the promise of a public hearing. Yet in the letter there was an equally important word as John of Chlum lovingly suggested that 'God has visited you by his afflictions solely for your great good.'[21] Hus was a great and courageous man of God. But there were still rough edges to be planed off. In his imprisonment he was to suffer much – privation of company or the presence of hostile oppressive company, as well as many physical ailments and torments.

In one letter Hus can write in verse words which our twentieth century, with its clamour for instant healing, must find very hard to understand:

> He deigns kindly to look upon us
> And to endow us with wondrous gifts:
> A narrow prison, hard bed, plain food,
> Cruel boards, toothache, vomiting and fever.[22]

He saw these afflictions as part of the chastisement deliberately and specifically appointed by God. Nor was he constantly plunged into moroseness and gloom. When his enemies pounded him with the usual questions about Wyclif, he told John of Chlum that he was conscious of smiling as they relentlessly attacked him. The punning against the subtle theologian was not the only incident of this kind. Several times he refers to his need of 'constancy in Constance'. Referring to his book *Against a Hidden Adversary*, he is glad that 'the *Hidden* remains hidden'.[23] (In requesting more than once that certain books should be concealed Hus was not strictly truthful. God had to deal with him on this matter and over the fact that he once falsely denied having certain books.)

At other times he would scribble hexameters with impossible abbreviations in Latin and Czech to while away the time. Therefore one noble friend is entreated:

> Remember me, please,
> Whene'er you eat cheese.[24]

One wonders what he would have made of that. But, of course, he knew Hus well, as is plain from the letter. Early in March Hus had an unexpected encounter, the effect of which he describes simply: 'I blame myself that, seeing Master Christian unexpectedly, I was unable to restrain my tears, which gushed at the sight of my faithful master and particular benefactor.'[25] Christian of Prachatice had always been a particularly loyal friend of Hus.

Meanwhile, Hus was dreaming – it might seem logical to suggest that he had been eating too much cheese late at night, but in view of prison conditions this is hardly likely! He dreamed of the flight of Pope John XXIII before it happened and about the forthcoming imprisonment of his friend Jerome of Prague. He even dreamed of many serpents with many heads even in their tails which were, however, unable to bite him. Despite the fact that he went on to affirm that he did not see himself as a prophet or to exalt himself, he did have one dream which at least two of his very closest friends saw as significant. Here is his account of it: 'Explain to me tonight's dream: I saw that prelates wished to destroy all pictures of Christ in Bethlehem and actually were destroying them. I rose up the next day and saw many painters who were painting many and more beautiful pictures, on which I gazed with joy. The painters with a crowd of people were saying: "Let the bishops and the priests come and destroy these pictures of ours!" When it happened, many people in Bethlehem rejoiced and I with them. And awakening, I felt that I was smiling.'[26]

Hus, together with his two close friends, saw the obvious meaning. He explains it for us in another letter: 'Yet I hope that Christ's life, which I depicted in his own words in Bethlehem into the hearts of men, and which they wished to destroy in Bethlehem – first by the decree forbidding preaching in chapels as well as in Bethlehem, and thereafter that Bethlehem be razed to the ground – that life of Christ many preachers will depict better than I to the joy of the people who love the life of Christ. I also will rejoice at it . . . when "I awake", that is, when I rise from the dead.'[27] The preacher looked to the future. He believed that many more would hear the call and become faithful stewards of the Word. He saw the Word of God prevailing over all the schemes of men. He needed to have such dreams.

Some of Hus's convictions were becoming even more biblical at this time. When John of Chlum asked him for his opinion as to whether both the bread and wine should be taken at the eucharist Hus simply but clearly rejoined that both the gospel and the apostle Paul said that they should, as he had recently expounded in a little treatise. 'I know not what else to add, except that the gospel and St Paul's letter sound definite and that it had been practised in the primitive church,' he wrote.[28] To his friends he strongly deprecated the way the Roman church had overruled the apostle Paul. On this very matter he wrote, right at the close of his life, criticizing Havlik, his successor at the Bethlehem Chapel, who followed the Roman Catholic custom of forbidding the cup to the laity. Hus wrote, 'We ought not to follow custom, but Christ's example and truth.'[29]

Hus asked prayer from his friends that he might prove steadfast in the hour of trial, taking consolation from the promise of Christ that he would be given words and wisdom that none of his adversaries would be able to resist. As part of this deepening understanding we note that in March, in the third month of his confinement, he could write, 'Only now am I learning to understand the Psalter, to pray as I ought, to ponder upon the abuse of Christ and the sufferings of the martyrs. For Isaiah says: "Hardship alone gives understanding."'[30] But soon after this a new theme suddenly enters his letters as he writes, 'The council is in turmoil on account of the pope's flight.'[31] So great was the turmoil that it seemed that Hus might be deprived of even the little food he was allowed.

Pope John XXIII had not wanted to come to Constance. He had uneasily foreseen that a group of men who had deposed two popes at Pisa just a few years before could without any qualm of conscience easily dispose of another. And indeed that was quite evidently the intention of many at the council, including some of his leading cardinals. Sigismund was aware of the pope's temptation to flee. Some of their conversations must have been little more than complicated and elaborate skirmishings, as the king sought to convey gentle threats to the pope, telling him to stay.

Neither the pope nor Sigismund could have been taken in by the deferential and yet hypocritical compliments and assurances of friendship which each bestowed upon the other. Flamboyant and impressive though the ceremony of the pope's bestowal of the golden rose had been, it is unlikely that Sigismund had been unduly influenced by it. Nor would he be likely to be duped when the pope addressed him in fulsome terms as 'so worthy a son, and such an invincible athlete of the Christian faith'.[32] When the king was in hot pursuit of the pope, the latter might then have fervently wished that he was neither so athletic nor so invincible. We learn that on one occasion the king, upon visiting the pope, found him lying down. 'How are you, Holy Father?' inquired Sigismund. 'I am out of sorts,' answered Pope John, 'for the climate of this place does not suit me, and I cannot stand it.'[33] When the king alleged that there were many pleasant spots in the surrounding area and delicately urged that it would be foolhardy to leave such an attractive region, the pope seemed distinctly unconvinced.

Peter announces the flight of Pope John which took place on 20 March 1415 like this: '. . . At three o'clock at night (as it was said) Pope John XXIII fled disguised in lay clothing and secretly escaped from Constance . . .'[34] Richental even professed to know that he wore 'a grey cape with a grey cowl' and was heavily muffled up.[35] But soon other muffled and furtive forms were seen leaving the city as certain cardinals, clerics and servants followed in the wake of their fleeing master. Only three weeks before this Sigismund had thrown himself at the pope's feet and the *Te Deum* had been jubilantly sung as the pontiff offered to abdicate.

This was a crucial moment for the affairs of Hus in relation to Sigismund. As Hus announced to John of Chlum in a letter dated 24 March, 'All my guards are already leaving and I shall have nothing to eat.'[36] Indeed Peter points out that, as the jailers left, the keys of Hus's prison were delivered to Sigismund, who could then easily have released Hus and more faithfully kept to the terms of his safe-conduct, as he ought to have done.

The next stage is again sufficiently important to be included in the simple, faithful narrative of Peter himself: 'The king and the council accepted the keys and on Palm Sunday gave them to the Bishop of Constance, that he might take the master into his power. Indeed, at that time the king could have honourably freed him from the prison and thus could have honoured his own safe-conduct, had he acted justly in this matter.' But he did not do this, as Peter makes clear. 'The bishop ordered his armed guards the same night to conduct Master John to his fortress or castle. And they, taking the master at night, chained him and put him in a boat and went or sailed with him on the Rhine as far as the fortress of Gottlieben of the said Bishop of Constance, which was about a quarter of a mile distant from Constance.'[37] The consolation for Hus in this was that he was in 'an airy tower'. The drawback was that by day he had to walk in chains and at night he was fastened by iron handcuffs to a wall. Hus was cast down. But he was not forsaken.

Endowed with the worldly gifts of leadership and courtesy Sigismund might be. He yet lacked real inward warmth and regard for truth. There is, sad to relate, yet more treachery to record which will amply substantiate this judgement. Indeed, a contemporary who later became pope wrote of him: 'He made more promises than he kept, and often deceived.'[38] With regard to Sigismund, the words of John Milton, written about Belial, a fallen angel, are sadly appropriate:

> He seem'd
> For dignity compos'd and high exploit:
> But all was false and hollow.[39]

# 21.
# Violent and deceitful theologians

In the treatment he was receiving with regard to his safe-conduct, Hus could anticipate in some measure the lack of justice which would be in store for him at his trial, although it is certain that not even he, in spite of these experiences of enmity and betrayal, could fully know what lay ahead. Hardly any, if any, letters came from this new place of imprisonment. But it is possible that just one addressed to a Czech lord was written here. In it he significantly referred to the good and true Lord who never abandons his servant. This he contrasted with 'the unstable favour of men'.[1]

Later Sigismund, who was inundated with troubles over Bohemia because of his treatment of Hus, sought in a letter to vindicate himself from charges of treachery. Here is part of his plea: 'Had Hus accompanied me to Constance, instead of being there in my absence, his affairs would not have taken so ill a turn. God is my witness – and I cannot express myself on this subject with sufficient force – how much the misfortunes of Hus have affected me.'[2]

Not surprisingly his words fell on deaf or totally unsympathetic ears. Peter knew about the key being passed on to Sigismund who could then have acted. He was, after all, a man of action and indeed at this very juncture showed himself equal to the occasion, keeping the council in being when it was in danger of disintegration, and bringing back a shamefaced and humiliated pope after a series of firm manoeuvres and determined chases. Indeed Sigismund's resolution was particularly vital at this juncture.

One man, Peter de Pulka, writing from Constance in the aftermath of the pope's flight, speaks of the dangers on the roads and the state of war as Sigismund's troops massed to attack the lay patron of Pope John. He wrote, 'In truth, the dangers increase, especially here near Constance . . .'[3] Richental, concerned above all for the trade and profits of his beloved city, commented appreciatively on the prompt action of Sigismund to reassure people that the council was not disbanded and the great rejoicing and esteem for the king among the 'money-changers, apothecaries, tradesmen, merchants' and their ilk when they found that business was still as usual.[4]

After his own grovelling submission, John wrote to the king, reminding him how he had always felt great affection for him and how much he had contributed to his elevation to the place of emperor. Although he pleaded for a true return of love, he did not receive it, for as a contemporary writer commented, 'Men then beheld the confirmation of this expression of the Roman historian – that "there is but little security in majesty without power"; and the emperor acted towards the pope as suited the dignity of Caesar.'[5] All this but underlines the fact that Sigismund was very much in control of affairs at this time. He could have acted with the same resolution with regard to Hus as he showed in the case of the pope, but the desire was not there.

We must give full credit to the constant endeavours not only of John of Chlum but of a whole group of Bohemian lords over this next period of Hus's imprisonment. Peter gives in full the various documents which they brought before the council. They mentioned Hus's willingness to come to Constance and, of course, put much stress on the giving of the safe-conduct and the breach of faith by Sigismund. An interesting argument is the contrast which they drew between the dastardly and cruel treatment of Hus and the welcome afforded to the cardinals of the two Popes Gregory XII and Benedict XIII, who had been condemned as heretics by the Council of Pisa. We know from the diary of Cardinal Fillastre that when the cardinals of the former pope arrived there was 'a violent dispute as to whether they should be permitted to enter the city wearing their red hats'.[6] Such were the petty squabbles that constantly went on in the background. In the end the cardinals were permitted to enter with due ceremony. Some in the council argued that such lenity was more in accordance with the genius of Christ's church, which was bound as a mother to seek to reclaim her erring children. In the case of Hus such tactics were never even considered.

Soon we shall be hearing of the clamour which swamped Hus at his trial. It must not be thought that these were the only noisy sessions at the council. After the flight of the pope some cardinals contended that the council was *ipso facto* dissolved. Passionate disputing broke out. 'What they could not effect by reason', commented Dietrich of Niem, 'they attempted by their clamour.'[7] Richental draws our attention to more than one angry interchange between the various nations represented and Cardinal Fillastre's diary refers to violent disputes which broke out periodically.

The violent tone of the council revealed the absence of true Christianity among its leading members. We have already seen the moral decadence and pleasure-mania that gripped so many of the participants. The rows and wrangles are but another aspect of this terrible spiritual hollowness. A barely concealed cynicism was so often the order of the day. For example, Cardinal Fillastre, who kept a diary of proceedings, was present at a French national council some years earlier whan an abbot stood up and insisted that it was the pope's duty to pasture his flock, not to fleece them. Few overheard as the cardinal dryly retorted that 'He did not know what they did with sheep where the abbot came from; in his country, however, they sheared them.'[8] It will be recalled that Hus protested openly to the pastor who sheared the sheep of Prachatice.

In manly and Christ-like contrast to all this, the loyal and persistent Czech lords also drew attention to the fact that Hus was 'still kept so cruelly chained and reduced to so slender a diet that it is to be feared that, his strength being exhausted, he might be in danger of losing his reason'.[9] They went on to allude to the rumours that were being spread about to the effect that in Bohemia cobblers were now hearing confessions and administering communion, which was being carried about in bottles. Such slanders they strenuously denied.

It was during May that the above petitions were presented. Instantly a Bohemian bishop, who had long been an opponent of Hus, rose to affirm that such rumours were indeed well founded, that the country was a hotbed of Wyclifism and that a certain woman had snatched the communion from the hands of a priest and administered it herself. It was evidently the bishop's desire to show that Bohemia was in utter confusion and chaos because of heresy. This was an aspect which would particularly strike home to rulers who feared anarchy above all other things.

Further appeals presented by Peter reminded the council of the shocking treatment of Hus's representatives when he appealed over the excommunication and insisted that he had not been rebellious in face of the excommunication, but had appealed in the proper way. In response to certain charges that Hus had preached at Constance, Peter quoted the word of John of Chlum to the effect that Hus had never once left the house after his arrival. The Bohemian nobles also categorically denied the testimony of the Czech bishop in his allegation of disorders in the kingdom.

Alongside all these documents was reproduced the testimony of Nicholas, the officer responsible for enquiring into heresies, to Hus's orthodoxy. Poor Nicholas himself, who had probably produced these amazing documents under pressure, had appeared at the council, but been terrified upon being cross-examined. Merely because he had discoursed with Hus he was derisively called 'Nicholas-sup-with-the-devil'. It would seem that, having gratified the authorities by denying that Hus came freely to Constance, he was allowed to slip away, which he speedily did.

Among the plethora of documents which the lords kept showering upon an unimpressed council was one in which Hus himself testified to the orthodoxy of his faith, with special stress upon his belief in the Trinity, and his insistence that both in academic disputes and public preaching he wished humbly to submit to the sacred law of Scripture 'being ready to revoke whatever I said if I am taught that it is contrary to the orthodox faith and truth'.[10] The lords urged that Hus never meant to contradict the 'most holy Roman church and the catholic faith', argued that his teaching had been distorted, articles being taken out of his books inaccurately and out of their context, and they pleaded that Hus be given a fair hearing, that he might give his own explanations. Worried lest Hus should not prove equal to the occasion, even if granted a hearing, they also asked that he be freed to recuperate strength and thus acquit himself more ably. They, the lords, would stand as guarantors for him.

It is revealing to note that a council, convened under two masters of deceit and intrigue, and now about to try a man of artless sincerity, replied to this latter request through their spokesman to the effect that 'Even if a thousand such guarantors were offered, it is against the conscience of them, the deputies, to surrender such a man into the hands of the guarantors, for under no circumstances is he to be trusted.'[11] Snubbed by such a reply, the lords would nevertheless have been delighted to hear the spokesman say in the next breath that Hus would be given a public hearing on the following Wednesday, 5 June.

At this time Sigismund had been constantly inundated with requests that Hus be granted a public hearing and had even been confronted with scarcely disguised warnings that the breaking of his promise over the safe-conduct might affect the whole issue of the Bohemian crown to which he was heir. Yet there were other strains far more ominous for Hus himself. Possibly prompted by the subtle theologian who had earlier confronted Hus in prison, the King of Aragon sent Sigismund two letters pleading for the death penalty of a known heretic on the basis of Deuteronomy 13:6–9. These letters were sent in April. It was obvious from this what was the mood of some members of the council.

Yet there is an aspect to all this that demands more detailed comment. What some historians have found surprising is that Hus did not receive far more support than he did at the Council of Constance. One modern writer has put the issue like this: 'What is puzzling at first sight in these affairs is that neither Wyclifism or Hussitism was welcomed in a common cause by the conciliar reformers, but instead they were condemned as harshly in the councils as by the popes.'[12]

For several years there had been a group of men who were called 'conciliar reformers', who were very concerned about the abuse of power by the papacy and who wanted to see the absolute power of the pope curtailed and many abuses corrected, and who believed that this could be done through godly men meeting together in councils – hence the description 'conciliar' reformers. The schism between the rival popes, while it gave weight to these voices calling for reform and true unity, also brought a problem. One of the earliest members of the group, Conrad of Gelnhausen, writing in the very first days of division, put it like this: 'It is impossible for a general council to be held or celebrated without the authority of the pope. But to convene such a council in the present case the pope cannot step in, because no person is universally recognized as pope.'[13] For those who accepted papal supremacy as scriptural and legitimate it was, of course, a seemingly insuperable problem. To be sure we must be careful not to condemn the conciliar movement outright and *en bloc*. There had been many advocates of conciliar reform over a period of some thirty years of the schism and these included men of differing types of spirituality. Nevertheless the representatives at the time of the Council of Constance do stand in striking contrast to John Hus himself and also in clear and determined opposition to him. This was so despite the fact that at certain points they seemed to speak very much as he did. Why was there then not real unity between Hus and these conciliar reformers?

In order to explore this further, we shall take three examples of representative figures of the conciliar movement. The first is someone we have already met – John Gerson, the Chancellor of Paris University, a man of many gifts, whose opinion was universally respected at this time. The second is another Frenchman, Cardinal D'Ailly, the Cardinal of Cambrai, who features prominently in the trial of Hus. Variously called 'the eagle of France' and 'the hammer of the heretics', in 1411 he wrote a treatise on *The Reformation of the Calendar* of which one writer has said that 'Its chief defect was that it was before its age. From reading his work on geography, Columbus first gained the idea of a north-west passage to India.'[14] He was a man of obvious talent. Our third figure is a writer we have often quoted. Dietrich of Niem, secretary to many of the popes, had not the soaring talents and high academic standing of his colleagues. His mind was more run of the mill but none the less thoroughgoing and able. In his way he was a model civil servant, with years of inside knowledge of the workings of the curia.

It must be conceded that certain complaints made by these men could easily be mistaken for the voice of Hus himself. For example, Gerson, thinking of the likely deposition of the pope, wrote just prior to the council, 'If we should withdraw ourselves from every brother who walketh disorderly, how much more from a perverse and unjust superior, by whose example the commonwealth is corrupted and the church disgraced.'[15] D'Ailly himself was hardly less forthright. He asserted, 'That as there is joy in heaven when a sinner repents, so then there is joy in Rome when a prelate dies. His benefices are the carcass around which the eagles exult to gather.'[16] Furthermore Dietrich of Niem was yet another voice confirming many of the strictures of Hus when he wrote, 'In that very *curia* you will find a thousand officials for the procuring of money from benefices, but probably you will not be able to seek out one for the preservation of virtue. There, every day the conversation is of castles, land, cities, different men of arms, and money. Rarely, if ever, is mention made of chastity, almsgiving, justice, faith, or holy living.'[17] Even more than in the case of the two Frenchmen, quotations could be multiplied, for Dietrich had a detailed and intimate knowledge of the careerism, simony, deceit and cruelty of many popes.

D'Ailly had been appointed cardinal by John XXIII only in 1411 but he was by no means subservient, as was shown by the sermon he preached soon after the council opened, on 28 December 1414. His text was from Luke 21:15: 'There will be signs in the sun, moon and stars,' whereupon, wholly disregarding the context, he applied this passage of Scripture to the pope (the sun), the king (the moon) and the council (the stars), reaching the conclusion that the stars were going to become increasingly influential and dominant! The sermon was in fact a clarion call of the conciliar movement. Such had been the constant reasoning of his friend Gerson, who in a famous work had claimed that a council was superior to a pope and could in cases of necessity depose the pope. He and many others boldly argued these positions and their views triumphed temporarily, as we see from the deposition of John XXIII and also from the decree *Sacrosancta* which was issued on 6 April during the imprisonment of Hus.

Although in this case D'Ailly did not follow his colleagues, there were many, including Dietrich of Niem, who did believe in the virtual infallibility of the council.[18] Dietrich did not believe in the infallibility of the pope, who was for him 'a man, born of man, subject to sin, a few days ago a peasant's son; how is he to become impeccable and infallible?'[19] Yet in his work *Ways of Uniting and Reforming the Church* (1410) Dietrich anticipated what the council itself would say when he wrote, 'The pope cannot change the acts of a council; indeed he cannot interpret them or make dispensations contrary to them since they are like the Gospels of Christ . . .'[20] We have now moved from the infallibility of the pope to the infallibility of a council. Out of the frying-pan into the fire would not be an inadequate assessment.

On 23 March 1415, soon after the pope's flight, Gerson delivered a celebrated sermon on this text from John 12:35: 'Walk while ye have the light, lest darkness come upon you.'[21] In the sermon he proclaimed that ecclesiastical union depended on the one and only Head, Jesus Christ, and that it existed through a secondary ruler called the supreme pontiff or the pope. But while the church possesses in Christ a husband so completely inseparable that no divorce can be given, the same cannot be said of the relationship with the pope. There are, he argued, a variety of causes upon which a council may depose a disobedient pope.

Obviously Gerson, like Dietrich, did not believe in the infallibility of a pope. Without the removal of John there could be no reformation in the church – this he clearly saw. The popular voice must be heard. His fellow-countryman D'Ailly agreed with this point. 'Promotion to the papacy did not make a man holy. Peter was not impeccable', he asserted.[22] Such republican sentiments were not uncommon at this time. They had a long pedigree and they found forthright expression in the decree *Sacrosancta.*

This decree of 6 April 1415 boldly affirmed that 'This holy synod, constituting the General Council of Constance . . . lawfully assembled in the Holy Spirit, constituting a general council and representing the catholic church militant, it holds power directly from Christ; and that everyone of whatever estate or dignity he be, even papal, is obliged to obey it in those things which belong to the faith, and to the eradication of the said schism, and to the general reform of the said church of God in head and members.'[23]

Even Pope John XXIII was in the end compelled to acknowledge the inerrancy of the council, for when he was eventually brought back crestfallen, browbeaten and thoroughly humiliated, he determined to ingratiate himself with his captors by stating that 'He repented with all his soul of having so shamefully quitted Constance: he would rather have been struck dead than have caused the scandal of that act: he had no intention to oppose the resolutions of the council, which he recognized as just and *infallible*: his sentence might be sent to him, and he would receive it with all submission and bareheaded . . .'[24]

However John Hus, for one, in no wise consented to the above position. With scathing fervour Hus in one of his letters refers to the about-turn in the approach of the members of the council: 'It nonetheless did err: first, by adoring John XXIII on bended knees, kissing his feet, and calling him the most holy, although they knew that he was a base murderer, a sodomite, a simoniac, and a heretic, as they declared it later in the condemnation of him.'[25] Hus forthrightly criticized the notion of the infallibility of councils. It was this council which condemned him to burn! Hus specifically says that the council did err. With regard to his own condemnation, he tells 'all faithful Czechs' not to be terrified by their decrees. 'They will fly away like butterflies and their decrees will turn into a spiderweb.'[26]

In another of his last letters Hus summed up how far apart he stood from many who had condemned John when he wrote, 'These men have condemned and anathematized the seller, while they themselves remained buyers and middlemen and continue to sell at home.'[27] He was inferring that many had outwardly consented as they spoke or voted, but at heart they were still greedy and untruthful like the man they had condemned. And this is the sad conclusion we must reluctantly draw. It is no surprise that Gerson, D'Ailly and Dietrich of Niem were so fervently opposed to Hus.

His firmness and independence of thought was bound to annoy those who felt that the success and significance of all they had done depended on the ready acceptance of the supreme authority of the council. Having dealt so summarily and decisively with the majestic person of a pope, it was hardly likely that proud, self-sufficient men of authority and position would let a nonentity like Hus stand in their way.

We have already noted Gerson's vehement opposition to Hus in letters that he wrote. When Gerson arrived in February 1415, armed with arguments against Hus, the latter wrote from prison, 'Oh, that God would grant me time to write against the lies of the Paris chancellor, who so daringly and unjustly, before such a large multitude, was not ashamed to accuse a neighbour of errors!'[28] Hus expected God to reply to Gerson on the Day of Judgement if he did not have the opportunity to do so on earth. He saw the gulf there was between them in matters of doctrine.

Gerson, like so many others, had never read the works of Hus properly and then had twisted the little he had read out of all recognition. Although some have interpreted his relative silence in the later stages of the trial of Hus as indicating a change of heart, and although there is evidence that he thought that Hus could possibly have been freed, if he had been more adequately defended, yet during the trial of Jerome Gerson was the man who insisted that heretics who recanted were not to be trusted and were therefore to be kept in prison. He was also the man who had written, prior to the council, that in an emergency it might be right to deprive the pope of 'even his life'.[29] Gerson finished up a disappointed man, feeling in the end that all the attempts of reform within the council had been thwarted.

Cardinal D'Ailly featured constantly in the final trial of Hus and always as a bitter opponent. He distorted the views of Hus, was cruel in his methods and took mean and unfair advantages. It has been said that, for all the fervour of his thought, he was a rich man and would naturally hate Hus's condemnation of simony. Furthermore, while wrongfully condemning Hus's orthodoxy with regard to the sacrament, D'Ailly himself concealed the fact that he held far from orthodox views on this matter. With regard to the death of Hus, D'Ailly, far from showing compunction, displayed zeal and gloating cruelty. D'Ailly gradually drifted, even during the council itself, from being a reformer to an official reactionary.

In equally startling contrast to the stance of Hus was the whole tone of Dietrich. When the church was in danger, as it was with three popes all claiming allegiance, then in his view it was freed from the observation of moral law. This is how Dietrich put it: 'The end of unity sanctifies all means: craft, deception, violence, bribery, imprisonment and death. For all law is for the sake of the whole body, and the individual must give way to the general good.'[30] Not surprisingly, Dietrich, who probably had not even read Hus's work, wanted him imprisoned, degraded and handed over to the secular arm without any time-wasting. He claimed that Hus's work on *The Church* was as harmful as Mohammed's writings had been. It was he who referred to Hus as a 'squat yokel'.

Enough has been said about Hus for us to know that he could never have written in the way that Dietrich and others wrote. He did not believe that men should be killed for wrong views. Above all he was passionately concerned with truth at every turn. His philosophy was never 'Let the truth of God abound through my lie'. Because he was so decided a Christian, whose conscience was formed by reverence for Holy Scripture, he sought fervently to be truthful in every way. Apart from the vital fact of their inability to recognize a Christian kinsman in Hus, the great cleavage to which we must draw attention is indeed Hus's great fervour for, and submission to Scripture and his opponents' empty lip-service to it, which veiled a basic indifference. For example, a very clever piece of writing came from the pen of D'Ailly as early as 1381. In this letter from the devil he assumed the same role as did C. S. Lewis in the *Screwtape Letters* and, writing as Satan himself, ridiculed the attempts to heal the schism. But although he infers that the laws of Justinian and the codes of Gratian are to be preferred (from the devil's angle) to those of Scripture, yet the authority of Scripture is not affirmed. The deadly enemy of Satan is seen to be not the Word of God but the general council –

this speaks volumes about the views of the author. Not surprisingly, during the trial of Hus, D'Ailly rarely showed spiritual understanding of the Scriptures cited by the man on trial.

Likewise in the case of Gerson, when he wrote in 1409 a tractate on the *Unity of the Church*, the appeals to Scripture are superficial and the main arguments are taken from circumstances and from common sense. One of his most powerful quotations is in fact from Cicero. Most telling of all is the fact that Gerson did not even believe that men should have the Bible in the vernacular.[31] The same could be said of the tract of Dietrich of Niem on a similar theme to that of Gerson. The appeals to Scripture are again peripheral and quite unlike the way in which Hus himself wrote, seeking to establish every point from the Word of God itself.

To give but one example, both D'Ailly and Dietrich used Matthew 18:15–20 as applicable to the calling of a general council, and its right to deal with rebellious popes.[32] Yet neither of them really investigates the passage in any depth. By contrast, in *The Church* Hus discussed this same passage in considerable detail and pointed out, with telling reference to his own unfair treatment, that far from describing some vast nebulous body, able to pronounce on all matters, the passage should compel local investigation of an alleged fault among witnesses who know the parties concerned.[33] This, of course, was not done in his case.

Furthermore, even on the purely human, pragmatic level it must be pointed out that the work of the conciliar reformers was doomed to failure. There were two insuperable obstacles in the way of such reform. One was that the only thing the popes of this period could be trusted to do was to break their word! This made it impossible to deal with them in any long-term way. The second obstacle in the way of implementation of decrees was that a pope could easily outwit a body of men who met only every six or seven years. Before the council itself had ended the famous decree *Sacrosancta* had indeed become a dead letter as, once more, one man, the new pope, was able to outwit a body of men who by this time were all ready to pack their bags and go home. This, after all, had been a long period of lodging-house fare for the ecumenical globe-trotters of the day.

# 22. A mockery of a trial

'Here follow the So-called Hearings, but in Truth not Hearings but Jeerings and Vilifications' is the title which Peter gives to the section of his work which deals with the actual public trial of Hus. It was a very apt title indeed. There was in fact very nearly no public hearing at all. It would seem that the spiritual lords were going to deny Hus even this until Sigismund intervened. There are sentences in Peter's account which may not be matchless prose but which do indicate matchless love, and the following is one such example, even though at first sight it may read more like a cryptic puzzle: 'They then attempted to condemn all those articles before he, Master John, was heard. When U., who stood near the reader, perceived this, he ran out and told it to P., and P. ran to the lords W. and J., in order that they might report it to the king.'[1] A servant Ulrich ran to inform Peter, who in turn told the two lords, Wenceslas and John, who were so close to Hus. This in fact is how Sigismund learned of the council's plans and was able to intervene.

At the opening of the first hearing on 5 June verses from Psalm 50 were read. These included sentences such as 'To the sinner then God said: why do you expound my justice, and why do you take my covenant into your mouth? You indeed hate discipline and have cast my words behind you. If you saw a thief, you ran with him; and with adulterers you took your portion. Your mouth abounded in malice, and your tongue concocted deceit.'[2] Words less appropriate for the man on trial and yet more fitting for his judges could scarcely have been devised.

Then, in an increasingly familiar but nevertheless sad pattern of distortion, they went on to read what purported to be a letter which Hus had left behind when he rode from Bohemia to Constance. 'If I should happen to abjure, you should know that even though I confess with my mouth and abjure, I do not agree with these things in my heart' was the fabrication foisted on the council. Peter's heartfelt and loyal ejaculation at this point was the only appropriate response. He simply wrote, 'What a lie, Almighty God!'[3] In his narrative Peter then included a copy of this letter which showed that nothing of the kind was said or even implied.

The next problem for the friends of Hus was the fact that so many articles had been 'falsely abstracted' from his books. Their response to this was to offer three of their own copies of his major treaties, including the volume on *The Church*, to the council for their inspection, taking care at the same time to ask that the books be returned. Hus himself took the books and owned that they were his own.

On many occasions throughout the trial Hus was bombarded with noise, hoots of derision and outbursts of sarcastic laughter. And all this despite the decree which the pope had announced at the very outset of the council, when, after an allusion to James 1:26, it was commanded that 'Whatever is discussed in the sessions of members or proposed by a party bringing an accusation shall be expressed in the mildest words, that the minds of the hearers be not confused with contentious voices or the vigour of their judgement shaken by tumult'![4]

As far as Hus was concerned, this was a rule more honoured in the breach than the observance. Peter brings incident after incident of the three days' trial vividly before our eyes. Sometimes it is the familiar figure of Cardinal D'Ailly interrupting, taunting or seeking to crush the reformer. Sometimes it is a more fleeting glimpse – of a monk 'dressed in a black cape over which was draped something shiny black' vehemently warning them against the deceiver; of a 'fat priest, sitting in the window, clad in an expensive tunic' yelling for Hus's condemnation; of a 'certain old and bald bishop from Poland' tersely exclaiming that the treatment for heretics was plainly laid down.[5]

Occasionally the Emperor Sigismund himself steps to the

forefront of the picture to express his own disapproval of Bohemia's disobedient son. But more often than anything it was the clamour of many strident, indistinguishable voices, for Hus was shouted down times without number. On the first day, as Hus tried to explain about his books, 'immediately they shouted: "Leave off your sophistry and say 'Yes' or 'No'." And others mocked him.'[6] While he went on struggling to explain, they continued to shout him down. When he grew silent, because he simply could not make himself heard, some then construed this as tacit admission of guilt. Either way he was guilty.

Hus never lost his initial surprise at being treated in such a way by a supposedly Christian assembly. In his last letter to 'The Entire Christian World' he declared, 'What clamour then, what mocking, jeering, and reviling arose against me in that assembly is known to Lords Wenceslas of Duba and John of Chlum and his notary Peter, the most steadfast knights and lovers of God's truth. Hence even I, being often overwhelmed by such clamour, spoke these words: "I had supposed that in this council would be greater reverence, piety, and discipline."'[7]

At this first hearing little emerged, except that Hus, confronted by copies of his writings, again said he would humbly amend what was wrong if he were properly instructed. After all the din and shouting, Peter narrates that Hus left, 'blessing the people, smiling and merry, joyfully walking despite that mockery'.[8] Nevertheless he could not have been unaffected, for on the day of the second hearing, 7 June, he wrote to friends, saying, 'I am suffering with toothache and at the castle I suffered with vomiting of blood, headache, and the stone.'[9]

In his recollections of that first ordeal Hus observed that he heard Michael de Causis calling out for the burning of his writing. Apart from one or two individuals, he seemed to have no friends among the council. However he had little time to reflect on his experience, for on Friday 7 June, after an almost total eclipse of the sun, he was once more brought before the council, under an escort of guards armed with swords, crossbows, axes and spears.

Despite his repeated and unvarying assertions to the contrary, he was once more told that he believed in remanence, or the view that the substance of the material bread remained unchanged after the consecration. Cardinal D'Ailly, who belonged to a different theological school, simply assumed that Hus could not believe as he did. Others brought forth rumour and innuendo, charging Hus with views which were certainly held by some of his fellow reformers, but not by himself. One cardinal intervened to state that if so many people, about twenty in all, witnessed against him then he must be wrong. Another, D'Ailly, sank to the level of telling Hus that Stephen Páleč had been more kind than he might have expected in abstracting articles from his books, and then appeared terribly shocked that Hus should have the effrontery to oppose Gerson, 'than whom surely no more renowned doctor could be found in all Christendom'.[10]

Soon after this the council was involved in the inevitable tangle of the relationship of Hus and Wyclif, as the accusation was made that Hus had defiantly defended the forty-five articles of Wyclif which had been condemned. Once more Hus, while making it clear that he did not follow Wyclif at every point, nevertheless affirmed that he could not in conscience say that all these articles were heretical. The members of the Council of Constance repeatedly linked Wyclif and Hus together. Invectives flew about during the sessions. The 'Missal of the Wyclifists', as it was called, left no doubt as to what many thought of this association of names. It ran: 'I believe in Wyclif, the lord of hell and patron of Bohemia, and in Hus, our only begotten son, our nothing, who was conceived by the spirit of Lucifer, born of his mother and made incarnate and equal to Wyclif . . . ruling at the time of the desolation of the University of Prague, at the time when Bohemia apostatized from the faith, who for us heretics descended into hell and will not rise from the dead or have life eternal.'[11] It may not be the very cleverest of parodies, but it does at least show the hatred which was felt towards Wyclif and Hus.

Furthermore Hus was alleged to have said, 'If the pope or priest is in mortal sin, then he neither transubstantiates, nor consecrates, nor baptizes.' He denied this and stated that although such men did celebrate unworthily themselves it was still a proper sacrament from which the recipient could draw spiritual benefit. Hus also managed on this rare occasion to demonstrate to the council that this was what he had actually said in his book.

In a series of exchanges on almsgiving and tithes and yet more references to Wyclif and the burning of his books in Prague, Cardinal D'Ailly and Stephen Páleč were particularly prominent, the latter frequently being on his feet to recall utterances of Hus made during his ministry in Bohemia. After referring to his appeals and responses to the various excommunications, and admitting that he had not received any absolution from Pope John, Hus was then asked whether it was lawful for him to appeal to Christ as he did. 'He replied: "I here publicly assert that there is no more just or effective appeal than to Christ." They laughed a great deal at that saying,' reports Peter.[12] There are few incidents more typical of the tone and outlook of the council than this one. It is no surprise that we find a moment later that Hus was accused of demanding that his adversaries be cut down with the sword after the example of Moses. Hus sought to enlighten them as to the difference between the sword of the Spirit, which he had meant, and the physical sword. It seemed a hopeless task. He faced widespread spiritual obtuseness.

The departure of the Germans from Prague, the conflicts within the nation and even the fact that Stephen Páleč had himself been sent into exile were all falsely attributed to Hus's instigation. When other outbreaks of violence were mentioned, Hus correctly pointed out that much of this had arisen because of conflict between the king and the Archbishop Zbyněk during the time when, after the Council of Pisa, they supported different popes. Where there had been seizure of property it had not been by Hus's command.

The hatred of Cardinal D'Ailly for Hus was constantly in evidence during this session. In the midst of the exchanges just mentioned Peter tells us, 'The Cardinal of Cambrai said: "Master John, you have recently in the tower spoken more patiently than you do now. And you should know that this is not in your favour." He replied: "Reverend father! Because then they spoke fairly with me; but here almost all shout at me. I believe, therefore, that they all are my enemies."'[13] It may seem incredible, but Peter then records D'Ailly's denial of the shouting, at which Hus reminded him of the decree issued at the beginning of the council that all speech should be mild and fair.

D'Ailly was soon speaking again and explaining that on a journey from Rome he had happened to meet people and to hear that in Bohemia clerics were being ill-treated and robbed of their property. Where such vital issues were at stake, so much was on the level of innuendo and hearsay.

Then, in an astute manoeuvre to discredit Hus with Sigismund, who liked to feel that he was all-powerful, D'Ailly reminded Hus of his claim that he came to the council freely and of his bold assertion that, if he wished otherwise, many a lord in Bohemia would have protected him and prevented anyone from taking him captive. Hus rose to the bait. He admitted that he had made these claims and added that he could have hidden in castles so that neither Wenceslas nor Sigismund could have compelled him to come. We are told that the cardinal then pulled a face as though indignant at Hus's effrontery. But not only Hus fell into this trap. 'And lord John said to those standing around, murmuring at it: "Indeed, he speaks the truth and it is true. I am but a poor knight in our kingdom, but I would have protected him for a year, whether it would have pleased or displeased anyone, so that he could not be seized. And there are many and great lords who love him, who possess the strongest castles, who would have protected him as long as they wished, even against both these kings."'[14]

The incident says much for the loyalty and love felt for Hus, but it must no doubt have grated on the ears of Sigismund. For example, when the king had triumphed over the particular noble who had aided Pope John in his escape, he did not miss the opportunity of displaying his power. After the reading out of an abject submission, Richental says, 'Our lord king turned back to the envoys of Milan and of the Genoese, the Florentines and the Venetians and looked at them as if to say: "See how mighty a prince I am over all lords and cities."'[15] Therefore, although Sigismund did admit that Hus had come freely, the remarks made by Hus and Lord John would not have pleased him.

It was almost time for Hus to be led back to prison, but before he left Cardinal D'Ailly urged him to submit to the correction and instruction of the council, and Sigismund in a long speech admitted the giving of his safe-conduct, which he now construed as merely guaranteeing a public hearing so that Hus might answer for his faith. This, according to Sigismund, had been done as promised. He added that the council should be thanked for this, although he added that some had said that he could not grant a safe-conduct to one suspected of heresy.

Urging Hus not to be obstinate and counselling him to throw himself on the mercy of the council, Sigismund went on, 'But if you wish to hold all that obstinately, then indeed they know well what they must do with you. I told them that I am not willing to defend any heretic; indeed, if one should remain obstinate in his heresy, I myself would kindle the fire and burn him.'[16] He then renewed his plea that Hus should cast himself on the mercy of the council, and with that Hus was led away in his chains.

This time there was no interval, not even of one day, for Hus as the final day of the trial was on the morrow, 8 June. It began ominously with excerpts being read from books (which, as Peter correctly insisted, were often read out in a distorted form) and Cardinal D'Ailly, fresh from his exertions of the previous day, crying out to Sigismund and others how dangerous these sentiments were. From this point onwards we must summarize as it becomes very complex, though Peter supplies most of the details. Some twenty-six articles were drawn from Hus's treatise *The Church*, some seven articles from a work written against the views of Stephen Páleč and a further six articles from another controversial work. These were debated at length, with Hus intervening at many points. We shall just concentrate on the central issues in the debate.

Although it must be said that Hus was in part condemned for views which he did not hold, such as the doctrine of remanence, and although it must be conceded that he was repeatedly quoted in an inaccurate way, yet the council rightly recognized the kernel of his doctrines as truly evangelical and their detestation of this is blatantly obvious. Thus among the articles condemned the first four were strong avowals of the doctrine of predestination, which Hus supported by quotations from Scripture and Augustine. The fact that Hus admitted that in the visible church there are mere professors as well as true saints was virtually ignored. While Hus's adherence to the doctrine of the final perseverance of the saints clearly emerged, it would seem that he did not accept a very strong view of personal assurance.

His articles and ensuing discussion made it clear that in his view false teachers should be exposed, despite Cardinal D'Ailly's pleas for moderation. This interchange is worth giving. The cardinal said to him, 'You do not observe moderation in your preaching and writing.' He was referring to the frequency of Hus's attacks on the false clergy. To do this was 'to scandalize the layman', the cardinal added. So Hus was faced with the familiar accusation that it is wrong to hang out one's dirty washing in public. In the view of the cardinal such attacks tended to 'destroy the status of the church'. Hus's reply was a classic and can indeed still be applied to many situations today. He answered, 'Reverend father, I have dealt with such matters because my sermons were attended by priests and other learned men, in order that both the present and future priests would know beforehand what to guard against.'[17] In this Hus was both biblical and right.

Other articles affirmed that Christ, and not Peter, is the rock on which the church is built, that there should be no death penalty for heresy (or did Hus waver at this point?) that there should be no abandonment of preaching in the face of an unjust excommunication, that most aspects of the interdict were unscriptural, and that Wyclif should not be condemned categorically and completely without proper scriptural refutation.

The articles were read laboriously. There do not seem to have been comments at every point. We just highlight some of the significant and dramatic moments. When Hus argued that the heretic should be corrected patiently from the Scriptures, passages were read from one of his books where he blamed the ecclesiastics, namely the Pharisees and scribes, for causing Jesus Christ to be handed over to the secular arm to be killed. 'Thereupon instantly with a great tumult and noise they shouted at the master,' narrates Peter.[18] Clearly the appeal of Hus directly to Christ rankled deeply with many. Their ready and vociferous spokesman

D'Ailly inferred that by doing this Hus wished to be above St Paul who, when wronged in Jerusalem, appealed not to Christ but to Caesar. Hus was convinced that Paul had done this by divine revelation, having already been instructed by Christ that he must go to Rome. An interesting discussion of the way in which the man justified by faith is wholly transformed, in which D'Ailly significantly showed himself unable to understand Hus, was again broken off by shouting.

Upon his being challenged about the view that he must preach, regardless of an unjust excommunication, without fear of eternal damnation, an interesting interchange took place: 'And they objected (as was said) that such an excommunication was a blessing. The master responded: "That is true; yet I say that an excommunication unjustly suffered by a man is for him a blessing before God, according to the prophet: 'I will curse your blessings and will bless your cursings.'"'[19] Presumably Hus was here testifying to the way in which God had upheld and even blessed him despite the unjust actions of men.

There was a tense moment when they were discussing an article drawn from the treatise against Stephen Páleč, which read in their version: 'If a pope, bishop, or prelate is in mortal sin, then he is not pope, bishop, or prelate.' This again involved the point made by Hus that, although the sacrament might validly be received from such men and in that sense God uses them, yet they are no true ministers. However, Peter describes the dramatic sequel: 'When that article was concluded, the master said: "Indeed, he who is in mortal sin is not a worthy king before God, as appears from IV Kings 16, where the Lord said through the prophet Samuel to Saul, who should have killed Amalek but did not: 'For this, that you have rejected my word and did not kill Amalek, I will also reject you from being king.'"'[20] (The reference should be to 1 Samuel 15:26.)

At once there were excited cries that Sigismund, who was leaning out of the window of the refectory talking to friends, should be summoned. As he came one ecclesiastic was loudly muttering that there had never been a worse heretic than John Hus. Hus was then compelled to repeat his remarks to the king, who said, 'John Hus, no one lives without sin.'[21] Eager to blacken Hus, Cardinal D'Ailly then said, 'It was not enough for you to despise the spiritual order by attempting to overthrow it by your writings and teachings, and now you also wish to overthrow the status of the royal order and of kings?'[22]

Páleč too sought to underline Hus's error and after commenting on the incident of King Saul pointed out that 'pope', 'bishop' and 'king' were names of offices and that someone might be a true pope, bishop or king although not a true Christian. With quiet drama Peter writes, 'And Master John, after a pause, said: "Indeed, this is clear in regard to the already deposed Pope John XXIII, who is now called Balthassarre Coxa or Cossa: if he had been true pope, why was he deposed?"'[23]

At once Sigismund, failing to perceive the import of the remark and Hus's implied challenge to the council's theology, declared that John had been a true pope but because of his notorious crimes the council had deemed it fit to depose him. But, as Spinka points out, if Páleč had been right and a man had the right to office regardless of his life then the council had no right to depose John XXIII. Later Hus again returned to this point and asked the council point blank whether they deemed John a true pope. 'And they, looking at one another, derided him, saying: "Indeed, he was a true pope."'[24] It would seem that the council found it impossible to address Hus without derision or mockery. In this case, however, their derision masked their obvious irritation at his exposure of their inconsistency.

After discussion of yet another article, again closely bearing on the issue of justification by faith, in which Hus championed the evangelical view, Peter continues, 'When this article was finished, Master John said: "Indeed, I do not know the ground for calling the pope the most holy, since it should suffice him that he both be called and be holy. For it is read concerning Christ: 'You alone are holy, you alone are Lord,' etc. And him I call truly the most holy . . ."'[25] This was indeed the nub of the whole controversy. It was for his adherence to Christ as only Saviour and supreme Lord that Hus suffered.

Indeed, much of the discussion in the closing stage of the trial centred on Christ as the true and only Head of the church. Shortly before the debate was concluded Hus affirmed, 'I say that the church at the time of the apostles was infinitely better ruled than it is now ruled. What deters Christ from not regulating it better without such monstrous heads as there have been now, through his true disciples? And see! now we have no such head and yet Christ does not desist from regulating his church.'[26]

How vehemently they again derided him! They knew that this was indeed a different gospel from that of Rome. It was time for D'Ailly to beseech him to throw himself on the mercy of the council and defer to the views of the 'great and enlightened men' present.[27] Spelling this out in detail, he said that Hus should, firstly humbly acknowledge his error, secondly, recant these errors and promise never to teach them again, thirdly, publicly revoke them and, fourthly, preach and expound the opposite.

Amid shouts and cat-calls Hus again argued that he could not 'abjure' opinions which he had never held. Sigismund sought to persuade him to abjure, whether he had held such views or not, but Hus retorted that the king was not using the word in its correct sense. As Hus continued to plead for further hearing and more opportunity to explain, Sigismund voiced the prevalent view that already sufficient testimony had been brought against him.

Still the session dragged itself along, more references being made to events in Bohemia, including the beheading of the three men, with other opponents attributing comments made by Hus's friends to Hus himself. Peter aptly captures the suffering, as Hus was further bombarded with questions: 'And from so great a harassment he already grew very pale, for – as those said who knew about it – he had spent the whole night without sleep because of toothache and headache, and began to be shaken with fever.'[28] Yet again Wyclif's name was introduced. It was said that Hus had publicly read in a sermon a letter brought from England commending Wyclif. It was recalled that one Bohemian had even brought a stone from the grave of Wyclif himself which the Praguers venerated as a relic, and that Hus himself was aware of all this.

After a lull, when there had actually been silence for a while, and no doubt consciences were stirring uneasily,

Páleč rose to say that in no way had he acted with malice, and Michael de Causis followed suit. As though playing the part of chorus, Cardinal D'Ailly then commended them for treating Hus so kindly. The only comment of Hus was 'I stand before God's judgement, who will judge justly both me and you according to merit.'[29] As he was led out Lord John of Chlum, faithful to the last, reached out his hand to console him.

The drama of the day was still not quite over. Unknown to Sigismund, the two Czech lords and Peter were still in the building. Turning to some leaders, Sigismund expressed the view that Hus should be condemned, continuing, 'Therefore, if he will not recant his errors and abjure and teach the contrary, let him be burned, or deal with him according to your knowledge of your laws. And be sure, that whatever he would promise, whether he intends to recant or whether he actually recants here, you do not believe him; nor would I believe him.'[30]

Sigismund expressed then his conviction that Hus should in no wise be allowed to go back and confirm people in error and that there should be a determined effort to extirpate the errors from the lands of Bohemia and Poland where they had taken such strong root. 'The king said again: "Indeed I was still young when this sect had its origin and inception in Bohemia, and see how much it has grown and multiplied!" Then they left the refectory, parting from one another and rejoicing.'[31] At this juncture the loyal friends of Hus could see little reason for sharing in the mood of the king and his companions as they sadly left the building. The fate of Hus was evidently a foregone conclusion. But was it not also divinely foreordained?

# 23.
# On fire for God

Satan launched many a dart at this faithful warrior of Christ. So far Hus had triumphantly come through testing from individuals, committees and a vast council. There had been the unedifying and evil spectacle of outright bullying and lying. His imprisonment had been harsh. Another account, which claims to be contemporary, narrates how during one stage of his imprisonment 'he was put in a prison-chamber which was so narrow that he could hardly stretch himself, and which had but a small window, so that he could obtain a small quantity of water or wine, for in those countries there is no beer'.[1] Hus was to spend a further month in prison before the final dénouement took place, for the council had still not ended its endeavours to win him over. The next attempt was through an unnamed prelate of the council whom Hus called 'Father'. There was a satanic subtlety in this approach and we cannot agree with those who would describe this attempt as 'kindly'. The prelate had sent to Hus a formula of recantation in which he might affirm that, although some things were ascribed to him which he never thought, yet he did in fact recant and abjure all that was there set down. Hus replied as follows, 'I am most grateful for your kind and fatherly grace. Nevertheless, I dare not submit to the council in accordance with the proposed terms, because I should thus either have to condemn many truths they call scandalous, as I have heard from themselves; or I should fall into perjury, if I recanted and confessed that I had held the errors. I should thereby scandalize a great many of God's people who have heard me preach the contrary.'[2]

The 'father' then wrote to Hus, urging that he should not rely upon his own wisdom but rather should trust in the 'many knowledgeable and conscientious men at the council'; that he should realize that such perjury would not be counted as sin in him but in those who exacted it and that he should follow the example of Paul who was lowered in a basket down a wall to procure a better end. Here we have a prime example of Roman Catholic reasoning from the Scriptures! Unpersuaded by these specious arguments, Hus again replied, concluding his letter in this way: 'How could I, who have for so many years preached about patience and constancy, fall into many lies and perjury and give offence to many sons of God? Be it far, far from me! For Christ the Lord will abundantly reward me, granting me at present the aid of patience.'[3]

Hus was to need that divine aid of patience during those last few weeks. There are aspects that cannot be told. Two references in his letters hint at what he endured. Just two and a half weeks after the trial he wrote to the two faithful Czech lords saying, 'I cannot describe what I have passed through this night.'[4] And the very last phrase of the very last letter addressed to 'The Entire Christian World' reads, 'And immediately the council rose up. God knows what great temptings I suffered afterward!'[5] In a somewhat fuller reference, written one day after the former brief allusion, Hus said that God had granted him a 'long-drawn-out and great testing' so that he might recollect his sins better and truly repent of them and might also meditate more profoundly on the sufferings of Christ and thereby himself 'suffer more gladly'.[6] It would seem that Hus entered even more deeply into what the Greek liturgy calls Christ's 'unknown agonies' during this last month. We can say no more than this.

Hus still had things to learn. The desire to puncture the theologian through with Scripture during those first days at Constance illustrates the element of spiritual buccaneering and sabre-rattling that was still within him. God had to mellow him even in these last days. He would seem to have done this particularly in his relationship with Stephen Páleč. It hardly needs underlining that Hus felt the poignancy of Páleč's betrayal and frequently spoke about it. Just after the trial had concluded he wrote this to his friends in Constance: 'Páleč visited me in my gravest illness in the prison. He thus greeted me before the commissioners: "Since the birth of Christ, except Wyclif, no more dangerous heretic has arisen than you!"'[7] John Hus answered, 'May God not account this to thee as a sin, for thou hast preached the gospel from the same pulpit as I, and thou hast preached the true faith.'[8] This was what weighed most heavily on Hus – the fact that Páleč had deserted the faith he had once so clearly professed. Páleč then further charged Hus with infecting many with heresy, upon which Hus asked what the reaction of people in Bohemia would be if he [Hus] were burned, obviously implying that Páleč would never dare to show his face there again. Thus Hus added, significantly, 'This, perhaps, I should not have written, so that it would not appear that I hate him sorely.'[9]

Had Hus realized that he had mentioned these acts of treachery too frequently, dwelt on them too bitterly and refused to commit them sufficiently to God alone? Surely through all these events God was dealing with Hus and mellowing within him a true spirit of forgiveness. In this connection we know that a short while before the end Páleč visited Hus, urging him to recant. In this interview, which was at Hus's request, for he had asked for Páleč as his confessor ( a role which Páleč did not in fact fulfil) the latter wept and they had a moving conversation. In particular Hus asked Páleč to forgive him if he had spoken 'any reproachful word, and especially that I had called him a deceiver [*fictor*] in writing'.[10] The differences remained. Many points of disagreement were actually mentioned in this interview. No true or final reconciliation seems to have taken place. But at least Hus asked forgiveness, not for his theological convictions but for any belligerence or unkindness of tone.

Another aspect of this growth in ability to forgive is the way in which Hus wrote of King Wenceslas, just before his death. As we have seen earlier, although Wenceslas had given Hus a real measure of support, largely for nationalistic and political reasons, in the end he more or less abandoned him. Yet from prison Hus wrote, 'I thank all the lords, knights, and squires of the kingdom of Bohemia, and particularly King Wenceslas and the queen, my gracious lady, that they have dealt affectionately with me, have treated me kindly, and have striven diligently for my liberation.'[11] More realistic and more in tune with the spiritual reality of the situation are the two letters (one written on the last day of his life) where he mentions the queen alone. 'Give my thanks in my behalf to the queen, my gracious mistress, for all the good she has done me,' was a fully deserved tribute.[12] In a letter a week earlier Hus had urged that she be given especial greeting and urged 'that she be constant in the truth'.[13]

We must also consider the possibility that there was initially in Hus a somewhat overconfident spirit, even a wrong desire to seek martyrdom. This is rarely, if ever, mentioned in books about Hus but we feel that we should draw attention to it. It comes out in his rather foolish request, when locked in debate with hostile theologians, that both sides should undergo some kind of ordeal by fire. It comes out in the frequency with which he mentions his own death. For example, out of the many illustrations we could draw on, we take this one from a letter to Christian of Prachatice, to whom Hus wrote, 'I hope, however, with God's grace, if needs be to oppose them until I am consumed by fire. If I cannot liberate the truth in all, at least I will not be an enemy of the truth and by my death refuse consent.' He went on to say, 'He who fears death, loses the joy of life. Truth conquers all things.'[14]

Much of this is admirable. To balance what we have just said, it could be claimed that the fact that Hus acted with full consciousness of the likely outcome makes his martyrdom in some ways more courageous and perhaps more significant than many other martyrdoms. But it must be admitted that in the event God did not permit Hus to preach dramatically and declare the truth to the council as he himself had envisaged. It was only after a long, gruelling period of confinement that he ultimately came forth, broken in body and weary in mind, to proclaim the faith amid constant jeers and interruptions. In his mid-forties, he was now a pale thin man in shabby clothes. He was described by one as being so weak that the bones seemed to cling to his skin. Smelling of prison, he came from a long spell in close confinement, not from one of the brilliant receptions so lavishly and regularly laid on by the council. For him there had been no banquets, only hard prison fare. He had only been given medical attention that he might be kept alive to suffer publicly. It was God's way and plan for the great Bohemian preacher. For Hus gave a mighty testimony even in his weakness, and out of his weakness grew increasingly strong in Christ Jesus in ways of which he had never conceived. Yet it was not the stirring, challenging, eloquent evangelical sermon that he had planned out in his own mind and even sketched on paper. Moreover in that overwhelmingly hostile assembly there were no fervent, guttural 'Amens' to what he said. Hus was still preaching – but in a different way. Hus had triumphed over another assault of Satan.

The devil often attacks us at our strongest points and this was so in one of the final attacks he launched at Hus. Hus was rich in personal friendships. He had many loyal followers. Could they not be used to weaken his resolve? Thus on 5 July, about a month after the trial, four bishops, in the company of the two Bohemian lords who had been so faithful to Hus, were sent by Sigismund to visit Hus in prison in order to secure a recantation with regard to the articles brought against him at the council. This was a last endeavour to break his resolve. Perhaps Lord John of Chlum hardly fulfilled the persuasive role that Sigismund had hoped, for apparently his address to Hus was as follows: 'Look, Master John! We are laymen and know not how to advise you; therefore see if you feel yourself guilty in anything of that which is charged against you. Do not fear to be instructed therein and to recant. But if, indeed, you do not feel guilty of those things that are charged against you, follow the dictates of your conscience. Under no circumstances do anything against your conscience or lie in the sight of God: but rather be steadfast until death in what you know to be the truth.'[15]

The reply of Hus was made with humility and weeping as he rejoined, 'Lord John, be sure that if I knew that I had written or preached anything erroneous against the law and against the holy mother church, I would desire humbly to recant it – God is my witness! I have ever desired to be shown better and more relevant Scripture than those that I have written and taught. And if they were shown me, I am ready most willingly to recant.'[16] This was ever Hus's stance. It is manifestly the evangelical position. Writing to the members of the University of Prague after his three public trials, he said, 'The council desired that I declare that all and every article drawn from my books is false. I refused unless they should show its falsity by Scripture.'[17] Not even the pleas of close friends could dissuade him from this resolute stance.

There is yet another aspect to this question of friendship. True friends must have helped Hus much but as by his imprisonment he was deprived for periods of their immediate assistance he was facing a new situation. Right through his ministry both in Prague and in rural Bohemia he had ever seemed surrounded by a loyal band of supporters, many of whom held him in deep affection and esteem. Now was the time for him to discover at a yet deeper level the friendship of the greatest and truest Friend of all. His faith in Christ was to shine forth in all these trials. Passages in the Gospels which describe the sufferings of Christ or where the Saviour promises a cross to his followers are constantly quoted in his letters. But there is one little incident which clearly illuminates his faith. At the council he needed someone to plead his cause. Yet, as we know, this was turned down. Writing to John of Chlum he says, 'I also inform you that I asked the commissioners before witnesses and notaries in the prison that they assign me a procurator and an advocate. They promised me to do so but later refused to grant it. I commit myself to the Lord Jesus Christ that he himself act as the procurator, advocate, and judge in my cause.'[18] Of course, in terms of Scripture Hus could not have procured himself a better advocate. His plea would be heard and he himself vindicated!

Moreover, through all the conflict in his life Hus had come to see doctrinally that Christ was the sole Head of the church. Now the doctrine was to be to him a living experience. In the opening section of the next quotation, which is from a letter written one month before his death, Hus is alluding to the removal of Pope John from office. 'Now faithful Christendom exists without a pope, a mere man, having Christ Jesus for its head, who directs it the best; for its heart, which vivifies it, granting the life of grace; for the fountain which irrigates it by the seven gifts of the

Holy Spirit; for the channel in which flow all the streams of graces; for the all-sufficient and unfailing refuge to which I, a wretch, run, firmly hoping that it will not fail me in directing, vivifying, and aiding me; but will liberate me from the sins of the present miserable life, and reward me with infinite joy.'[19]

Jesus Christ is set forth so clearly in the above letter as the source of every good. Still nearer to his death, Hus wrote again of his consolation through meditating on the Saviour's sufferings, adding with regard to the question of rejoicing in tribulation, 'It is easy to talk about it and to expound it, but difficult to fulfil it.' He ends this particular letter with a very moving prayer: 'O most kind Christ, draw us weaklings after thyself, for unless thou draw us, we cannot follow thee! Give us a courageous spirit that it may be ready; and if the flesh is weak, may thy grace go before, now, as well as subsequently. For without thee we can do nothing, and particularly to go to a cruel death for thy sake. Give us a valiant spirit, a fearless heart, the right faith, a firm hope, and perfect love, that we may offer our lives for thy sake with the greatest patience and joy. Amen.'[20]

In the afore-mentioned interview when John of Chlum made his half-hearted plea, the four bishops were as unimpressed by Hus's stand for Scripture truth as they would have been by these prayers. They only saw him as an obstinate heretic. The following day, 6 July, Hus was brought to the cathedral where Sigismund was presiding, wearing his crown. On a table lay the various priestly garments prepared for the unfrocking of Hus, who fell to his knees and prayed for some time. In apt symbolism of the evil incompetence of the Roman authorities who condemned Hus, a bishop then delivered a sermon on a text again taken wildly out of context. It was based on Romans 6:6: 'that the body of sin be destroyed'. The bishop coupled Hus with Arius and Sabellius in his address, placing schism in the first rank of evil, asserting that heresies were widespread and blaming much of the iniquity and vandalism of the day onto them.

Turning to Sigismund, he declared that he was called particularly to heal the schism and put an end to heresy. He thus addressed the king, 'To the performance of so holy a work, God has conferred upon you the wisdom of divine truth, the power of royal majesty and the justice of right equity. As the Most High has said (Jeremiah 1.) "Lo, I have put my words into thy mouth by imparting wisdom, and I have placed thee over the nations and kingdoms by conferring power, that thou mightest root up and by executing justice." So mayest thou destroy heresy and error; and especially this obstinate heretic, by whose malign influence many regions have been infected with the pest of heresy, and by reason of whom many things have gone to ruin.'[21]

Later in the proceedings Sigismund was observed to blush when Hus alluded to the pledge of a safe-conduct which had proved so empty a promise. In a letter Hus also mentions Christ, who deceives no man by a safe-conduct. Faced by the bishop's empty panegyric, Sigismund might well have blushed earlier, yet it would seem that he readily accepted all the compliments as due to him. However, the moment when he blushed was not to be forgotten. When, at the celebrated Diet of Worms, the enemies of Luther pressed Charles V to have him seized, in contempt of the safe-conduct which he had given him, his reply was very revealing. 'No', he said, 'I should not like to blush like Sigismund.'[22]

When the charges were read out, Hus attempted to reply but was silenced several times as he sought again to protest that views were still being ascribed to him falsely. When his entreaties to be heard were bluntly rebutted, Peter says, 'He fell upon his knees, and clasping his hands and lifting his eyes to heaven, he prayed most devoutly, committing his cause to God, the most just Judge. He did this repeatedly.'[23]

After Hus had stood up and yet again denied that he held the view of remanence with regard to the sacrament, he found himself facing the new and farcical charge that he claimed to be the fourth person of the Godhead. The council refused to name the source of this wild charge. Therefore Hus simply affirmed his faith in the blessed Trinity. The council's continued condemnation of his appeal to Jesus Christ in face of papal excommunications elicited from Hus a further appeal to the Saviour, which he ended as follows: 'I continue to declare that there is no safer appeal than to the Lord Jesus Christ, who will not be suborned by a perverse bribe, nor deceived by a false testimony, but will render to each one what he deserves.'[24]

The same items which were dealt with in the council were read out by an old, bald man and the charge of obstinate heresy was made yet again. Then Hus's books suspected of heresy were commanded to be burned. Once more Hus himself would not be silenced, as he protested, 'Why do you condemn my books, when I have ever desired and demanded better scriptural proofs against what I said and set forth in them, and even today I so desire? But you have so far neither adduced any more relevant Scripture in opposition, nor have shown one erroneous word in them.'[25] Furthermore many of the works, as Hus reminded them, were in Czech, which hardly any of his judges could read.

Hus continued then to pray as the sentence was read and Peter again catches a poignant moment: 'Master John Hus again knelt and in a loud voice prayed for all his enemies and said: "Lord Jesus Christ, I implore thee, forgive all my enemies for thy great mercy's sake; and thou knowest that they have falsely accused me and have produced false witnesses and have concocted false articles against me! Forgive them for thy boundless mercy's sake!" And when he said this, many, especially the principal clergy, looked indignantly and jeered at him.'[26]

At the command of the seven bishops who assisted at his unfrocking, he had then to dress in the altar vestments. Upon which he said, 'My Lord Jesus Christ, when he was led from Herod to Pilate, was mocked in a white garment.'[27] At every point Hus was upheld by the example of Christ himself. He still rejected the commands to abjure, whereupon many remarked how exceedingly great his wickedness was. Then we read in the moving words of Peter: 'After he descended from the table, the said bishops at once began to unfrock him. First they took the cup from his hands, pronouncing this curse: "O cursed Judas, because you have abandoned the counsel of peace and have counselled with the Jews, we take away from you the cup of redemption." He replied in a loud voice: "I trust in the Lord God Almighty, for whose name I patiently bear this vilification, that he will not take away from me the cup of his redemption; but I firmly hope to drink from it today in his kingdom."'[28]

After undressing him and pronouncing various curses, his enemies then began to disagree among themselves as to how they should get rid of his tonsure (the bare patch on the head of a priest). Some wanted to shave the rest of his head. Others wished to cut off the remaining hair with scissors. But all were united in their wish to make him look a fool and humiliate him. This was also undoubtedly the intention of those who went on to place on his head the paper crown which showed a picture of three horrible devils about to seize a soul and tear it to pieces with their claws.

However, once again, Hus himself recalled an incident from the crucifixion of his Lord and said, 'My Lord Jesus Christ on account of me, a miserable wretch, bore a much heavier and harsher crown of thorns. Being innocent, he was deemed deserving of the most shameful death. Therefore I, a miserable wretch and sinner, will humbly bear this much lighter, even though vilifying crown for his name and truth.'[29] It is amazing how throughout, Hus was repeatedly sustained by remembering what happened to Jesus Christ himself in his crucifixion.

As Hus was led from the church, the scene of his humiliation, he smiled as he saw a bonfire of his own books. Almost the whole of the city turned out to watch him on the road to his death and, as Peter says, many of the lay people instinctively knew that Hus was a good man. He was tied to a stake with ropes, a sooty chain was put round his neck and the wood piled round him up to his chin. At this point Hus was again urged to recant and he again refused, asserting that the main intent of all his preaching and writing was to 'turn men from sin'.[30]

Peter goes on: 'When the executioners at once lit the fire, the master immediately began to sing in a loud voice, at first "Christ, thou Son of the living God, have mercy upon us," and secondly, "Christ, thou Son of the living God, have mercy upon me," and in the third place, "Thou who art born of Mary the virgin." And when he began to sing the third time, the wind blew the flame into his face. And thus praying within himself and moving his lips and the head, he expired in the Lord.'[31]

Other accounts emphasize the courage of Hus throughout all this. Well does a contemporary analyst exclaim, 'He was to take leave of his cell, not of his constancy; of his life, but not of his faith!'[32] Especially interesting also is the comment of Aeneas Sylvius, who later became pope and who knew all the circumstances of the deaths of Hus and Jerome (who was to die in the same way, though not without some wavering beforehand, almost a year later). He wrote, 'They went to their punishment as to a feast. Not a word escaped them which gave indication of the least weakness. In the midst of the flames they sang hymns uninterruptedly to their last breath. No philosopher ever suffered death with such constancy as they endured the flames.'[33] This is indeed an amazing tribute.

Richental, who claims that he was present, reports on the immensity of the crowd and gives himself an important role in the whole enactment. Quite clearly he gives some details inaccurately. According to his account the white mitre, which he said had inscribed on it 'Heresiarch' or 'Archbishop of all heretics', was still intact after Hus himself had been consumed. This must be false as we consider the power of the flames. However, Richental does describe how Hus as he was led there called out, 'Jesus Christ, Son of the living God have mercy upon me!' and how he sought to preach but was prevented from doing so.[34]

Apart from the element of spectacle and pageantry, Richental showed very little interest in the death of Hus. He was not the only member of the council of this mind. Cardinal Fillastre says in his diary little more than that Hus was 'condemned and degraded for heresy' and then 'conducted by the secular court outside the city and burned, impenitent'.[35] But perhaps the classic instance of scribal indifference is the entry in the journal of the papal notary Cerretano. It simply reads: 'July 6. Fifteenth session. Condemnation of errors of Wyclif and Hus. Sentence and execution of Hus. July 15, seventeenth session. Farewell to Sigismund.'[36] On with the normal business!

However, his enemies knew that not all were so indifferent to what happened to Hus. Therefore they were determined to obliterate his remains as far as this was possible and Peter continues by describing how 'the executioners pulled the charred body along with the stake down to the ground and burned them further by adding wood from the third wagon to the fire. And walking around, they broke the bones with clubs so that they would be incinerated more quickly. And finding the head, they broke it to pieces with the clubs and again threw it into the fire.'[37]

After finding the heart, they likewise made sure that this was burned to ashes, and then someone, realizing that his clothing might be venerated and treated as relics by his followers, checked that this was thoroughly consumed by fire. 'So they loaded all the ashes in a cart and threw it into the river Rhine flowing nearby.'[38] A later account, possibly also by Peter, adds at this point, that they were 'wishing to destroy, as far as they could, his memory among the faithful'.[39] It was a futile endeavour. God had other purposes.

For this we may be sincerely thankful. Above all we must be deeply grateful to God for the labours of Peter of Mladoňivice, in particular. It is through his fidelity, concern and love that we are able to reverence the memory and recall 'the death and agony of the celebrated Master John Hus, the eminent preacher of the evangelical truth', to quote Peter's own words.[40] May it be, to use his words again, that 'his memory might be vividly recollected'.

# Appendices

# Appendix 1: The historians' view of Hus; Luther as a corrective

Of course, it is by no means universally acknowledged that Hus was a great Christian martyr. It is true to say that there is a wide variety of opinion about him. For some, amazing though it may seem, he was little more than a crypto-Communist. For others he was one who foolishly and unsuccessfully rebelled against pure Roman Catholic truth and who is best forgotten. For others he was one who was still a Roman Catholic at heart. For others, still more amazingly, he was an ardent nationalist of the worst type, even a forerunner of Hitler and his ilk. For others he was a somewhat wavering, inconsistent reformer who disappointingly failed to emerge with sufficient clarity into full-blooded evangelicalism. For yet others he was a Christian of sterling conviction, balance and warmth who has been one of the most Christ-like sufferers in the annals of the church.

It is ironical that Hus should have been seen as a crypto-Communist. Obviously the land where he once laboured for the gospel is now firmly in the grip of atheistic Communism. An edition of the *National Geographic* which dealt with Czechoslovakia vividly brought out this aspect. Everywhere one could see the red flags, the lantern jaws and the unsmiling comrades. A marriage ceremony shown was emphatically a purely secular event. A brief mention of Hus in the article informed the reader that he was a national hero who led 'an unsuccessful revolt'. With his own beloved country so grimly overshadowed by organized atheism, does this not seem true? Yet it must be emphasized that this article was not typical of the general Czech attitude. For them he is not a forgotten figure, a failure of yester-year. He is the first and foremost among the comrades!

A book published in Prague in 1958 on the Hussite movement in general has revealing chapter headings: 'The crisis of feudal society', 'The roots of the revolutionary movement in Bohemia', 'The defeat of the poor in Tabor' and a final concluding chapter on 'The significance of the Hussite revolutionary movement' which begins like this: 'This short survey of the history of the Hussite revolutionary movement shows that Hussitism was up to its time the most powerful anti-feudal struggle of the mass of the people in the medieval period.'[1] Undoubtedly the book draws on features of Hus's own teaching which are authentic and which must not be ignored. Admittedly it is dealing with the Hussite period as a whole. We concede that some references are made to Christian convictions and truth but the whole emphasis is distorted. One further quotation will show that the stand of Hus is not valued for what makes it most worthwhile and truly Christian: 'The Czechoslovak people value the Hussite tradition not only as an inspiration of their revolutionary and patriotic struggle and a treasury of national culture, but also because it shows the importance of peaceful cooperation among nations.'[2]

A book by an English Communist from which we have drawn much valuable material makes the same kind of points. Taking what is an increasingly familiar attitude among historians, the author tells the reader that 'Towns have ever been the forcing grounds of social progress and political revolution,' as he interprets much of the Hussite movement as little more than a reflection of social conditions.[3] 'The Bohemian reform movement was part of the general European middle-class revolution' and 'though the Czech reform movement was fundamentally a social phenomenon, it was of course not consciously so,' are two other judgements that he expresses in this vein.[4] By this simple device all the intense Christian fervour of Hus is simply explained away. His fervour was but the product of social and environmental forces.

In these books Hus and his followers have become little more than pawns in a game of Communist propaganda. Of course, Hus, with all his knowledge of injustice stemming from his peasant background and biblical insight, was deeply concerned about social righteousness. To refer back to that earlier comment of a Communist we must insist that the religious movement was not just a question of whether the divine body could be eaten with or without sauce. Hus was very much aware that man does not live by bread alone. He would have approved of the modern definition that the preacher is but one beggar telling other beggars where to get bread, but he would not have understood this as a reference to material bread. When a Roman Catholic writer, Pastor, also says that Hus 'declared war on the social order' this we must also label as false.[5] Hus only declared war on the evil within the social order. He did not seek to topple the social order itself. Even the Communists admit this, though some seem to feel he sowed the seeds of its overthrow!

Yet, oddly enough, the other key feature of the article in the *National Geographic* mentioned earlier was Roman Catholicism. Ritualism was evidently in full sway. There were pictures of shrines and picturesque village churches and the very mention of Hus's 'unsuccessful revolt' was attached to a picture of a Roman Catholic shrine. Since the battle of Hus was ultimately very much against the dominance and error of Rome, must he again on this account be deemed a failure?

As further illustration of this aspect we may take the Church of our Lady of Týn which dominates one square in Prague. Its history is perhaps typical of many. For a time the church followed Hussite doctrine. In fact it still preserves the arms of John of Rokycany, the last bishop of Hussite conviction to minister there – a star and a horse's hoof. A gilded chalice, symbol of the Hussite demand for communion with both bread and wine, once stood between the two towers. However, when the reformers were defeated and the Roman Catholics regained control, the Jesuits had this melted down and used it to make a crown, sceptre and halo for the statue of the Virgin and Child now in the gable. Yet the Roman Catholics, too, found that the memory of Hus has not been so easily obliterated. Even today many still regard him as a national hero although they do not follow him in doctrine. It was to counter this that the shrine and legend of John of Nepomuk were devised.

Moreover, as we think of the plethora of shrines, it is interesting to note that one earlier biographer of Hus, travelling in the country in the early years of the century, made this observation: 'At my last visit in St Vitus, 1913, after being shown by the verger the tombs of St Wenceslas and other shrines, I said: "Well, why haven't you a shrine to John Hus? He was a famous patriot." "So he was," replied our guide most good-naturedly, "but there was nothing left for a shrine. His ashes were all thrown into the lake of Constance."'[6] Hus needs no shrine as a memorial. His memory will not be obliterated so easily but it does need preserving in the proper way, since there is another Roman Catholic distortion to face.

That Hus was really a Roman Catholic at heart is the conclusion of De Vooght in his monumental book on Hus. He concedes that Hus was rightly condemned for heresy and pinpoints his work *The Church* as particularly harmful, while commending him for his early protests in the Wilsnack enquiry and much of what he wrote during the indulgence controversy. He finds fault with Hus's intemperate language and in particular the way he discussed themes in front of the common people and roused them to fury and action against false pastors. It is De Vooght who commended those at Constance who delivered similar strictures because they did it in Latin and to a very confined audience. In his view Hus was narrow and obsessed with the vices of the clergy, blowing up their faults out of all proportion.

The nub of his charge is that at vital moments Hus lacked the true courage of a reformer. He singles out the fact that he left Prague at the announcement of the interdict saying, 'For an authentic reformer, who had already, in spirit, broken with the church, the inconveniences of the interdict – after all, temporary – would have seemed light.'[7] He also contends that during the last months Hus was ever seeking to submit to the church, even falling at the feet of John XXIII, asking for a confessor and reciting the creed. He acknowledges Hus's courage and the fact that he was in the main ardent for truth, although he does accuse him of being guilty of small evasions which, ultimately, he completely surmounted and relinquished. He has much admiration for his final act, ironically conceding that he was condemned for the same heresy as Constance itself displayed – namely believing it could dispense with the pope.

His conclusion is that *despite himself* Hus was a Protestant but *at heart* he was always a Catholic. That the contrary is in fact the case we have sought to prove in this book. When De Vooght speaks of the three heads of church as being just an accidental ('The accident is not the rule!') and D'Ailly and Sigismund as being basically favourable to Hus he only betrays other aspects of his false reasoning.[8]

That Hus should be linked with Hitler is perhaps the most astounding suggestion of all. However, it has been made in all seriousness. For example, one writer can see the Hussite movement as 'in many ways the forerunner of German National Socialism'. He then adds, 'It may be left an open question to what extent Hussite elements worked upon Hitler.'[9] That this can be an open question to any writer must lead one to doubt whether he has ever opened any book by Hus.

Admittedly there were nationalistic elements in Hus's protests and teaching. This is true of most great men. But they were peripheral to his main emphasis and in no way sufficiently dominant to justify the assertion of yet another modern historian who states, 'It is genuinely difficult to say of Hus, as it is genuinely difficult to say of Luther, whether he is a national leader masquerading as a religious reformer or a religious reformer skilfully making use of national sentiment.'[10]

There is no genuine difficulty at all in this matter. Hus loved his country. He spoke with fervour about it. As we have seen, he was involved in a significant clash with the German element. But we have seen that he personally shed his misplaced nationalism. Perhaps the two things which finally shattered this false notion that gospel and country are always one were the welcome he received from Germans on the way to Constance and the fact that at Constance it was his own countrymen who were the foremost instigators of proceedings against him. Yet, prior to that, as he saw in Bohemia that a Czech could indeed be a heretic, he had already changed considerably. Of course, it cannot be gainsaid that his unwise utterances may have left an unfortunate and unscriptural legacy among some of his less spiritual or even unspiritual followers. This may be seen in the protest which certain nobles sent to Constance after his death and which stated that the condemnation of the Czech peasant's son was an insult to 'the most Christian Czech kingdom'.[11] Nevertheless Hus did receive the recognition of perhaps the greatest of all Germans, as we shall see in a moment.

In some ways the saddest aspect of all is the failure of evangelicals to do justice to Hus. For example, this excerpt from an admittedly brief article called 'Reformers before the Reformation' is far from adequate. The writer states, 'Despite his insistence that Scripture was the judge between truth and falsehood, Hus himself never approached Wyclif in his understanding of the truth. In fact, even where Scripture was concerned, Hus could speak of the relative inspiration of the Old Testament alongside the New Testament, and said that the Christian had as his guides "God, the apostles, the holy doctors of the church, and the catholic church."'[12] Another brief contemporary sketch of his life, which is, in the main, good and helpful, tells us that 'Hus never attained to the grasp of truth that was characteristic of Wyclif.'[13]

The former of the two writers draws heavily for his own brief survey on another evangelical history, which is undoubtedly in many ways a helpful book.[14] It is precise, scholarly and well-documented. Yet the tremendously sad thing is that in its pages Hus scarcely emerges as a man of real flesh and blood. It is as though his letters, which reveal him so clearly in his varied moods, his positive fervour and his deep biblical conviction, did not exist. In so many treatments of this period the historical 't's are carefully crossed and the theological 'i's are all carefully dotted as the movements of the curia and the decisions of the Council of Constance are meticulously recorded, but the only man who is worth studying in depth, worth imitating and worth thanking God for merges anonymously into the background of a welter of real but mostly insignificant facts and figures.

Where evangelical scholars follow such a path they come perilously close to the judgement of a modernist such as Harnack who wrote, 'The Wyclifite and the Hussite movement must be taken as the ripest fruitage of the reform movement of the Middle Ages, and although it loosened the ground and prepared the way, yet it brought to expression no reformatory ideas.'[15] It is not surprising when

Harnack fails to acknowledge men of great evangelical conviction in the past. It is tragic when evangelicals themselves fail to discern the features of a great reformer.

However, we may be thankful in this connection that Luther, a German and himself a man of towering evangelical conviction and fervour, knew a man when he saw one. Above all, he knew a man of God. He could readily and humbly recognize a man of passionate evangelical conviction, a man worthy of imitation, a man needing to be studied. The testimony of Luther is vital at this point, for he clearly saw and increasingly asserted what so many have failed to see and assert, that Hus in all essentials stands gloriously and unambiguously in the evangelical succession.

It is important to realize that Luther did not form his views about Hus without considerable struggle. As a student at Erfurt, he read Hus's sermons, but, as he was then a staunch Roman Catholic, his reaction was predictable. Let Luther tell his own story: 'When I was studying at Erfurt, I found in a library of the convent a book entitled *Sermons of John Hus*. I was seized with a curiosity to know what doctrines this heresiarch had taught. This reading filled me with incredible surprise. I could not comprehend why they should have burned so great a man, and one who explained Scripture with so much discernment and wisdom.'[16]

However, it was not yet God's time for light to dawn fully and Luther drew back from the right conclusions. He continues, 'But inasmuch as the very name of Hus was such an abomination that I imagined that at the mention of it the heavens would fall, the sun be darkened, I shut the book with a sad heart. I consoled myself, however, by the thought that perhaps he wrote it before he fell into heresy; for, as yet, I knew nothing of the doings of the Council of Constance.'[17] There was still much deep-seated prejudice to be overcome.

The next big step in Luther's change would seem to be the Leipzig debate of July 1519. Here Luther was confronted by an extremely skilful adversary, Eck, who succeeded in drawing the admission from him that some of Hus's views condemned by the Council of Constance had been good and Christian. Luther was manifestly uncomfortable. He sought, it would appear, to evade the issue and change the subject. Here he is replying to the charge of Eck: 'The eminent Doctor has just called my attention to the articles of Wyclif and John Hus. He has also spoken of Boniface, who condemned them. I reply as before that I neither want to nor am in a position to defend the Bohemian schism.' But Luther added almost immediately, 'Secondly, it is also certain that many of the articles of John Hus and the Bohemians are plainly most Christian and evangelical.'[18]

During the debate Eck kept on pressing this matter. Apart from the fact that Luther seemed to be verging on heresy, the ground was especially treacherous at Leipzig because Bohemia was nearby. It was still within the memory of some that the later followers of John Hus had ravaged the Saxon lands. So Eck gloatingly dwelt on the fact that Luther 'asserts in unchristian fashion that the most evil errors of the Hussites are Christian'.[19]

Under this incessant pressure Luther was driven more and more into the open. He openly agreed with the article that 'It is not necessary for salvation to believe the Roman church superior to all others', even if it came from Hus or Wyclif. Inaccurately he asserted that the Council of Constance did not say that all the articles of Hus were heretical. (Here Luther was implying his own agreement with assertions that Hus had made, while refusing to acknowledge that Rome had thoroughly condemned them.) Luther also went on to declare that councils sometimes err and contradict each other.

'But this', said Eck, 'is the Bohemian virus, to attach more weight to one's own interpretation of Scripture than to that of the popes and councils, the doctors and the universities.'[20] In this Eck saw more clearly than did Luther himself the direction in which the reformer was moving. At the Council of Worms Eck was to bring up this issue yet again when he charged, 'You do nothing but renew the errors of Wyclif and Hus.'[21] By this time it was clear that the charge was to all intents and purposes true. Just before this famous diet was held another representative from the papal side spoke sneeringly and accusingly of 'John Hus, whom Luther has recently proclaimed his saint' and then set out to prove, employing words borrowed largely from a papal bull, that

Luther was 'a heretic who brought up John Hus from hell and endorsed not some but all of his articles'.[22] These accusations, which were substantially accurate, show how far Luther had moved between Leipzig in 1519 and Worms in 1521.

In 1520 Luther was writing furiously and step by step he was moving more into line with the views of Hus. He was becoming bolder. Thus in the *Pagan Servitude of the Church* we meet with this pronouncement: 'I shall not give an ear, nor pay any attention, to those who cry out that my opinion is Wyclifite or Hussite heresy, and contrary to the decrees of the church.'[23] In *An Appeal to the Ruling Class*, composed earlier the same year, he can even contemplate joining with the Hussites and urges that such a course be pursued. Although still not totally clear he can declare, 'I have no desire to justify at this stage John Hus's propositions or defend his errors, although to my way of thinking he wrote nothing erroneous.'[24]

Luther goes on to argue that, if there is union with the Hussites, they must not be 'compelled to abandon taking the sacraments in both kinds, for that practice is neither unchristian nor heretical'.[25] Yet even in this tract he still has some reservations. He is still oscillating. 'I am not to be understood as meaning that John Hus was a saint or a martyr, as certain of his fellow-countrymen maintain. But I do declare my belief that he suffered a wrong, and that his books and his teaching were wrongly condemned,' he writes.[26]

Soon Luther was to become completely clear as to his closeness to Hus. At about this time some Hussite followers sent him a copy of *The Church* by Hus. Also in June 1520 a bull condemned some forty-one errors of Luther, one of them being that Luther had claimed that certain of the articles of Hus condemned at the Council of Constance were in fact Christian, true and evangelical. Luther commented on this aspect of the bull as follows: 'I was wrong. I retract the statement that certain articles of John Hus are evangelical. I say now, "Not some but all the articles of John Hus were condemned by Antichrist and his apostles in the synagogue of Satan." And to your face, most holy Vicar of God, I say freely that all the condemned articles of John Hus are evangelical and Christian, and yours are downright impious and diabolical.'[27] The support of Luther for Hus was now without reservation or qualification.

From this position Luther never swerved. In fact his enthusiasm for Hus deepened and grew. He could write to Spalatin as early as February 1520 in this vein, 'Shamelessly [unawares] I both taught and held the teachings of Hus: in short, we were all Hussites without knowing it.'[28] 'Behold the horrible misery which came upon us because we did not accept the Bohemian doctor for our leader!' he fervently exclaimed.[29] Writing to Melanchthon in 1530, he could link his own cause quite firmly with that of Hus. He urged his troubled friend, 'With all my heart I hate those cares by which you state that you are consumed. They rule your heart, not on account of the greatness of the cause but by reason of the greatness of your unbelief. The same cause existed in the time of John Hus and many others, and they had a harder time of it than we do. Great though our cause is, its Author and Champion is also great, for the cause is not ours.'[30] With some justice Luther saw the cause of Hus as even greater than his own. These were memorable words.

In 1537 Luther supplied a preface to some letters of Hus and had opportunity not just to express doctrinal agreement but also to voice the warmth of his affection. He did so powerfully. 'If he, who in the agony of death, invoked Jesus, the Son of God, who suffered on our behalf, and gave himself up to the flames with such faith and constancy for Christ's cause – if he did not show himself a brave and worthy martyr of Christ – then may scarcely anyone be saved.'[31]

All this was a far remove from what Luther had once somewhat arrogantly declared, very much in the vein of those who suggest that Hus was an incomplete reformer: 'John Hus attacked and castigated only the pope's abuses and scandalous life; but I . . . have attacked the pope's doctrine and overthrown him.'[32] It is an even further remove from a yet earlier opinion: 'I used to abhor the very name of Hus. So zealous was I for the pope that I would have helped to bring iron and fire to kill Hus, if not in very deed, at least with a consenting mind.'[33]

We may safely believe that Luther had the insight to

recognize clearly and enthusiastically one of his greatest forerunners, though a thousand modern scholars seek to deny it in a thousand monographs or obscure it by a thousand footnotes! What is far more important still is that Luther was not half-hearted. He was unashamedly enthusiastic. 'Oh, that my name were worthy to be associated with such a man!' was his exclamation in one letter.[34] It was a truly God-given aspiration.

We must raise again here the whole question of apostolic succession. Most of us at some time or other have been confronted with the question: 'Well, once we were all Roman Catholics, weren't we?' Then we begin to wonder whether for fifteen hundred years everybody was a Roman Catholic and we tend to think that only with the protest of Luther did evangelicalism emerge. Some have seen Luther as desperately and almost dishonestly seeking forbears. The Roman Catholic Ronald Knox wrote sneeringly of Luther's attitude as follows: 'That Protestantism had no pedigree was a sore subject; and reunion with the heirs of John Hus will have attracted Luther just as marriage into some decayed aristocratic family has been known to attract the *nouveau riche*.'[35] How little Ronald Knox, who himself had turned his back on the evangelicalism of his youth, understood of the biblical view of apostolic succession!

If God had left the church in fifteen centuries of unrelieved darkness it would seem that the promise of Christ that the gates of hell would not prevail against his church had failed. We have already seen that this was not true, in that some of the darkness had only recently arisen and for centuries there had been faithful groups. But more should be said. There is great significance in the fact that Hus himself lived over a hundred years before Luther nailed his theses to the door of the church. But this fact alone does not tell the whole story. Hus in a real way reaches back into the past and into the future. He was greatly influenced by Wyclif, and his final attitude seems illustrated by the fact that a week before his death he told Peter to choose any works of Wyclif from his own library that pleased him. This was intended as a generous gift of something that was precious to the giver. However, his own fully balanced attitude comes out in a statement he made one year before his death in 1414, when he declared, 'Whatever truth Wyclif has taught I receive, not because it is the truth of Wyclif, but because it is the truth of Christ.'[36]

We have already seen that there was much contact between the Lollards and the Hussites. We have seen how Richard Wyche, a priest who was himself to be burned at the stake some twenty-five years after Hus, wrote to the Bohemians to encourage them. Nor did the interchange stop with the death of Hus. Prominent in the leadership of the Hussites several years after the burning of Hus was an Englishman called Peter Payne. Moreover, in 1433 a Hussite missionary was put to death – in Scotland! There was much to-and-fro traffic in the gospel even in those days.[37]

After Hus, despite the existence of wild extremists and also those who idolized him as a man without truly submitting to Scripture, there was a constant succession of Bible-believers, such as Jakoubek of Stříbro, Peter of Chelcicky and Luke of Prague. If we were to trace this line we would find that figures as diverse as John Bunyan and many of the Puritans in the past, and in our own day Georgi Vins' father and Aida of Leningrad, have been influenced by Hus's teaching and example.[38]

When we think of the question of apostolic succession and the influence of one mind upon another, Hus himself has some very wise words to say. He is again writing to his own congregation from prison and he probably realizes the danger of idolizing his person: 'I pray that you hold that truth of God which I have drawn from the law of God, and have preached and written from the teachings of the saints. I also beseech you that if anyone has heard at my preaching or in private anything contrary to the truth of God, or if I have written it anywhere – which, I trust God, there is none of it – that he does not hold it.'[39] Just a month before his death he wrote to the Praguers beseeching them 'to be kind toward Bethlehem as long as the Lord God will be pleased that the Word of God be preached there'.[40] Support was to be not merely for tradition's sake, but out of loyalty to Scripture alone. This is true apostolic succession.

# Appendix 2: Some contemporary applications

We have already drawn on the music of Smetana as an introduction to the beauty and grandeur of the Bohemia which Hus so loved. But Smetana was not the only great Czech composer to draw on Hussite themes as background for some of his greatest music. His equally famous compatriot Dvořák sought to do likewise. It is interesting to note that when the latter, who was a Roman Catholic, went in 1857 to stay in Prague he lodged at the Bee Inn in Hus Street. He also intended at one time to write a vast work on the Hussite period.

In the end only the *Husitska Overture* or *Hussite Overture* was completed. This is a work of force and lyricism with mounting dramatic passion. It has been said of it that 'It is a work which is truly Hussite in its harshness and unyieldedness, which justifiably sounds to a foreigner as "fanatic, as if in places it had been orchestrated for scythes, flails and spiked clubs."'[1] Such emphasis on harshness is not our view of the true quality of Hus's own life, whatever may be said of the later Hussite period, but it is none the less an interesting insight.

The somewhat inconsistent and wavering comments of one music critic, Alec Robertson, are particularly fascinating in this connection. Initially he contends that 'In this overture Dvořák solves a problem which still eludes theologians by quoting both a Hussite and a Catholic tune, and pointing the moral by ending with the national anthem.'[2] Here the writer is obviously suggesting that Dvořák succeeded in doing what the ecumenical movement so far has failed to do, in bringing about a synthesis of Protestant and Roman Catholic elements.

Yet later, as Alec Robertson describes in more detail

the attempt of the composer to blend the Hussite chorale tune and the Czech Roman Catholic song of St Wenceslas, he recounts how the Hussite chorale receives the full weight of the brass, the urgent, compelling beat of the timpani and the excited rushes of the strings and then informs us that 'The result is a slight feeling of anticlimax and a conviction of the triumph of Hus.'[3] If we view the triumph of Hus as a triumph of the true church of Jesus Christ we say, 'Amen', to this.

There must be no blurring of the issues. We mention this because it so often happens. We have seen that there are those who seek to portray Hus as a crypto-Communist or forerunner of Fascism. We trust that this book has given the lie to these libels. There are academic historians who say that Hus ought to be left where he belongs, hidden away in the complicated period of the medieval papacy. 'The whole subject is too complicated to be presented to the average reader,' they argue. We hope that in some small and imperfect measure this book helped to dispel that myth.

We must therefore ask what are the clear lessons that emerge from this study of the life of God's servant John Hus. *The first lesson is that Hus stood in firm and decided opposition to the evils of the papacy because of his unswerving allegiance to the Word of God.* Of course, not all would agree that the papacy as a system was, or is, evil. Or, if they agree that it was once evil, they cannot believe that it is still so today. Therefore we must summarize the issues as succinctly as we can. It is an issue of great importance.

There must be no whitewashing. This must be stressed because there are those who seek to explain or excuse the evil of some of the characters in our drama by stressing the pressures of the situation in which they found themselves and also by emphasizing the generally low standards of that particular era. For example, one scholarly writer infers that there are indeed many good things to be said for Pope John XXIII, Sigismund and others.

'It is perhaps pertinent to remark here,' says this writer, 'that the principal actors in the scene we are now about to view have often been judged as foolish or malintentioned by those who have written for the popular taste. The record, however, gives clear evidence that, while the principal actors of the conciliar epoch were but men, they were serious and interesting ones, above average for that or any other age.' A little later we read, 'Men of the time believed that Sigismund had something of the hero about him. In spite of his personal fallibilities and his admittedly grand defeat, we are hard put not to agree with them . . . True, John XXIII's personal life was more suitable for a secular prince than for a pontiff, though the libellous exaggerations of his enemies are clearly to be discounted. But he was a man of energy and decision, even of good will until overwhelmed by circumstances.'[4] While we have conceded that Sigismund, as well as being unswerving in loyalty to the Roman Catholic Church, showed courtesy, wit and prompt presence of mind, we must say that this verdict is evidently that of a person who cannot call evil by its proper name.

The greatest characteristic of Sigismund was showmanship, but he was also immoral, deceitful and proud. Apparently, in 1437, as he was conscious of his approaching death he put on his imperial robes and, with the crown on his head, he attended High Mass. When the service was over at his command grave-clothes were thrown over the imperial vesture. Then, taking his seat on his throne, he awaited death. The same evening he died. He was left seated there for three days as he had commanded 'that men might see that the lord of all the world was dead and gone'.[5] He was flamboyant to the last – in this life at least: there is a world to come.

The writer who so praises Sigismund also seeks to exonerate Gregory XII and Benedict XIII from real blame, arguing that the former was learned, even saintly, and the latter quick-witted. But we must assert that all who seek to usurp the place of Jesus Christ commit great evil. The simony, deceit and cruelty are but additional evils – real, but small in comparison with the blasphemous claims and unscriptural attitude of those who claimed sole obedience on earth of the faithful and anathematized all who dissented from them.

Of course, it should have emerged clearly during the whole of this book that the claims of Rome are spurious. It was not merely that there were many evil men in the papal chair. That in itself is bad enough. But it must again be emphasized that throughout the whole lifetime of many people it was not known by millions who was the real head of the church. For there to be one head he must be clearly recognizable. Even a twentieth-century Roman Catholic writer admits that 'An entire generation had known only a church rent asunder, popes who preached crusades against one another, governments that haggled over the price of their loyalty.'[6]

Since the same writer also states that both the groups involved in the original schism could make claims with some degree of legitimacy, we are entitled to ask how the ordinary man could be expected to sort out their rival claims. Interestingly enough, the pope whom the present Roman church acknowledges as representing the true line, Gregory XII, had in the end the smallest following. It is also interesting that contemporaries punning on the Latin form of his family name, Correrius, irreverently but relevantly called him '*Errorius*' (the foremost in error).[7] Many a true word is spoken in jest.

It may, of course, be argued that this era was a particularly bad and thoroughly untypical period for the papacy and we may therefore be urged to share the relief of many at the council itself that in the end the confusion was dispelled, the rival popes were deposed or resigned, and Martin V was appointed with glad acclaim and the allegiance of the Roman Catholic communion at large. Many indeed rejoiced that unity had been restored. Ought we to have rejoiced with them?

There are simple answers to this. Firstly, we point out that Martin V was not only one of the very cardinals who fled in support of John XXIII when he made his secret escape from the council, but was also in fact the last to desert him. Presumably he felt real kinship with John XXIII. Secondly, we remind ourselves that Martin V more or less fobbed off the council with a few generalizing promises of reform and then refused to carry them out in any thoroughgoing way. We recall that Gerson felt that the reformers had been defeated on all accounts. 'It has been said of Constance that the Council defeated Pope John XXIII, but Pope Martin V defeated the Council,' comments a modern author.[8] But for our third and most important point we can do little better than quote the verdict of an older historian, whose writings have been so helpful in the preparation of this book. He wrote, 'Thus many seemed to see in Martin V, a John XXIII *redevivus.* The man might die, but the system lived.'[9] This is a most perceptive comment. It is not without significance that John himself ended his days as a wealthy cardinal and as Dean of the Sacred College under Martin V. His mortal remains were laid to rest in a magnificent tomb that is still admired by visitors to Florence.

The system indeed continues to live many centuries after all these events. In fact, within the lifetime of many readers of this book there has been yet another Pope John XXIII. This is because the present Roman Catholic Church, tracing the succession through Urban VI and Gregory XII, does not acknowledge Pope John XXIII of Hus's day as a true pope. 'It is Catholic practice to blot away an undesirable pope,' comments one author.[10] The implication in the choice of a man with an identical name is that the earlier claimant is best forgotten and that there is no true continuity between these two men. Is this in fact so? Has the papacy a new heart as well as new face?

Pope John XXIII of the twentieth century does seem a startling contrast to the Pope John XXIII of Constance. While the former was an utter rogue, the latter would seem to have been a genuinely devout Roman Catholic. He was widely liked as a jovial, out-going personality. Indeed, although Pope John Paul II has for many widened the appeal of the papacy to an unimagined extent in our day, Pope John XXIII was the man who initially sent some Protestants starry-eyed with misguided ecumenical euphoria. His pioneering role must not be forgotten. Men spoke of a transformation in the attitude of the papacy after his appointment. The man had undoubtedly changed. But had the system changed? This is the vital question. We can check on the recent John XXIII's views by looking at his book *The Journal of a Soul.* This will show us how far he really differs from the popes of Hus's day.

We briefly draw attention to John's desire (symbolized for him in the visit of Edward VII, 'a heretical King of Protestant England', to the Vatican) to see 'a slow but real and sincere return of the nations to the arms of their common Father who has long awaited them, weeping over their foolishness'.[11] We note his assertion of the role of the papacy, uttered before his own elevation: 'In days of uncertainty and sadness St Alphonsus used to say: "The Pope's will: God's will!"'[12] Even before the dogma of the bodily assumption of Mary was promulgated he had believed it. He refers to her constantly. She is, in his estimation, 'the glorious Virgin, the Queen of Peace, and Peacemaker of the whole world'.[13] The book is full of ejaculations in an adulatory vein to Mary Immaculate.[14] It may incidentally be said that, although Hus held some wrong views about Mary, he never spoke about her in this idolatrous way.

But what is the most worrying factor of all and, indeed the most damning one in connection with one who claims to speak in the name of Christ in a special way and with a God-given authority above all others, is the early entry in the *Journal* to the effect that, after several years of being a priest, he at last felt a strong urge to study the Bible! He then mentions that he is beginning to read the Scriptures. But later with dismay we read another entry informing us that he had not in fact read much of the Bible.[15] And Rome talks of the ignorance of the common people! What do we make of such terrible admissions from the supreme guide? And if a love of God's Word is one sign of true conversion, what do we infer about his spiritual state? We assert that ignorance of the Scripture is in fact a constant and typical mark of Rome. The system does not change.

In our own time popes have come in all shapes and sizes. Some have been withdrawn, austere and apparently devout, like Gregory XII. Others have been quick-witted and courageous as Benedict XIII undoubtedly was. Others, without sharing the terrible vices of the first John XXIII, have yet been out-going and flamboyant, with dramatic flair and a feeling for occasions. Yet all alike have been products of the same antichristian system, earnestly proclaiming doctrines that are contrary to Scripture and staying strangely silent on matters that lie at the heart of the evangelical faith.[16]

In the light of all this, we must further ask, Why is there today the utterly foolish and completely unbiblical stress on dialogue with Rome? Why are so many people today ashamed of the word 'Protestant'? Various denominational groupings have for a long time now been entering into serious dialogue with Rome. They do this with the full knowledge of all the growth of Roman error since the time of Hus. Although it would at times seem that some of the conciliar reformers were opposed to the papacy, or at least intent on limiting papal powers and reforming the office, the judgement of one historian is apposite when he says that in reality the council's task was not to 'kick the pope when he was down; rather their job was to help him get up again'.[17] This was true then and it will always be so. In any compromise solution the papacy will always prove the victor. In next to no time all the decrees of Constance limiting papal power were a dead letter. It will likewise be found today that unity with Rome can only be attained by the sacrifice of biblical truth.

Sadly many have failed to recognize the penetrating nature of Hus's criticism of the papacy. Therefore a modern historian misleadingly writes that 'Hus's revolt, however, was ethical rather than theological, and he yearned for a reform in morality rather than a revolution in the church.'[18] This is a woefully insufficient judgement – little more than a blurring of the issue. Hus went much deeper than the criticisms of people's outward lives. Many other people did this without being burned at Constance. Hus was supremely concerned with doctrine. Luther ultimately recognized this after his initial false assessment. The Roman Catholic writer of a biography of Gerson was much nearer the truth when he asserted, 'Hus sought to revolutionize, Gerson sought to revise.'[19] Step by step, Hus moved relentlessly towards biblical reformation and revolution.

Hus refused not only to submit to the Archbishop of Prague and the whole galaxy of cardinals, but also to the pope where the truth was at stake. How wrong it would be to criticize Hus for any tardiness in rejecting Rome's claims! He lived in days before many of the worst papal doctrines had been promulgated. There was no formal dogma of papal infallibility in his lifetime. Unlike us, he did not have the hindsight of the period of the Reformation. Only in the course of his own conflict did he find how unreformable Rome was. Yet we have seen how powerfully he did eventually write against the pope's claims. Some of his last pronouncements clearly point to his conviction that ultimately there could be no true fellowship either with Rome or with the ecumenical council. The only way he could prove this to future generations was not by writing a long tract but by bequeathing to us the legacy of his blood. How far are we benefiting from the legacy bequeathed by this man?

*The second lesson is that Hus stood in firm and decided opposition to the evils of the ecumenical council because of his unswerving allegiance to the Word of God and also because of his experience of true conversion.* This obviously leads us to ask further questions about the role of people like Gerson, D'Ailly and others. What relevance today is there in the particular study of their conflict with Hus? It is again an issue that has much contemporary relevance. Although we have dissented from the judgement of the historian quoted earlier in the chapter, to the effect that Sigismund and Pope John XXIII were good men, yet we would concur with his judgement that many of the participants in the council were, as he says, 'above average'. This is beyond dispute. Another writer has argued that 'Such a gathering of notables was unparalleled in the history of the great councils of the church, while the assembly numbers were so countless as the drops of water in the sea.'[20] In other words, it would be very hard to summon anywhere today a more outstanding and distinguished ecumenical gathering. We have in no wise glossed over the seamy side, but we must pause to underline that the place was bristling with outstanding scholars and clergy, that D'Ailly and Gerson were really the top-ranking theologians of their day, and that some, such as Aenias Sylvius and Poggio, the famous humanist, who both admired the way Hus and Jerome died without in any way sharing their beliefs, were undoubtedly men of culture and literary powers.

Yet how false is the judgement of the one who wrote, 'Indeed, the tragedy of the conciliar fathers was that Hus and Jerome insisted upon dying'![21] The implication is that Hus either was misunderstood or misunderstood himself and that there really was not a wide cleavage between his views and those of Gerson, D'Ailly and others. Hus knew how far apart, indeed how irreconcilably apart, they were.

Moreover the aforementioned Roman Catholic biographer of Gerson rightly points out that, unlike Wyclif and Hus, Gerson, despite the assertions of some, was no true precursor of the Reformation.[22]

Hus submitted his judgement constantly to Scripture. He had no time for the belief in the infallibility of a council of mere men – and very ungodly men at that – and said so. One little scene at his trial underscores this vividly. One learned doctor urged his submission saying, 'If the council told me I had but one eye, I would confess it to be so, though I know I have two.'[23] Hus was impervious to such nonsensical and indeed satanic reasoning. He would not tamely follow the majority vote in any council or conference or synod or assembly when this was opposed to Scripture. Nor would he defer to a group of theologians merely because of their number or reputation.

Two comments of Hus sum up the vast cleavage in belief between Hus and the conciliar reformers. In one letter he mentioned how the Council of Constance had consigned some of his writings to the flames. He drew a parallel with the experience of the prophet Jeremiah, whose books had been burned by the people of his day. However, it consoled Hus to reflect on the fact that those who burnt the prophecies did not thereby escape the word which God had spoken. Jeremiah, at God's command, wrote it all down again, adding some further words against the opponents of God's truth. 'Having these things before your eyes, do not allow yourselves to be terrified into giving up the reading of what I have written or into surrendering your books to them to be burned,' Hus concluded.[24] The writer of this book has sought to answer this appeal. Hus's other comment concerns the way in which his enemies diligently perused his books. Hus drew a clear lesson from this by showing a contrast. 'I am glad that they were obliged to read my small books, which openly reveal their wickedness. I know that they have read them more diligently than the sacred Scriptures, desiring to find errors in them,' he caustically wrote.[25]

An incident which happened at the council in February 1415, while Hus was languishing in prison, epitomizes the difference between the two incompatible theologies. We give the incident in the words of Richental, who told how scholars came from Norway, Sweden and Denmark to show 'how some time previously there had been in their realms a holy queen, named Bridget, who at God's behest had visited many lands and taken with her a devout master of holy theology and two proved and devout priests, to whom she imparted all her revelations and by whose counsel she governed herself before God in all things. Both in her life-time and after her death, she performed many great miracles, as a veritable saint should do.'[26]

As they declared their convictions that she had truly performed miracles, and called for her canonization as a saint, Richental was delighted with the council's positive reply. 'Then an archbishop of Denmark celebrated mass and during mass a figure of the queen, like a doll, was set up on the altar and she was canonized, that is, made into a saint, with due sanction and customary rites,' records our chronicler.[27]

Imagine how the man who had exposed the fraud at Wilsnack would have reacted to all this ecclesiastical mumbo-jumbo! Imagine how he would react to books today which purport to narrate how in a certain country more miracles are being performed than took place in the whole era of the Acts of the Apostles! Hus was not the man to believe miracles or new revelations just because a large number of contemporaries accepted them. He believed that the Word had been given once for all. Those who demand new miracles were, in his view, not men of deep faith but men of little or no faith. In the aftermath of the Wilsnack investigation Hus had berated priests who 'worship the devil' and 'for the sake of a full moneybag manufacture relics and "bleeding" hosts'.[28] There was no room for compromise on this matter. Nor is it surprising that men interested in new miracles and spiritual sensationalism had no real interest in a man who had a deep commitment to the whole of Scripture, but who ploughed so lonely a furrow and who was himself delivered by no miraculous intervention. The same would be true today.

This indeed was one of the essential points of difference. The conciliar fathers and the pope used Scripture in a super-ficial, even blasphemous way. Despite their interest in religious wonders and the fact that God was 'doing a new thing' in Scandinavia, Scripture was for them but an appendage, a source of interesting quotations rather than an absolute God-given rule. For Hus its truthfulness was a matter of life and death. The Scripture demanded whole-hearted submission. Hus quoted it extensively, had it at his fingertips in debate, but above all held it in his heart and was prepared to die unless he were properly corrected by it. It is not even fair to say, as many do, that Hus was almost equally influenced by the traditions and fathers of the church as by Scripture itself. Like Wyclif before him and Calvin after him, Hus had a deep love of the writings of Augustine and many others, but he never set the commentators above the sacred Word itself, however much he profited from them. Therefore inevitably both pope and council had to show themselves consistent opponents of one who was not only prepared to study Scripture in seclusion but was prepared to the cost of his own life to apply the Word of God to every aspect of the church's life, both to the false claims of the papacy and of the council itself.

Above all it was the fact that they were confronted with a converted man that infuriated the council and earned the contempt of the pope. How wild they were! Says Luther, describing a scene at the council, 'All worked themselves into a rage like wild boars; the bristles of their back stood on end; they bent their brows and gnashed their teeth against John Hus.'[29] It may be imaginative but it is surely not a false picture. Glance back at the chapters dealing with the trial and you will find that, although there were misunderstandings and it could be said that Hus was burned for some beliefs he did not hold, yet this does not alter the fact that the council recognized that he had another source of authority to that of his judges, another quality of life burning in his own breast, another church to which he held allegiance and ultimately, it would seem likely, another destination. For Hus was on trial both for his belief in the Word of God and also for his own personal faith and holiness of life.

Hus's opponents, both papal and conciliar, were supremely at home with precise procedures, pettifogging committees, time-wasting subcommittees, rowdy sessions, incessant referrals back, futile sub-clauses, meaningless 'points of order', and all that goes with ecumenical electioneering and empty protocol. As we have seen, Richental loved it all. At worst the pope and the fathers of the council were only too familiar with bribery, intrigue, cruelty and lies. The contrast of Hus riding into Constance 'openly and with uncovered face', as he himself described it, and Richental's description of the ignominious secret flight of the pope, furtive and muffled, is too glaring to miss. It epitomizes the difference. Hus was a converted, holy man. Few of the council appear to have been such.

The council was right in that it recognized truth though it also hated it. Thus the first four articles brought up from Hus's writings for condemnation were on the glorious theme of predestination, or the power of divine grace. The council as a whole seemed not to understand this teaching at all in any real, personal way. Long after the council was over, when Gerson was both writing and lecturing against the Hussites, he seemed to have a particular dislike of aspects of Hus's emphasis on predestination. Likewise in matters that touched on justification by faith D'Ailly simply seemed nonplussed and out of his element. But perhaps the most revealing illustrations of the lack of conversion experience in members of the council was the furious way in which they reacted whenever Hus mentioned the name of Christ in any warm personal way. We recall one of the moving sentences of Peter: 'Hus replied: "I here publicly assert that there is no more just or effective appeal than to Christ." They laughed a great deal at that saying.'[30]

Everyone who is themselves converted makes every effort to bring others to know the Saviour. Hus was specifically called to preach. Rome hates biblical preaching. Through the pulpit in the Bethlehem Chapel Hus influenced countless multitudes. Rome desired to demolish this 'soul-trap'. God protected it and extended its influence for, wherever there is such true gospel preaching, God normally calls others to such work. Indeed Hus rejoiced in his prison that others were being raised up to follow in his steps. He went to Constance convinced that they would allow him to preach. He had to learn the hard way that Rome might tolerate ecumenical orations but she has always detested true gospel preaching and fervent gospel preachers.

But although the devil thus sought to limit his congregation, Christ, who is always victor, greatly extended it. Hus preached his last great message as the flames lapped around him.

Yet still today the ecumenical juggernaut rumbles on its way. There are those who still shelter timidly behind the decrees and commands of the council or conference or synod or assembly and tamely follow the guidelines of ecclesiastical hierarchies who have no deep, heartfelt concern for scriptural truth. There has obviously been a major shift of attitude towards the pope. In England both Established Church and Free Church leaders have had conversations with Rome. The remark of Dom Gregory Dix is so apposite in this connection. 'It is no accident that the symbol of a bishop is a crook, and the sign of an archbishop a double-cross,' he declared. The same could legitimately be said of much denominational leadership. Hus himself put his finger on it when, on the occasion of the condemnation of Pope John XXIII, he shrewdly observed that while the seller had been condemned, the buyers and the middlemen remained free. He was, of course, inferring that it was not sufficient to condemn the pope on scriptural grounds and yet remain under the leadership of an assembly of men who were opponents of biblical truth. Both must be shunned. Hus constantly appealed to his contemporaries to take a stand in this way.

*The third lesson is that Hus stood in firm and decided opposition to the tragic compromise of the erstwhile evangelical because of his deep love of the church of God.* And here we must look again at the sad figure of Stephen Páleč. Hus informs us that Páleč 'had said in the prison before the commissioners that "since the birth of Christ no heretic, except Wyclif, has written more dangerously against the church than you"'.[31] On this one writer, with reference to Páleč himself, understandably but perhaps somewhat too strongly says, 'The fact was that since the arrest of Christ there had been no such Judas.'[32]

Indeed Stephen Páleč was at one time more zealous for some points of evangelical doctrine than was Hus. He was far more radical in his criticism. But then he turned back. It must be conceded that there are some who appear in their youth fiery evangelicals. They may adopt a cause – evangelicalism. They may love (perhaps overmuch) a bout of theological fisticuffs. They may zealously stand for a position. If evangelicalism is in the ascendancy, they appear zealous. Yet when suffering is called for and a real stand for Christ is the need of the hour they fall smartly back into denominational line. Was Páleč in this category?

Or did Páleč tell himself, like so many today in such conditions, that he was going to fight for truth within the denomination, within the system? Perhaps the few feeble bleats he made when the indulgence-seller came were meant to be taken for resistance to error. They fooled nobody. The indulgence-seller was not put off. Páleč did not really salve his conscience. And Hus happened to be awkwardly at hand, to remind him that he whispered about the truth 'in corners' but said nothing in public, where the battle-lines were actually drawn.

Very soon Páleč was to be seen seeking to stifle public debate on the issue. The next stage was one of fierce opposition to the evangelical gospel and a satanic desire for its total suppression. Such was his attitude at the trial of Hus. Such is the sad story that has been repeated in many ages of the church. The neutral position cannot be held. If a man does not stand for Christ, he will soon be ranged against him. And in many ways the muffled voice of the erstwhile evangelical who had once stood for truth is even more tragic than the muffled form of an escaping pope.

The last glimpses we have of Páleč are sad in the extreme. Was he just sadly and terribly backslidden and compromised? Certainly he had not displayed the total callousness of Michael de Causis. Páleč had at least wept with Hus at the memory of a lost friendship and perhaps at the tragedy of abandoned convictions. Nevertheless any true summary of the life of Páleč must state that he was ranged against Hus with de Causis the money-grubber, and D'Ailly the theological verbal juggler. If he were a true Christian we must ask, as the prophet Jehu asked godly Jehoshaphat, with regard to his alliance with evil Ahab, 'Should you help the wicked and love those who hate the Lord?' (2 Chronicles 19:2). If he were but a sad apostate, we must reluctantly say that he was in the right company. The final judgement on this as on all else must belong to God alone.

Apart from the clear message that we must always remember to ask of a man who once stood for evangelicalism whether he still stands firm, there are further lessons to be learned from Hus's cleavage with Páleč in particular. We feel that it is proper and indeed essential at this point to stress Hus's loyalty to the local church and the bodies of believers that he knew so well. It is only in the local church that the reality of many of our beliefs can be embodied and fully understood and experienced. A man may present interesting historical papers on church issues at conferences for the whole of his life but never once seek to implement the lessons from them in the local church setting. Hus was not such a one.

That Hus had reached in his thinking the truth that the vital unity in God's plan on earth was the local church, we have earlier sought to prove. We illustrate this in three ways. Firstly, we note again his emphasis that the man in the pulpit must be one who is known locally and approved by the local people. He must not be appointed, with the passing to and fro of considerable fees, by some remote, ignorant, unwieldy body or some avaricious pontiff. Moreover, the local people, who should have the spiritual discernment to recognize a wolf, should only support the upkeep of and attend the ministry of a true shepherd. Always Hus gave the local church a positive, active role. They were not a mere rubber stamp for denominational decrees. He personally rejoiced with some fervour that in his own congregation laymen and laywomen were so active and loyal.

Yet can it be said categorically that Hus embraced the separatist position? It cannot legitimately be said that he did. For example, during his exile he wrote to a pastor in this vein: 'As for your exchange, it seems to me in all conscience that you should not pass it by. I hope that you are there a shield against the Antichrist. It is my judgement that God so ordained it: since that church was served by a pastor who was the greatest enemy of the Word of God, so God on the contrary ordains you to be a friend of the Word of God. As for the parishioners who do not wish to accept it gratefully, having all spiritual superintendence, you have for your excuse the plain statement in Ezekiel, chapter 3: read it.'[33]

Here we have the not uncommon situation where an evangelical is to be foisted, it would seem against the desire of many of the local people, on a congregation which had previously been served by a man of very different outlook. Hus was very much in favour of seizing this opportunity. Of course, it hardly needs saying to readers of this book that Hus would not expect him to be a silent evangelical, mumbling timidly in the background and quite content to be overruled by the local bishop or chairman after some token protest. Those who would be happy to quote Hus in favour of staying permanently in an unbiblical situation should go back over the pages of this book and note how incessantly and courageously he spoke out on issue after issue, firmly contending for the truth of God's Word against all comers. If this is done consistently as Hus did it, either the church will truly and substantially be reformed according to God's Word, or separation will inevitably result. The reformer's vision was of a local church active and responsible before God and free from major doctrinal error or compromise.

Secondly, the whole issue of excommunication illustrates how his earlier convictions on the vital role of the local church were reinforced by what happened. On the one hand, Rome thundered forth excommunications in a harsh, unscriptural manner, and threw out interdicts, sometimes punishing a whole community for what she saw as the fault of one man, for reasons which were quite unjustified. She also applied cruel and totally unbiblical measures, such as burning by fire, to a man whose writings she had refused to read properly and whose arguments she never once refuted by plain Scriptures.

On the other hand, men like the legates of the other two popes who had been condemned for heresy were suddenly acceptable again, not because of any genuine change of heart but merely because of ecumenical manoeuvring and church politics. It is interesting that Gerson in his pre-Constance writings was above all else interested in the question of the rank which a deposed pope should be given![34] Among such people it was human wisdom and strategy rather than humble submission to divine truth which were the order of the day. This is why there was so much chaos and evil.

At the Second Vatican Council one man spoke out forcibly about this wrongful element of coercion. He was Cardinal Beran, who as Archbishop of Prague had been imprisoned by both Nazis and Communists. He eventually died in Rome, having been released to attend the council but having been refused permission to return. He expressed himself as being opposed to all persecution and asserted that 'Everywhere, and always the violation of liberty and conscience gives birth to hypocrisy in many people.'[35] Then he went on to say this, 'So, in my country, the Catholic Church at this time seems to be suffering expiation for defects and sins committed in times gone by in her name against religious liberty, such as in the fifteenth century the burning of the priest John Hus and during the seventeenth century the forced reconversion of a great part of the Czech people to the Catholic faith . . .'[36] These were brave words. They underline the far-reaching effects of these events. But has the Roman Catholic Church ever formally acknowledged the sin of these deeds? And, even more important still, has a proper biblical discipline been instituted?

This issue is in no wise a dated one. The Roman church today, along with many among the denominational groupings, would never dream of applying discipline in the proper scriptural way as taught by our Lord in Matthew 18:15–20 and by the apostle Paul in 1 Corinthians 5. Even those who claim to be evangelical who are trapped in such denominational situations are content to study the subject as one of merely antiquarian interest. But these are Scriptures that are meant to be applied.

In this way the I.R.A. or Protestant bombers are rarely properly disciplined by publicly being put out of the church and declared to be outside the kingdom of Christ unless true repentance is shown. In this way the avowed homosexual clergyman is just shunted from one parish or pastorate to another where he is not known, or is even welcomed back with acclaim by his own people. In this way the opponent of Scripture and the heretic are often not only permitted to reside comfortably in the body of the church, but also to occupy its pulpits and share in its councils, even to teach its new generation of theological students.

Hus saw that discipline should be applied and that it could

only be carried out properly by local people who knew the situation. He had obviously seized on an essential mark of the church. The Lord Jesus Christ only mentions the word 'church' twice and on one of these occasions he gives clear teaching about local church discipline. Many of the reformers argued that there were three marks of a true church: the pure preaching of the Word, the right administration of the sacraments and the proper use of church discipline. This is not to be rejected by a casual rejoiner that excommunication is a Roman Catholic or medieval dogma and a few muttered phrases about 'bell, book and candle'. Nor is it to be lightly tossed aside by saying, 'Who are we to judge?' Christ has told the church to obey him in this way. Hus embraced this truth.

The third aspect of Hus's fervent and practical belief in the local church is evidenced in his love of countless people from all ranks of society. He was not the kind of man who moved easily among the hierarchy and nowhere else. From his early ministry among the cobblers, tailors, priests, barons and knights at Prague to his close friendship as a prisoner with the three gaolers and their wives, he was approachable, warm and ever ready to add to his circle of friends. His letters show how much friendship mattered to him. He expected laymen to stand firm for truth. Many did not disappoint him. Three of those who were most loyal to Hus were, of course, Jerome of Prague, who was himself to be burned for his faith almost exactly one year after Hus himself, and two noblemen called John of Chlum and Wenceslas of Duba. What must have delighted Hus most of all was that when he stood condemned before an almost totally hostile audience, John of Chlum, who was present, strode across the room and took him by the hand. In a letter, Hus later recalled this incident. He remembered this act of loyal kindness. 'Oh, how comforting was Lord John's stretching of his hand to me . . . a poor, rejected heretic, in bonds and cursed by almost all.'[37] The unswerving loyalty and sacrificial friendship of John of Chlum in particular cannot be praised too highly.

How much friends meant to Hus at this period of his life is summed up movingly in the following excerpt from a letter to two of the closest of them – Peter who wrote the description of his trial and John Cardinal of Rejnstejn, a faithful preacher. Hus writes, 'Oh, how consoled I have been by your letters which, along with mine, will, I hope, by the grace of God, benefit the people! As long as I am aware that you and the lords are in Constance, so long it is a consolation to me, assuming that I should already be led to death. I take it for certain that God has given you as angels to me, comforting me, weak and wretched, in greatest trial.'[38]

Having befriended Wyclif as a true brother in Christ Hus could not and would not lightly abandon him. It was because he loved Páleč so dearly that the wound caused by the other's treachery was so long in healing. Of course, Hus is still making friends. Across the centuries brother clasps the hand of brother. There is in the University of Prague an old Hussite hymn book. In it are three pictures. They beautifully illustrate what the evangelical believes about apostolic succession and also issue a challenge to the people of God today. In the first picture, John Wyclif is seen striking sparks from a stone. In the second, John Hus is depicted as kindling coals from the sparks. In the third, we see Martin Luther standing brandishing a flaming torch. There is a call of God to each reader to be among those who brandish aloft this flaming torch of gospel truth in our day.

# Notes

In order that the notes may not be too bulky a series of abbreviations have been used for books used frequently in this study. They are as follows.

*L.* John Hus, *Letters of John Hus,* translated by Matthew Spinka, Manchester University Press, 1972.

*TC.* John Hus, *De Ecclesia. The Church* (Translated with notes and introduction by David S. Schaff), Greenwood Press, Westport, Connecticut. 1974.

*AR.* Matthew Spinka (ed.), *Advocates of Reform,* Library of Christian Classics, S.C.M., London, 1953, Vol. XIV. ('On Simony' by Hus is on pp. 196–278, but there are other writings by contemporaries included in this work.)

*P.* Matthew Spinka, trans., *John Hus at the Council of Constance,* Columbia University Press, 1965. 'Peter of Mladoňovice: An Account of the Trial and Condemnation of Master John Hus in Constance' is on pp. 89–234, but the book includes other relevant documents.

*Lo.* John Hine Mundy and Kennerly P. Woody eds, *The Council of Constance – The Unification of the Church,* translated by Louise Ropes Loomis, Columbia University Press, New York & London, 1961.

*B.* R. R. Betts, *Essays in Czech History,* The Athlone Press, London. 1969.

*G.* E. H. Gillett, *The Life and Times of John Hus,* Boston, 1863. Reprinted AMS Press, New York, 1978. (2 vols indicated as i and ii)

*Lz.* Count Lützow, *The Life and Times of Master John Hus,* J. M. Dent, London. 1909.

*S.* Matthew Spinka, *John Hus – A Biography,* Princeton University Press, 1968.

*JHCC.* Matthew Spinka, *John Hus's Concept of the Church,* Princeton University Press, 1966.

*JHCR.* Matthew Spinka, *John Hus and the Czech Reform,* The University of Chicago Press, 1941.

*W.* H. B. Workman, *The Dawn of the Reformation,* Charles Kelly, London, 1901.
Vol. i, *The Age of Wyclif,* Vol. ii, *The Age of Hus.*

*WL.* *The Letters of John Hus,* translated by H. B. Workman and R. M. Pope, London, 1904.

For other books, full details will be given of each book the first time it is mentioned. After this unless it is otherwise stated it will be referred to by the author's name, or a shortened version of the title.
q. = quoted in.

## Introduction

1. See Ernest Roth, *A Tale of Three Cities,* Cassells, London, 1971, p. 95.
2. Introduction to Act IV of *Winter's Tale.*
3. q. Count Lützow, *The Story of Prague,* J. M. Dent, London, 1907, p. xv. (Henceforth referred to as *The Story of Prague*).
4. Friedrich Heer, *The Holy Roman Empire* (translated by Janet Sondheimer) Weidenfeld and Nicholson, London, 1968, p. 113.
5. See Norman J. G. Pounds, *Eastern Europe,* Longmans, London, 1969, p. 400.
6. *L.*, p. 209.
7. q. Geoffrey Moorhouse, *Prague,* Time-Life Books, Amsterdam, 1980, p. 11.
8. q. *TC.*, p. xviii.
9. Geoffrey Barraclough, *The Medieval Papacy,* Thames and Hudson, London, 1968, p. 167.
10. John Burke, *Czechoslovakia,* B. T. Batsford, London, 1976, p. 49.
11. František Bartoš, *Bedřich Smetana, Letters and Reminiscences* (translated from the Czech by Daphne Rusbridge) Artia-Prague, 1955, p. 265. For other comments on the music see John Clapham, *Smetana,* J. M. Dent, London, 1972.
12. q. Burke, pp. 45–6.

## Chapter 1

1. *L.*, p. 171.
2. q. *B.*, pp. 196–7.
3. q. Joseph Macek, *The Hussite Movement in Bohemia,* Orbis-Prague, 1958, p. 17. (Henceforth referred to as *Hussite Movement*).
4. John Martin Klassen, *The Nobility and the Making of the Hussite Revolution,* Columbia University Press, New York, 1978, p. 11. See also pp. 8–10.
5. q. *JHCC.*, p. 322. See also *AR.*, p. 225.
6. q. *Hussite Movement,* p. 15.
7. *AR.*, pp. 235–6.
8. *L.*, p. 9.
9. *L.*, p. 8.
10. *L.*, p. 11.
11. q. *JHCC.*, p. 61. See also *AR.*, pp. 225, 230 and 244.
12. *AR.*, p. 197.
13. *AR.*, p. 219.
14. q. *JHCC.*, p. 305 (note 53).
15. q. *B.*, p. 56 (note 15).
16. *AR.*, p. 217.
17. *AR.*, p. 238.
18. *AR.*, p. 247.
19. *AR.*, p. 230. See also Joseph Macek, *Jean Hus et Les Traditions Hussites,* Librairie Plon, 1973, p. 66. (Henceforth referred to as *Les Traditions*).

20. q. *JHCC.*, p. 294.
21. *L.*, p. 4.
22. q. *W.* ii, p. 96.
23. Jean Gimpel, *The Medieval Machine,* Futura Publications Ltd, London, 1979, p. 97.
24. *AR.*, p. 226.
25. See Ruth Hurst Vose, *The Connoisseur Illustrated Guides: Glass,* The Connoisseur, London, 1975, pp. 10, 26 and 58.
26. Burke, p. 82.
27. q. Count Lützow, *Bohemia. An Historical Sketch,* revised and extended by H. A. Piehlder, J. M. Dent, London, 1939, p. 76.
28. q. *Lz.*, p. 65.

## Chapter 2

1. q. *S.*, p. 22.
2. *AR.*, pp. 255–6.
3. *AR.*, p. 256.
4. As above.
5. *AR.*, p. 250.
6. q. Paul Roubiszek and Joseph Kalmer, *Warrior of God,* London, 1947, p. 23.
7. q. Morris Bishop, *The Horizon Book of the Middle Ages,* Cassell, London, 1969, p. 265.
8. q. *The Story of Prague,* p. 15.
9. q. Brian Knox, *Bohemia and Moravia – An Architectural Companion,* Faber and Faber, London, 1962, p. 21, and Heer p. 115.
10. Moorhouse, p. 82.
11. q. Emanuel Poche, *Portrait of Prague,* Hamlyn Books, London, p. 9.
12. See Jan Herben, *Hus and his Followers,* Bles, London, 1926, p. 18.
13. q. Heer, p. 114.
14. q. *Czechoslovakia. Travel Guide,* Nagels Publishers, Geneva, 1966, p. 42.
15. Anthony Rhodes, *Art Treasures of Eastern Europe,* Weidenfeld and Nicholson, London, 1972, p. 73.
16. Knox, p. 22.
17. William Wordsworth, *Poetical Works,* Oxford University Press, 1956, p. 214.
18. See Cedric Jagger, *The World's Great Clocks and Watches,* Hamlyn, London, 1977, p. 67, and E. H. Gombrich, *The Story of Art,* Phaidon, London, 1967, pp. 155–7.
19. q. *The Story of Prague,* p. 17.
20. q. *Lz.*, p. 68.
21. q. Count Lützow, *Lectures on the Historians of Bohemia,* Henry Frowde, London, 1905, p. 24.
22. q. *G.*, i, pp. 51–2.
23. q. D. S. Schaff, *John Huss,* London, 1915, p. 82.
24. *L.*, p. 55.

25. q. *W.*, ii, pp. 100–1.
26. q. *B.*, p. 22.
27. J. F. N. Bradley, *Czechoslovakia – A Short History*, University Press, Edinburgh, 1971, p. 38. See also S. S. Laurie, *The Rise and Early Constitution of Universities*, Kegan, Paul, Trench and Co., London, 1886, pp. 255–263.
28. Hastings Rashdall, *The Universities of Europe in the Middle Ages*, ed. F. M. Powicke and A. B. Emden, Oxford, 1936, vol. II, p. 223.
29. Marjorie Rowling, *Everyday Life in Medieval Times*, Carousel Book, London, 1973, p. 184.

## Chapter 3

1. See Barbara W. Tuchman, *A Distant Mirror – The Calamitous 14th Century*, MacMillan, London, 1979, p. 482, and E. Denis, *Huss et La Guerre des Hussites*, Paris, 1878, p. 55.
2. q. Bishop, p. 376.
3. q. Klassen, p. 53.
4. q. *B.*, p. 26.
5. M. D. Lambert, *Medieval Heresy – Popular Movements from Bogomil to Hus*, Edward Arnold, 1977, p. 283.
6. q. *B.*, p. 6.
7. q. Rhodes, p. 75.
8. John Hale, Roger Highfield and Beryl Smalley (eds) *Europe in the Late Middle Ages*, Faber and Faber, London, 1965, p. 424. See also Klassen, pp. 21–3.
9. q. *Lz.*, p. 69 (note 2).
10. R. W. Seton-Watson (ed.) *Prague Essays*, Oxford, 1949, p. 24.
11. q. *S.*, p. 28.
12. q. *Les Traditions*, p. 76.
13. Knox, p. 41.
14. See article on Bohemia in the *Larousse Encyclopedia of Music*, Geoffrey Hindley, ed., Hamlyn, London, 1947, and William Anderson, *Castles of Europe from Charlemagne to the Renaissance*, Elek, London, 1970, p. 251.
15. q. Heer, p. 114.
16. q. *B.*, p.117.
17. q. *S.*, p. 199.
18. q. *S.*, p. 50.
19. q. *G.*, i, p. 73.
20. q. *Lz.*, p. 53.
21. q. *B.*, p. 122. See also *JHCC.*, p. 15.
22. q. *B.*, p. 114.
23. q. *B.*, pp. 71, 99 and 73.
24. q. *G.*, i, p. 32. See also *B.*, pp. 33–4.

## Chapter 4

1. q. *S.*, p. 29.

2. q. *The Story of Prague*, p. 67.
3. q. *S.*, p. 38.
4. q. Schaff, p. 110.
5. *S.*, p. 31.
6. q. *JHCR.*, p. 23.
7. q. Emile de Bonnechose, *Reformers Before the Reformation* (trans. Campbell Mackenzie), Reprinted AMS Press, New York 1980, p. 29.
8. q. *G.*, i, p. 48.
9. *L.*, p. 121.
10. See Bishop, p. 203. See also G. C. Coulton, *Chaucer and his England*, Methuen and Co. Ltd, London, 1930, p. 274. (Henceforth referred to as *Chaucer*).
11. q. *S.*, p. 45.
12. *AR.*, p. 255.
13. H. J. R. Murray, *A Short History of Chess*, Oxford, 1963, p. 32.
14. As above, p. 31.
15. *AR.*, p. 239.
16. *AR.*, p. 238.
17. *AR.*, p. 250.
18. *AR.*, p. 247.
19. *L.*, p. 121. See also *S.*, p. 44.
20. *L.*, p. 121.
21. J. Huizinga, *The Waning of the Middle Ages*, Penguin Books, London, 1955, p. 251. See also pp. 271–2.
22. *AR.*, p. 262.
23. As above.
24. q. *S.*, p. 45.
25. *AR.*, p. 263.
26. *AR.*, p. 248.
27. *AR.*, p. 247.
28. *AR.*, p. 262.
29. *AR.*, p. 277.

## Chapter 5

1. q. *W.*, ii, p. 120.
2. q. Lambert, p. 284.
3. q. *Hussite Movement*, p. 21.
4. q. *S.*, p. 76.
5. q. *S.*, pp. 76–7.
6. q. *Lz.*, p. 77.
7. q. *Lz.*, p. 295.
8. q. *JHCC.*, p. 10. See also pp. 9 and 41.
9. *JHCR.*, p. 7.
10. *L.*, p. 46.
11. *L.*, p. 119.
12. q. *S.*, p. 52.
13. *TC.*, p. 273.

14. q. *JHCR*., p. 7.
15. q. Schaff, p. 61.
16. q. *JHCC*., p. 45.
17. q. *JHCC*., pp. 48–9.
18. *L*., p. 128.
19. q. *WL*., pp. 86–7.
20. As above.

## Chapter 6

1. G. W. H. Parker, *The Morning Star*, Paternoster Press, 1965, p. 55.
2. q. *Lz*., p. 18 (note 2).
3. q. David Fountain in an article in *The Manifold Grace of God*, Puritan and Reformed Conference Report for 1968, p. 42. See also *AR*., p. 48. For the contrary view see, for example, G. Lechler, *John Wycliffe and his English Precursors* (trans. by Lorimer and Green) Religious Tract Society, London, 1904, pp. 302–4.
4. q. Parker, p. 37.
5. q. Margaret Aston, *The Fifteenth Century – The prospect for Europe*, Thames and Hudson, London, 1968, p. 128.
6. q. *JHCC*., p. 22.
7. Tuchman, p. 339.
8. *AR*., p. 49.
9. q. G. M. Trevelyan, *England in the Age of Wycliffe*, Longman, 1899 (Reprinted 1972), p. 176.
10. q. *G*., i, p. 61.
11. V. H. H. Green, *Medieval Civilisation in Western Europe*, Arnold, London, 1971, p. 101.
12. q. Lechler, p. 411.
13. q. Lechler, p. 412.
14. q. *B*., p. 198.
15. q. *Lz*., p. 80.
16. q. *W*., ii, p. 124.
17. q. *Lz*., p. 80.
18. q. *S*., p. 64.
19. *L*., p. 4.
20. As above.
21. *L*., p. 5.
22. *L*., pp. 6 and 7.
23. *AR*., p. 235.
24. *AR*., pp. 244–5.
25. *AR*., p. 243.
26. *AR*., p. 244.

## Chapter 7

1. *L*., p. 22.
2. Bishop, p. 131.

3. Marzieh Gail, *The Three Popes,* Robert Hale and Company, London, 1972, p. 187. See also p. 83.
4. q. *Lz.*, p. 83.
5. q. *G.*, i, p. 88.
6. q. *JHCC.*, pp. 59–60.
7. q. *S.*, p. 69.
8. q. *W.*, ii, p. 131.
9. *L.*, p. 12.
10. q. *JHCC.*, p. 57.
11. q. *JHCC.*, p. 59.
12. q. *Lz.*, p. 297 (note 1).
13. q. *S.*, p. 138.
14. q. *JHCC.*, p. 148.
15. q. *Lz.*, p. 301.
16. q. *JHCC.*, p. 327.
17. *AR.*, p. 219.
18. q. *G.*, i, p. 287.
19. q. Roubiszek, p. 72.
20. As above.
21. q. *S.*, p. 204.
22. q. *S.*, p. 213.

## Chapter 8

1. q. preface in Schaff.
2. Aston, pp. 56–7.
3. Herben, pp. 209–10.
4. *L.*, p. 2.
5. *L.*, p. 3.
6. *L.*, p. 2.
7. *L.*, p. 7.
8. *L.*, pp. 8 and 10.
9. q. *Lz.*, p. 89.
10. *L.*, p. 13.
11. R. A. Knox, *Enthusiasm,* Oxford, 1950, p. 488. (Henceforth referred to as *Enthusiasm*).
12. q. Klassen, p. 23.
13. *L.*, p. 15.
14. *L.*, p. 16.
15. As above.
16. *L.*, p. 17.
17. Dorothy L. Sayers, *Unpopular Opinions,* London, 1946, p. 11.
18. *L.*, p. 18.
19. *L.*, p. 19.
20. Lambert, p. 272. See Klassen pp. 11 and 77.
21. *Coriolanus,* Act III, scene i, line 66.
22. *AR.*, pp. 231–2.
23. q. Stephen E. Ozment (ed.) *The Reformation in Medieval Perspective,* Chicago, 1971, p. 102 (note 3).

24. *L.*, p. 20.
25. q. G. C. Coulton, *From St Francis to Dante*, London, 1907, p. 97. (Henceforth referred to as *St Francis*).
26. Chaucer, *Canterbury Tales* (trans. Nevill Coghill), Penguin Classics, 1952, p. 302; (Henceforth referred to as 'Coghill').
27. Rowling, p. 85.
28. *L.*, pp. 128–9. See also pp. 120 and 170.
29. *AR.*, p. 257.
30. *L.*, p. 20.
31. *L.*, p. 21.
32. q. Schaff, p. 310.
33. q. *B.*, pp. 58–9.
34. q. *B.*, p. 81 (note 37).
35. Moorhouse, p. 83.

## Chapter 9

1. q. Schaff, p. 62.
2. q. S., p. 44.
3. See *Les Traditions*, p. 61. See also Paul de Vooght, *L'Hérésie de Jean Huss*, Louvain, 1960, pp. 477, 193 and 468–9.
4. Coghill, pp. 30–2 and 43–5.
5. q. Trevelyan, p. 106.
6. q. M. Creighton, *A History of the Papacy*, Longmans, London, 1882, Vol. i, pp. 262 and 263.
7. *AR.*, p. 213.
8. *AR.*, p. 238.
9. *AR.*, p. 207.
10. *L.*, p. 30.
11. Creighton, p. 308.
12. *Lz.*, p. 116.
13. *AR.*, p. 251.
14. See *AR.*, p. 253, *TC.*, pp. 280–2 and Huizinga, p. 162.
15. q. *JHCC.*, p. 37.
16. q. *Lz.*, p. 85.
17. See *Lz.*, p. 100.
18. *L.*, p. 22.
19. *L.*, p. 23.
20. *L.*, pp. 24 and 28.
21. *L.*, p. 29.
22. *L.*, p. 30.
23. *L.*, pp. 30 and 31.
24. *L.*, p. 34.

## Chapter 10

1. Herbert J. C. Grierson (ed.), *Metaphysical Lyrics and Poems of the Seventeenth Century*, Oxford University Press, 1952, p. 88.

2. See Green, pp. 108–9, *G.*, i, pp. 19–20 and ii, p. 86 and Loraine Boettner, *Roman Catholicism,* Banner of Truth, London, 1966, pp. 209, 243–6, 310–12 and 352.
3. Green, pp. 132–3.
4. As above, p. 135.
5. q. Gail, pp. 33, 36 and 38. See also Walter Ullmann, *The Origins of the Great Schism,* London, 1948 and G. Mollat, *The Popes of Avignon,* Edinburgh, 1963.
6. q. Gail, p. 71. See Tuchman, p. 331.
7. q. Gail, pp. 77 and 80.
8. q. *W.*, i, pp. 172 and 173.
9. q. G. J. Jordan, *The Inner History of the Great Schism of the West. A Problem in Church Unity,* Burt Franklin, New York, 1972, p. 31.
10. q. Gail, p. 102. See also Huizinga, p. 30.
11. Tuchman, p. 335.
12. q. Gail, p. 228.
13. q. *W.*, i, p. 175.
14. *TC.*, p. 181.
15. q. *JHCC.*, p. 61.
16. q. *G.*, i, pp. 98–9.
17. q. *G.*, ii, p. 276.
18. q. *S.*, pp. 86–7.
19. q. *W.*, ii, p. 137. See also *Lz.*, pp. 114–15.
20. *L.*, p. 36. See also *TC.*, pp. 155–6.
21. q. *B.*, pp. 203 and 204.
22. q. *B.*, pp. 22–3.
23. q. *B.*, p. 207.
24. q. *Les Traditions,* p. 60.
25. q. *B.*, p. 205.
26. *P.*, p. 177.

## Chapter 11

1. q. *B.*, p. 27.
2. q. *Lz.*, p. 106.
3. q. *W.*, ii, p. 128.
4. q. *Lz.*, p. 107.
5. q. *S.*, p. 102.
6. q. *S.*, p. 107.
7. q. *JHCC.*, p. 95.
8. q. *JHCC.*, p. 96.
9. q. *W.*, ii, p. 141.
10. q. *W.*, ii, pp. 141–2.
11. q. *G.*, i, p. 161.
12. q. *B.*, p. 109.
13. q. *Lz.*, p. 126.
14. q. *Lz.*, p. 128.
15. q. *Lz.*, p. 130.

16. q. *B.*, p. 214.
17. *L.*, p. 38.
18. *L.*, p. 39.
19. *L.*, p. 40.
20. *L.*, p. 41.
21. *L.*, pp. 41–2.
22. q. Bonnechose, p. 33.
23. *Hussite Movement*, pp. 16–17.
24. q. *Lo.*, p. 11.
25. *Lz.*, p. 97.

## Chapter 12

1. *L.*, p. 45.
2. q. *S.*, pp. 115–6. See also Klassen, p. 87.
3. *P.*, pp. 242–3.
4. q. *JHCC.*, pp. 107–8.
5. *L.*, p. 215.
6. *L.*, p. 46.
7. *L.*, pp. 46 and 47.
8. *L.*, p. 48.
9. *L.*, p. 43.
10. *L.*, p. 49.
11. *L.*, p. 52.
12. *L.*, p. 60.
13. *L.*, pp. 61–2.
14. *L.*, p. 62. See also *Les Traditions,* pp. 64–5.
15. *L.*, p. 61.
16. As above.
17. *L.*, p. 63.
18. As above. See *AR.*, pp. 198 and 199.
19. q. *B.*, p. 77.
20. As above.
21. *L.*, p. 56.
22. *L.*, p. 57.
23. *L.*, pp. 57 and 58.
24. *L.*, p. 58.
25. *L.*, p. 39.

## Chapter 13

1. Moorhouse, pp. 116–17. See also Poch, plate 66.
2. q. Gail, p. 205.
3. R. W. Southern, *Western Society and the Church in the Middle Ages*, Penguin Books, 1972, p. 138.
4. As above, pp. 138–9.
5. q. *Lz.*, p. 151.
6. q. *S.*, p. 135.
7. q. *JHCC.*, p. 113.

8. q. Bonnechose, p. 38.
9. As above.
10. q. *W.*, ii, p. 163.
11. q. Bonnechose, p. 40.
12. q. *JHCC.*, p. 111.
13. q. *G.*, i, p. 293.
14. *TC.*, p. 166.
15. q. *S.*, p. 140.

## Chapter 14

1. Lambert, p. 292.
2. q. *B.*, p. 215.
3. q. Bonnechose, p. 37.
4. q. *B.*, p. 216.
5. q. *B.*, p. 218.
6. q. *G.*, ii, p. 236. See also *Lo*, p. 135.
7. q. *Lz.*, pp. 156–7.
8. q. *Lz.*, p. 157.
9. *P.*, p. 219.
10. *TC.*, pp. 253–4.
11. *TC.*, p. 254.
12. *AR.*, pp. 206–8.
13. q. *B.*, p. 218.
14. q. *JHCC.*, p. 117.
15. q. Green, p. 115.
16. q. *JHCC,* pp. 114 and 306.
17. *P.*, p. 238.
18. *P.*, p. 240.
19. *P.*, p. 244.
20. *P.*, p. 245.
21. *L.*, p. 75.
22. *L.*, pp. 75–6.
23. *L.*, p. 104.
24. *L.*, p. 93.

## Chapter 15

1. Liam Nolan with J. Bernard Hutton, *The Pain and the Glory – the Life of Smetana,* Harrop and Co., London, 1968, p. 284.
2. See *JHCC.*, pp. 181 and 250.
3. q. *JHCC.*, p. 142.
4. q. *JHCC.*, p. 143.
5. As above.
6. q. *JHCC.*, p. 85.
7. q. *JHCC.*, p. 161.
8. q. *JHCC.*, pp. 191, 234 and 227, and *B.*, p. 56 (note 15). See also *JHCC.*, pp. 219 and 226.
9. *L.*, p. 102.

10. *L.*, p. 103. See also p. 99.
11. *L.*, p. 102.
12. q. *G.*, i, p. 227.
13. q. *JHCC.*, p. 242.
14. q. *JHCC.*, p. 239. See also p. 230.
15. q. *JHCC.*, p. 206.
16. q. *S.*, pp. 189–90.
17. See *L.*, pp. 15–16 and 79–80.
18. *L.*, p. 115.
19. See *AR.*, p. 197.
20. *AR.*, p. 249.
21. *TC.*, p. 72. See also pp. 104–5 and 132.
22. *L.*, p. 71.
23. *L.*, p. 73. See also pp. 82–3.
24. *L.*, pp. 97 and 99.
25. *L.*, p. 102.
26. q. Leonard Verduin, *The Reformers and their Stepchildren*, Paternoster, London, 1966, p. 168.
27. As above, p. 152.
28. See *G.*, i, pp. 11–12.
29. Philip Hughes, *A Popular History of the Reformation*, Hollis and Carter, London, 1956, p. 35. See also pp. 32–4 and 238–41.
30. *Chaucer*, pp. 99–101.
31. q. Boettner, p. 131.
32. q. *G.*, i, p. 159.
33. q. *St Francis*, p. 261.
34. Rowling, p. 77.
35. Coghill, pp. 330–1.
36. See *S.*, p. 202 (note 26) and Coghill, p. 38.
37. Green, p. 103. See also Trevelyan, p. 131.

## Chapter 16

1. *L.*, pp. 23 and 84.
2. *AR.*, pp. 216–7 and 221–2.
3. *TC.*, p. 55.
4. *L.*, p. 104. See also pp. 73–4 and 90–2.
5. *G.*, i, pp. 77–8.
6. Gordon H. Leff, *Wyclif and Hus: a doctrinal comparison.* Reprint from the Bulletin of John Rylands Library, Spring 1968, Vol. 50, no 2, p. 403.
7. Green, p. 171.
8. Aston, p. 127.
9. Schaff, p. 272.
10. q. Fountain, p. 38.
11. *L.*, p. 208.
12. *L.*, p. 84.
13. q. *S.*, p. 179.
14. *P.*, p. 246.

15. *L.*, p. 77.
16. *L.*, p. 108.
17. *L.*, p. 106.
18. *L.*, p. 83.
19. *WL.*, pp. 86–7.
20. *L.*, p. 112.
21. *L.*, p. 122.
22. *L.*, p. 72.
23. *L.*, p. 66.
24. *P.*, p. 237.
25. *L.*, p. 123. See also pp. 80 and 109.
26. *TC.*, p. 120.
27. q. Schaff, p. 309.

## Chapter 17

1. *AR.*, p. 205.
2. *JHCR.*, p. 75.
3. q. Gimpel, p. 141.
4. *L.*, p. 67.
5. q. *G.*, i, p. 288.
6. q. *S.*, p. 145. See *TC.*, pp. 11–12.
7. q. *JHCC.*, p. 325. See also pp. 385–8.
8. *TC.*, p. 83.
9. See *L.*, pp. 61 and 98.
10. *L.*, p. 100.
11. *L.*, p. 82.
12. q. *G.*, i, p. 276.
13. q. Bonnechose, p. 46.
14. *L.*, p. 41. See also pp. 96–9 and *TC.*, p. 87.
15. q. *S.*, p. 140.
16. See *P.*, p. 183–201. See also *AR.*, pp. 211–4 and 217–8.
17. *TC.*, p. 73.
18. *TC.*, p. 75.
19. *L.*, p. 96. See also pp. 88–9, and *TC.*, pp. 126–9 and 294–5.
20. q. *JHCC.*, p. 240.
21. *TC.*, p. 295.
22. *AR.*, p. 215.
23. *TC.*, p. 206.
24. *TC.*, pp. 206–7.
25. *TC.*, p. 2.
26. *TC.*, p. 139.
27. *TC.*, p. 63.
28. See *TC.*, pp. 248–50.
29. *TC.*, p. 158. See also p. 156.
30. *AR.*, p. 270.
31. *TC.*, p. 220.
32. *TC.*, pp. 16 and 45.
33. *TC.*, pp. 84–7.

34. *TC.*, p. 68.
35. *TC.*, pp. 68–9.
36. *AR.*, p. 247.
37. *AR.*, p. 240. See also pp. 217 and *TC.*, p. 124.
38. *TC.*, p. 4.
39. *TC.*, p. 41.
40. *TC.*, p. 59.

## Chapter 18

1. *AR.*, p. 222.
2. q. *W.*, ii, p. 134 (note 1).
3. *JHCR.*, p. 71.
4. *L.*, p. 199.
5. *P.*, p. 234.
6. *P.*, p. 89.
7. *P.*, p. 91.
8. *L.*, p. 119.
9. *L.*, p. 123.
10. *L.*, p. 169.
11. q. *G.*, i, p. 313.
12. q. Bonnechose, p. 44.
13. *P.*, p. 179 and 106.
14. *P.*, p. 94.
15. *L.*, p. 125.
16. See *AR.*, pp. 264–6 and *TC.*, pp. 210 and 238–40.
17. q. *G.*, i, pp. 267–8.
18. q. *JHCR*, p. 74.
19. *L.*, p. 126.
20. q. Rowling, pp. 117 and 118.
21. C. M. D. Crowder, *Unity, Heresy and Reform, 1378–1460. Documents of Medieval History 3*, Arnold, London, 1977, p. 130.
22. *L.*, p. 126.
23. As above.
24. *L.*, p. 132.
25. *P.*, p. 104.
26. q. *Hussite Movement*, p. 135.

## Chapter 19

1. q. *G.*, i, p. 538.
2. q. *W.*, ii, p. 79.
3. Edward Gibbon, *Decline and Fall of the Roman Empire* (with notes by the Rev. H. H. Milman), John Murray, London, 1888, Vol. xii, p. 363.
4. *Lo.*, p. 88.
5. q. *W.*, ii, p. 85.
6. *Lo.*, p. 90.
7. Martin Scott, *Medieval Europe*, Longmans, 1964, p. 389.

8. q. Eustace J. Kitts, *Pope John Twenty-Third & Master John Hus of Bohemia*, Constable, London, 1910, p. 85.
9. q. *W.*, ii, p. 206.
10. As above.
11. q. Gail, p. 216.
12. As above.
13. See Kitts, p. 86.
14. *Lo.*, p. 476.
15. Green, pp. 2–3.
16. *Lo.*, pp. 189–90. See also J. H. Wylie, *The Council of Constance to the death of John Hus*, Longmans, Green & Co, London, 1900, pp. 26–28.
17. *Lo.*, p. 190. See also Kitts, pp. 241–2.
18. Wylie, pp. 59–60.
19. See *Fodor's Germany West and East*, ed. by Eugene Fodor, Hodder and Stoughton, London, 1974, p. 281.
20. *Lz.*, p. 212.
21. *Lo.*, pp. 99 and 100.
22. *Lo.*, p. 103.
23. *L.*, p. 130.
24. *Lo.*, p. 98. See also p. 157.
25. *Lo.*, p. 113.
26. *Lo.*, p. 135.
27. As above.
28. q. Kitts, pp. 250–1.
29. *Lo.*, p. 110.
30. *Lo.*, p. 137.
31. *Lo.*, p. 147.
32. *L.*, p. 205.
33. *L.*, p. 196.
34. q. *St Francis*, p. 282.

## Chapter 20

1. *P.*, p. 100.
2. *P.*, p. 130.
3. *P.*, p. 101.
4. *L.*, p. 132.
5. As above.
6. *Lo.*, p. 204.
7. q. *W.*, ii, pp. 298–9.
8. *P.*, p. 113.
9. *P.*, p. 114.
10. *P.*, p. 115.
11. *Lo.*, p. 469.
12. *P.*, p. 116.
13. *L.*, p. 135.
14. *P.*, p. 119.
15. *L.*, p. 135.

16. *L.*, p. 136.
17. *P.*, p. 120.
18. *L.*, p. 138.
19. *L.*, p. 142.
20. *L.*, p. 143.
21. *L.*, p. 139.
22. *L.*, p. 156.
23. *L.*, pp. 151, 152 and 160. See also pp. 159 and 192. See also *W.*, ii, p. 275.
24. q. *W.*, ii, p. 296.
25. *L.*, p. 147.
26. *L.*, p. 149. See also p. 162.
27. *L.*, p. 150. See also p. 221.
28. *L.*, p. 140.
29. *L.*, p. 181. See also p. 179.
30. *L.*, p. 153.
31. *L.*, p. 154.
32. q. *G.*, i, p. 355.
33. q. Kitts, p. 294.
34. *P.*, pp. 120–1.
35. *Lo*, p. 117.
36. *L.*, p. 155.
37. *P.*, p. 121.
38. q. *W.*, ii, p. 206.
39. See John Milton, *Paradise Lost*, Book II, lines 110–2.

## Chapter 21

1. *L.*, p. 157.
2. q. *G.*, i, p. 391.
3. Crowder, p. 130.
4. *Lo.*, p. 118.
5. q. Bonnechose, p. 77.
6. *Lo.*, p. 208.
7. q. *G.*, i, p. 444.
8. q. *Lo.*, p. 29.
9. *P.*, pp. 124–5.
10. *P.*, p. 138.
11. *P.*, p. 141.
12. Parker, p. 91.
13. q. Maurice Keen, *The Pelican History of Medieval Europe*, Pelican Books, 1971, p. 287.
14. *W.*, ii, p. 210.
15. q. *G.*, i, p. 253.
16. q. *G.*, i, p. 366.
17. *AR.*, p. 168. See also E. F. Jacobs, *Essays in the Conciliar Epoch*, University of Notre Dame Press, 1963, pp. 24–43.
18. See *G.*, i, p. 400.
19. q. Gail, p. 233.

20. *AR.*, p. 160.
21. See Crowder, pp. 76–81.
22. q. *G.*, i, p. 365.
23. Crowder, p. 83.
24. q. Bonnechose, p. 77.
25. *L.*, pp. 177–8. See also pp. 190–1.
26. *L.*, p. 196.
27. *L.*, p. 190.
28. *L.*, p. 153. See also p. 148.
29. *AR.*, p. 146.
30. q. Ullmann, p. 182.
31. See Tuchman, p. 480.
32. See Crowder, p. 52 and *AR.*, p. 165.
33. See *TC.*, pp. 248–50.

## Chapter 22

1. *P.*, p. 164.
2. As above.
3. *P.*, p. 165.
4. *Lo.*, p. 205.
5. *P.*, pp. 205, 217 and 216.
6. *P.*, p. 166.
7. *L.*, p. 210.
8. *P.*, p. 167.
9. *L.*, p. 161.
10. *P.*, p. 171.
11. q. Schaff, p. 272.
12. *P.*, p. 175.
13. *P.*, p. 177.
14. *P.*, p. 179.
15. *Lo.*, p. 124.
16. *P.*, p. 180.
17. *P.*, p. 193.
18. *P.*, p. 194.
19. *P.*, p. 199.
20. *P.*, p. 202.
21. As above.
22. As above.
23. *P.*, p. 203.
24. *P.*, p. 206.
25. As above.
26. *P.*, p. 212.
27. *P.*, p. 214.
28. *P.*, p. 218.
29. *P.*, p. 221.
30. *P.*, p. 222.
31. As above.

## Chapter 23

1. q. *Lz.*, p. 375.
2. *L.*, pp. 173–4.
3. *L.*, pp. 176–7.
4. *L.*, p. 195.
5. *L.*, p. 211.
6. *L.*, p. 200.
7. *L.*, p. 161.
8. q. *Lz.*, p. 376.
9. *L.*, p. 162.
10. *L.*, p. 184.
11. *L.*, p. 180.
12. *L.*, p. 208.
13. *L.*, p. 205.
14. *L.*, p. 102.
15. *P.*, p. 224.
16. As above.
17. *L.*, p. 198.
18. *L.*, pp. 145–6.
19. *L.*, p. 178.
20. *L.*, p. 187
21. q. *G.*, ii, p. 48.
22. q. Bonnechose, p. 102.
23. *P.*, pp. 226–7.
24. *P.*, p. 228.
25. *P.*, p. 229.
26. As above.
27. As above.
28. *P.*, p. 230.
29. As above.
30. *P.*, p. 233.
31. As above.
32. q. *G.*, i, p. 548.
33. q. *G.*, ii, pp. 73–4.
34. *Lo.*, p. 133.
35. *Lo.*, p. 256.
36. *Lo.*, p. 499.
37. *P.*, pp. 233–4.
38. *P.*, p. 234.
39. *P.*, p. 234 (note 28).
40. *P.*, p. 234.

## Appendix 1

1. *Hussite Movement*, p. 93.
2. As above, p. 105.
3. *B.*, p. 88.
4. *B.*, pp. 91 and 93. See also pp. 180–1.

5. q. R. W. Seton-Watson, *History of the Czechs and Slovaks*, Hutchinson and Co, London, 1943, p. 52 (note 2).
6. Schaff, p. 263.
7. De Vooght, p. 478. See also pp. 61–2, 194, 460, 477 and 480–1.
8. As above, p. 468. See also p. 479.
9. Heer, p. 119.
10. Scott, p. 384.
11. q. Klassen, p. 68.
12. Article by David Boorman on 'Reformers before the Reformation' in *Adding to the Church* (Published by the Westminster Conference) pp. 96–7.
13. S. M. Houghton, *Sketches from Church History*, Banner of Truth, 1980, p. 69.
14. See Parker.
15. q. Schaff, p. 292.
16. q. *G.*, i, pp. 81–2.
17. As above.
18. Hans J. Hillerbrand (ed.), *The Reformation. A Narrative History related by contemporary observers and participants*, Baker, Michigan, 1978, p. 67.
19. As above, p. 68.
20. q. Roland H. Bainton, *Here I Stand. A Life of Martin Luther*, Mentor Book, New York, 1959, p. 90.
21. As above, p. 143.
22. As above, pp. 136 and 138.
23. John Dillenberger (ed.), *Martin Luther. Selections from his writings*, Anchor Books, New York, 1961, p. 266.
24. As above, p. 466.
25. As above, p. 468.
26. As above, p. 466.
27. q. Bainton, p. 128.
28. q. Schaff, p. 304.
29. q. E. H. Broadbent, *The Pilgrim Church*, Pickering and Inglis, London, 1963, p. 132.
30. *Luther's Letters of Spiritual Counsel*, ed. and trans. by Theodore G. Tappert, S.C.M. London, p. 146.
31. q. Schaff, p. 295.
32. q. Philip S. Watson, *Let God be God. An interpretation of the theology of Martin Luther*, Epworth, London, 1960, p. 29, note 20.
33. q. Gordon Rupp, *The Righteousness of God. Luther Studies*, Hodder and Stoughton, London, 1953, p. 3.
34. q. *TC.*, p. xxxvi.
35. *Enthusiasm*, p. 394.
36. q. *WL.*, p. 75.
37. See Parker, p. 71.

38. See, for example, *Works of Sibbes,* Vol. i, Banner of Truth, London, 1973, pp. 115–16; Vera Brittain, *In the Steps of John Bunyan,* Roch and Cowan, London, pp. 241–2; *Aida of Leningrad,* Michael Bordeaux, Xenia Howard-Johnston, Gateway Outreach, 1972, pp. 42–3; Georgi Vins, *Three Generations of Suffering,* Hodder, London, 1976, p. 37.
39. *L.*, p. 165.
40. *L.*, p. 167.

## Appendix 2

1. Otakar Sourek, *Antonin Dvořák. His Life and Work,* Orbis-Prague, 1952, p. 66.
2. Alec Robertson, *Dvořák*, J. M. Dent, London, 1969, p. 44.
3. As above, p. 152.
4. *Lo.*, p. 70.
5. See *W.*, ii, p. 207.
6. Bernard Guillemain, *The Later Middle Ages,* A Faith and Fact Book, London, Burns and Oates, 1960, p. 85.
7. Crowder, p. 49, note 32.
8. Gail, p. 263.
9. *G.*, ii, p. 356.
10. Gail, p. 207.
11. Pope John XXIII, trans. by Dorothy White, *A Journal of a Soul,* Geoffrey Chapman, London, 1965, p. 122.
12. As above, p. 177.
13. As above, p. 315.
14. As above, pp. 15–19, 56, 159, 163, 314, 361–73, 381, 391.
15. As above, pp. 173 and 272.
16. See especially Henry T. Hudson, *Papal Power. Its origin and development,* Evangelical Press, 1981.
17. Barraclough, p. 170.
18. David Christie Murray, *A History of Heresy,* New English Library, 1976, p. 117.
19. James L. Connolly, *John Gerson,* Louvain, 1928, p. 90.
20. Wylie, p. 48.
21. *Lo*, p. 43.
22. Connolly, p. 201. See also Steven Ozment, *The Age of Reform 1250–1550,* Yale University Press, 1980, pp. 168–9.
23. q. Barrows Dunham, *The Heretics,* Eyre and Spottiswoode, London, 1969, p. 224, note 1.
24. *L.*, p. 189.
25. *L.*, p. 201.
26. *Lo.*, p. 109.
27. *Lo.*, p. 110.
28. q. *JHCC.*, p. 59.
29. q. *G.*, i, p. 551.
30. *P.*, p. 175.
31. *L.*, p. 184.

32. Dunham, p. 225.
33. *L.*, pp. 103–4.
34. *AR.*, p. 146.
35. q. Peter Nichols, *The Pope's Divisions – The Roman Catholic Church Today*, Faber and Faber, 1981, p. 298.
36. As above, p. 299.
37. *L.*, p. 161.
38. *L.*, p. 192.